Above Tree Line

Mary C. Montanye

A MEMOIR

Above Tree Line

Mary P. Montanye

ISBN: 978-0-9887703-9-3

Cover and book design by Bobbi Benson, Wild Ginger Press
Author photo by Heather Taylor

Wild Ginger Press
www.wildgingerpress.com

For George

Perhaps then, someday, far in the future, you will gradually,
without even noticing it, live your way into the answer.

RAINER MARIA RILKE

CONTENTS

PROLOGUE

June 9, 2012

I am expecting Tony to call and give us the latest information on the wildfire that began southwest of Poudre Park and has moved rapidly toward us all day. It is late and I'm wandering around the house not sure what to do. Should I pack? Throw everything into the car even though Tony and George have assured me there is no way the fire can jump a mountain and travel eight miles before morning? Should I just go to bed?

Tony had called a few minutes ago to tell me he was going over to the firehouse to see what he could see from the second floor. He promised he'd call back; I told him I'd wait for his call before doing anything. George doesn't seem particularly concerned, sitting in his chair, flipping between television channels.

The phone rings and I pick it up fully expecting to hear Tony's calm voice assuring us that we can go to bed, that he will call if anything changes. It *is* Tony, but not the calm, assured, in-control Tony I know. He yells into the phone and I try to grasp the meaning of his words. Over and over he yells, "Get out! Get out! Now! Now! Now!" I try to interrupt him, get him to calm down and explain. He doesn't let me. He ends with "Get George and get out of there. Don't pack. Just leave. Got to go."

I look stupidly at the receiver in my hand for a second after Tony hangs up. Then I drop it onto the kitchen counter and turn to George. "We've got to get out of here. Now. We don't have time."

George stands, but he says, "Tony is being dramatic…"

"No. You didn't hear him. And Tony is never dramatic. We have to go *now*."

For a moment George looks as if he is trying to determine if what I'm saying is true. Then he turns to scoop Pepper off the couch. I look around for my shoes and purse and unplug my computer.

George hands Pepper to me. "Get the dogs in the car," he says. "I'll get the computers."

On the way down the front steps, I see my shoes and shove my feet into them. I find my purse on the desk by the garage door. I put Pepper onto the back seat of the convertible. Thank God the top is up, I think, and go back into the house for Chrissie, punching the garage door opener as I go by. I almost bump into George with Chrissie in his arms. He gives her to me and says, "Get out of here. I'll meet you at Ted's Place." I shove Chrissie into the back seat and before climbing into the car myself, glance back through the now open garage door. The entire hill immediately to the southwest of us looks as if it is on fire. The sky is as bright as day and glows red.

I am shaking badly and wonder if I can drive. I can't catch my breath and for an instant think I might faint. Shaking off the feelings and the thoughts, I turn on the car's ignition. Pepper tries to climb into my lap as Chrissie shivers on the floor under the dash. George has just carried a box out to our Jeep parked on the lawn and as he returns to the house he stops at the car.

"Do you have the dogs?" he yells in the open passenger-side window.

For a minute I don't understand. He knows I have the dogs because he handed them to me. Then I realize he's as rattled as I am and that he is yelling because it is unusually noisy for 11 p.m. in the canyon. There is the hum of cars streaming by on the road below us and an ominous low roar coming from the fire on the hill above.

"Yes," I answer. "Don't go back into the house. Let's just get out of here."

"Just go," he says. "Now."

I put the car into reverse and back out of the garage. Burning embers that look like tiny flames floating in the air fall around the car. Some land on the windshield and some on the lawn next to where the Jeep is parked. I turn the car and, as I do, look to see if George is coming out of the house. I don't see him but I know I need to go. All I can do is trust he won't do anything stupid like try to save any more of our stuff and endanger himself.

I pull out of the drive and turn right toward the mouth of the canyon and Ted's Place. I have to wait for a break in the long stream of cars— unusual for this time of night—heading in the same direction. In my rearview mirror I see the glow of the fire on the ridge above our house. Even though the smoke is dense I can see that George is not behind me. I can't wait for him. I pull out into the traffic and head east.

I look around as I drive. Thoughts go in and out of my mind: thoughts about dying; thoughts about whether or not we'll make it out. Pepper, whimpering, is still trying to climb onto my lap. I roughly shove her back onto the seat and then apologize to her. I'm so scared, but I talk softly to them, thinking how I need to keep them calm. Chrissie jumps from the floor under the dash to the back seat where she stands, terrified and shaking. I watch the taillights of the car in front of me. As we come up to each turn on the canyon road I worry about what is ahead. Will the line of cars stop? Has the fire traveled down from the ridge at some point and jumped the road? Has George left yet? Will I see him soon at Ted's Place? I push the thoughts away and say out loud to myself, "Don't think, Mary. Just drive. Don't think."

With so many cars on the road, the drive to Ted's Place takes twice as long as usual. Many of the canyon residents—my neighbors—are already there. They are out of their cars, standing in small groups and looking back toward the canyon. They talk quietly among themselves and point at the mountains. I look too. I can see the reflection of the fire against the sky.

I scan the line of cars coming out of the canyon for our red Jeep. *Where is George? Why wasn't he right behind me?*

When I finally see him turn into Ted's parking lot, I let out the breath I didn't know I was holding. He pulls up beside the convertible, turns off the ignition and jumps out of the car.

"You okay?" he says as he comes up to me in the crowd.

"Yes," I respond and take his hand. Together we look west, back at the mountain and the glowing sky.

The crowd is growing but it's not noisy. In fact, there is a hush. One man says, "No way in hell can our houses stand up to that. No way in hell…" His voice trails off and no one bothers to contradict him.

Now that we are all out of the canyon and safe for the time being, I realize that I am also worried about the house. But that is not what my heart aches over. It is the canyon itself—my beautiful, beloved canyon and its wildlife and evergreens and constantly flowing river. The fire is sweeping over them all and there is not one thing we can do to stop it.

ONE

The Beginning

November, 1991

On a chilly Saturday afternoon, I sat in a rental car in Colorado with my mother. We had the entire day spread out before us: nothing we had to do, nowhere we had to be—a situation very unusual for us both at the time. Earlier that morning I'd presented a paper at the annual conference of the National Association of Early Childhood Educators with my best childhood friend, Jacquelyn. I was a clinical social worker and she was a college professor. I'd flown to Denver for the conference from Southern California and Jacquelyn had arrived from Texas. My mother, impressed that we—two girls she'd known as flaky and average teenagers—were speaking in front of a national organization, had come to Colorado from her home in Illinois for the event.

Jacquelyn had more conference meetings to attend after she and I had presented our paper, but Mom and I were free for the rest of the day. As we drove away from the conference center, Mom turned to me and said, "What shall we do?"

Without pausing to think, I said, "Let's drive up to Fort Collins and then up to Poudre Canyon. I'd like to see the cabin again where Grandmother used to live."

I've always been quick to follow my intuition. Often I leap before looking, despite all warnings, admonitions or even opposition from others. Mostly my intuition leads me to the right person or place or best option for me. Sometimes, following my intuition means nothing more than buying a book I happen upon in a bookstore or seeing one movie instead of another. But sometimes, following my intuition has life-changing results. Though I didn't know it when I casually suggested we drive up to Poudre Canyon, this would turn out to be one of those times.

My grandmother had lived in that particular canyon, one of several in north central Colorado, during the 1950s and '60s, and both she and my mother had intimate connections with that place. Poudre Canyon was woven into our family history and my own personal mythology and I'd spent time there on several occasions as a little girl. But the road that led me to a deeper, more sustained relationship with the place—one might even call it a love affair—began that day in the autumn of 1991.

My mother, quite spontaneous and intuitive herself, thought driving up to the canyon was a fabulous idea and without further discussion we traversed the 70 or so miles north on Interstate 25. The mouth of Poudre Canyon is located northwest of Fort Collins, a town directly north of Denver along what is informally referred to as the Front Range, a swath of land lying just east of the Rocky Mountains that also includes Denver, Colorado Springs, Boulder and Longmont. The Front Range is relatively flat and treeless, but a wall of brown-, white- and green-streaked mountains rises up directly to its west.

In the Colorado sky you can often see through one shimmering layer of white, like sheer curtains, to a sheet of blue above. Beyond the blue might be a cluster of grayish-pink clouds above which might be another layer of blue sky. As we drove north, the air that winter day was clear and dry and cold, and the sky a deep blue.

My mother and I stopped at Perkins Restaurant on North College Avenue in Fort Collins for lunch before heading the rest of the way up the canyon. As we walked into the restaurant, Petula Clark was singing her old hit *Downtown* through the overhead speakers and I said to my mother, "Something good is about to happen. That song is a sure sign." Whenever I hear Petula Clark singing that song on the radio, a huge blow-you-out-of-the-water kind of event occurs in my life. It works 100 percent of the time and cannot be explained away as coincidence, but I have to hear the song completely at random. In high school I used to test this by playing *Downtown* over and over on my stereo whenever I wanted a specific good incident to happen, like a phone call from a particular boy or a good grade on an important test. It never worked. But I heard it right before I met George, my second and current husband. I heard it shortly before I found out I was pregnant with Brad. And I heard it the day I was accepted into graduate school. Whatever was about to happen here in Colorado was going to be big.

After lunch we headed north out of town on Highway 287. As I drove, with the tune of *Downtown* still playing in my head, Mom directed me as if she'd been there only the previous week. As far as I knew she hadn't been back to Colorado since her mother had died some 18 years before.

Unbeknownst to us at the time, the canyon was working its magic on us. It was as if something happened to Mom and me as we headed toward the canyon. The lives we both lived in far-away cities faded and tiny seeds took tentative root in the soil of our subconscious minds, soil that had been well-prepared by losses and needs, hopes and possibilities. My mother and I were on a path that had its beginnings long before the conference in Denver or this side trip to Poudre Canyon. We were following a lead of which we were not yet aware.

We wound around the northwestern tip of Fort Collins, a somewhat shabby area of town with trailer parks, liquor stores and rent-by-the-week motels mixed in with farm implement dealers, bait-and-tackle shops and kayak and rafting companies. We were so close to the foothills now we could no longer see the mountains west of them. We curved around to the right on what is called the La Porte Bypass, going north toward—as the sign said—Laramie, Wyoming.

My mother knew exactly where to enter the canyon. The landmark for the turn is a modern gas station that everyone calls—and that even shows up on some road maps as—Ted's Place. This looked nothing like Mom's memory of it. It had gone from being a quaint square building with a peaked roof to being a nondescript, modern, low-slung convenience store. Perhaps this was a sign of change to come. Change for Mom and for myself.

I was excited. I was returning to the place where my grandmother had lived by herself between 1949 and 1963. She had moved here after the death of her second husband, Jack, and left when poor health forced her into a nursing home. I'd been to the canyon as a toddler, but my first real memories of it stemmed from the time I was eight and my mother, my younger brother Paul and I lived with Grandmother for a while. Colorado was still the Wild West then and the romance of it had mesmerized Paul and me for one full, magnificent summer.

We rarely returned to Colorado and the canyon after that. Instead we spent our family summer vacations much closer to home in a cabin by a lake in Wisconsin. Grandmother stayed with us each winter in Illinois, so it wasn't necessary for us to go all the way to Colorado to see her. Slowly, in my mind, the Poudre Canyon turned from a real location into a mythical place: mysterious and magical and sacred.

Now here Mom and I were—in a real place, not mythical at all—about to enter the great mass of granite that is the canyon. We would be cradled, dwarfed and engulfed by it. We would travel through it by way of an artery naturally cut out of rock by the Cache La Poudre, a river thought to be two million years old.

After turning left at Ted's Place, we were only a mile from the mouth of the canyon. My mother and I were silent, each with our own thoughts and memories as we watched the mountain open before us. Like other canyons up and down the Front Range, this is a doorway into the Rocky Mountains, the greatest mountain range in the Northern Hemisphere. Each canyon is unique; each has its own distinct feel and outward appearance. My mother used to say that no matter how many times you entered

Poudre Canyon it always looked a little different from the way it looked the last time, as if it was a living organism with a changeable personality all its own. Sometimes it is bathed in cool shadow. Sometimes autumn sunlight and the Chinook winds make the yellow aspen and cottonwood leaves twinkle. In winter the soft snow clings to every branch and twig and bush, and the river rocks turn into fluffy white lumps.

We entered the canyon by driving over a bumpy cattle gate. A cattle gate is a man-made ditch in the road with steel pipes across it, designed to keep cattle in one area without using fences. An old cowboy once told me that cows stop when they come to a cattle gate because when they look down between the pipes across the ditch they see what looks like a bottomless pit and this scares them. The cattle gate here prevented cows from wandering down the road to busy Highway 287. A road sign farther up the canyon warned us to watch for cattle on the road. In many areas of Colorado open range laws were then still in place and cattle could wander at will. I loved the idea of cows wandering free and I wanted to see a few; I eased my foot off the gas pedal and looked around.

As we drove into the canyon, my senses felt more attuned to the world around us, perhaps a little like the senses of the forest animals that make this place their home. I was aware of the rugged beauty encircling our little rental car. Although it was only November, unblemished white snow blanketed everything except for the road, which had been recently plowed. The sky was deep Colorado blue and the evergreens swaying a little in the wind smelled the way only evergreens can. The cottonwoods by the river had dropped their leaves and the Poudre had more rocks in it at that time of year than water.

Nine miles up the canyon we passed a sign that said we were entering Poudre Park. In the Rockies, the flat grassy meadows between cliffs or mountains are often referred to as parks: North Park, Estes Park and Red Rocks Park are three of such named valleys in Colorado. My grandmother's house was in Poudre Park.

We passed the Columbine Store, a low wooden building that used to have working gas pumps. When I was a child, the people who owned the store built five one-room cabins down by the river out back for out-of-towners and fishermen to rent. They were pretty little cabins and clean back then as I remembered. My mom and dad had rented one of those cabins for the four of us once when Grandmother had a family reunion at her place and there wasn't room enough for my uncles' families and us. In the knotty pine, one-room cabin, with the fragrant mountain air drifting in through the open window, I lay on my back on a narrow bed shoved against the wall and listened to the river. Even then I was happier and more at home in the canyon than I was anyplace else—more at home than in my own frilly pink-and-white bedroom in Winnetka, Illinois.

Although they were now obviously rundown, the cabins were still there. And on the one-plus acre between them and the road, stood ten or so junky, dilapidated but obviously occupied mobile homes too.

Just past the Columbine Store my mother leaned forward in the passenger seat and motioned me to slow down. We were nearing my grandmother's house. We crossed a tiny bridge over a dry and rocky gully and turned right onto Poudre River Road, a dirt bypass that curves down to the river and back out again to the main highway. There were only about 15 houses on the entire road, not many more than had been there in my grandmother's time.

Grandmother's old house was the first of three on the left: a brown single-story log cabin with one stone porch attached to its front and another on its side. We stopped and introduced ourselves to its current owners. Very friendly and clearly excited to meet us, they showed us around their home, which now seemed tiny to me, almost doll-like in size. I remembered clearly the covered stone porch attached to the south side of the house and facing the mountain across Highway 14. Every night during the summer of 1958, my grandmother, brother and I put food on that porch for a family of skunks. We watched deer wander down from the mountain, cross the highway and pass Grandmother's house on their way to the river for water. As I thought about the summer we'd lived here with my grandmother, the owners talked about current residents and old neighbors whom Mom and Grandmother might have known.

When my mother mentioned how sorry she was that she'd had to sell the house after Grandmother moved into the nursing home, they suggested we take a look at the property next door.

"Next best thing to having your mother's house again," the woman laughed. "Just went on the market. You've got to see it. The owners are in California visiting friends, but I've got the key. It's here somewhere." She rummaged through a drawer looking for the key while we protested that she shouldn't go to any trouble for us. She finally found the key and took us next door.

It was a terrible house, one room slapped onto another in a ramshackle, drunken-builder fashion. My mother and I looked around quickly, talked awhile longer and, after hearing about monthly potlucks and the local church and its pastor, returned to our car. We continued on down the dirt road.

There was one more "for sale" sign in the Park. It stood in front of another small house, this one backing up to the river. I pulled over onto the side of the road and Mom and I looked at each other. Should we knock on the door? See if the owner would be willing to show it to us? Up to that moment neither of us had mentioned or even admitted to ourselves the possibility of buying a second home in the canyon. We were not the kind of women to make such an extravagant and impetuous purchase. We were only intuitive and spontaneous up to a point; mostly we'd conformed to the customs of the culture in which we were raised. For Mom and me, these customs included letting the men in the family make all major decisions, such as where to live and what homes to buy.

We were also not the type of women who talked much about our feelings, about our wants and needs and regrets, nor were we the type to dwell on the past. My mother had always been very uncomfortable with blatant displays of intense emotion. And though my dad was the more emotional parent, he had picked up from Mom that emotions were best kept under wraps, a lesson that probably did him no good in the long run. If my brother or I cried or raged over anything other than physical pain, Mom would repeat some stock phrase like "no use crying over spilt milk" or "if you can't control yourself, go to your room." So Mom and I had never talked about our pain when Grandmother died or how she felt when she and her brothers needed to sell Grandmother's house, a place in which we'd both experienced so much pleasure and comfort, in order to pay Grandmother's expenses at the nursing home. Instead we shoved it all down and covered it over with lots of activity and other not-so-healthy coping mechanisms. Now, as I sat with my mother in front of that tiny blue-and-white bungalow on the Poudre River, I was only aware of an intense longing to have a place in Poudre Park and to have a reason to come back again. I didn't understand then that the longing I felt was connected to a sense that this little town had the power to make me safe and happy, the way it had when I was eight years old. I certainly didn't consciously connect Poudre Park to my *current* need for safety and calm. And though I didn't recognize this at the time, I understand now that the same thing was happening to my mother.

Thirty years before, when she, Paul and I arrived in Poudre Park planning to spend the summer with Grandmother, Mom was frightened and unhappy. But Mom hid those feelings from us then—perhaps even from herself and Grandmother—just as she was now doing with her fears about Dad's illness and her own aging. She probably needed something happy to think about, something to take her mind off Dad and his precarious health. But I doubt that she recognized her hidden agenda any more than I recognized mine. We certainly didn't talk about any of these things. We merely sat, looking at the house and its "for sale" sign, trying to decide whether to get out of the car and knock on the door or forget the whole thing and drive away.

The decision was made for us when a short, round, middle-aged man with an immense belly stepped out of the bungalow and came around to my side of the car. He wore unlaced work boots and had thrown a thin jacket over his shoulders. He knocked on my window and when I rolled it down, he said, "Wouldn't you like to come in out of the cold?" He had a nice smile and didn't appear to question why two strange women were sitting in an idling car on a chilly November day, staring at his little home.

I looked at my mother, who nodded, and we got out of the car and followed him into the house. The main room was overly warm from a wood stove burning just inside the front door. He helped us off with our coats and after we'd made our introductions (his name was Timothy), asked us if we'd like something to drink. As he made tea in the tiny galley kitchen off the main room, he asked questions and answered ours. He wanted 60,000 dollars for his cabin, which sounded like a steal to the two of us, coming from expensive urban areas. Although he didn't really want to sell it, he told us, he thought it was time. He was a psychologist working with police officers on such issues as post-traumatic stress and most of his work took place in Denver, too far to be traveling back and forth several times a week. He was easy to talk to and his little house was comfortably furnished with well-worn furniture. There was only one fairly small main room, two tiny bedrooms facing the road, a bathroom and the galley kitchen. At the back of the house was an open, but covered porch. In the main room, a round battered table was positioned in front of a large picture window overlooking the river. My mother and I sat at the table sipping our cups of tea and looking out the window. Several large trees stood between the house and the river; beyond the river a forested hill rose dramatically. Timothy noticed we were looking at the hill and commented, "Deer come down from there to the river almost every morning and evening to drink. And in the spring, they bring the fawns."

Wonder and want filled a cavity within me that I hadn't realized existed until that moment. I wanted this place. I wanted it more than I had wanted anything in a very long time.

I'm not sure which of us said the words out loud first, but my mother and I were of one mind and one heart. We wanted this house and, losing all chance at any negotiation of price, we let him know just how much we wanted it.

"If you're really interested," Timothy said, "I should give you the name of a realtor friend of mine. Since you're from out of town and you're not going to be here very long, perhaps you should talk to him before you leave. In fact, if you'd like, you can call him from here."

I was excited but scared, too. What would Dad say? And George?

George and I had vacationed in Colorado two summers before on my 40th birthday. We'd noticed how many businesses and homes were on the market and had joked that the whole state was for sale. When we stopped at little ma-and-pa diners and stores, we laughingly asked the clerk or server if it was up for sale. The answer was always, "Depends. How much you offering?" It was a bad time for Coloradoans. My pragmatic husband and businessman father would not think buying something at this time was a good idea at all. But Mom and I had rediscovered the "home place," so to speak. Neither of us wanted to lose what we'd just found, even if the men we loved would surely think we'd lost our minds. At that moment, their approval and the money needed to buy the cabin seemed beside the point.

I called the realtor's number while Mom sat at the table sipping her tea and tapping her foot. Timothy walked around outside to give us a little privacy. The realtor's wife answered the phone and told me that her husband wouldn't be available until later in the evening, but that she, a realtor herself, knew Timothy and had been to the house. She answered my basic questions about earnest money and closing dates and assured me they could prepare a written offer and have it ready for me to sign first thing the following morning.

Mom had an early flight back to Chicago the next day so we had no choice but to return to Denver that Saturday night. Since Jacquelyn and I didn't have flights home until Monday we could drive up together on Sunday and I could sign the documents. I was excited to show Jacquelyn the house on the river that would soon be mine. The realtor assured us that after the initial contract was presented to and accepted by Timothy—and we had no reason to believe that he wouldn't accept our offer—the rest of the details and paperwork could be accomplished by mail.

On the way back to Denver, Mom and I constantly interrupted each other.

"Mary, the cabin will be our Shirley Valentine house!" Mom said. She was a bit obsessed at the time with Shirley Valentine, the character in a movie about a London housewife who, unhappy with her life, runs off to Greece where she has an affair and seriously considers never returning home.

I said, "Won't it be fun to have a place right on the Poudre?" I imagined tea and coffee and breakfast in our robes on the deck the following spring and how we would watch the fawns and their mothers descend the hill to drink from the river. Mom and I had always found water, whether lakes or oceans or rivers, to be particularly calming and now, with Mom concerned about Dad's health and me dealing with a challenging career, a sanctuary by water and the peace of mind we knew it would bring was what we both thought we needed. Even if we couldn't make the trip to the cabin often, the knowledge of its being there, belonging to us, waiting for our return, would be soothing in itself.

"I have an idea," Mom said. "I have some money from the sale of Dad's business. I am so sorry Paul, Dad and I benefited from the sale and you didn't. Why don't I buy the cabin for you? This would be a way for me to even things out."

"Are you sure?" I asked. "I don't think I lost out on anything. Paul worked in the business and negotiated the sale. He deserves his part of the money."

"Still, you are a member of this family and it was a *family* business. Besides, I want us to have the cabin."

And although we didn't actually say it out loud to each other then, we made the decision to buy the cabin with a portion of Mom's proceeds from the sale of the business. We sat silently contemplating the huge step we were about to take.

I hardly slept at all that night, filled with the anxiety and excitement that comes with any major life decision. And I wasn't thinking much past the buying of the house. I had no idea when I would actually *stay* in it for any length of time with career and family to consider and with Colorado so far from California. But I didn't care. I wanted a piece of Poudre Park and my grandmother again.

The next morning, after taking Mom to Denver's Stapleton Airport,

Jacquelyn and I drove back to Fort Collins. At Ted's Place, I used the pay phone to call the realtor. We had made preliminary arrangements the night before to meet at Ted's Place so I could sign the contract and take it up to Timothy for his signature. Before the end of the afternoon, Jacquelyn and I would be on our way back to Denver with a signed sales contract in hand.

Frank, the realtor, had bad news. Overnight, Timothy had decided not to sell the cabin. Apparently he'd talked to his girlfriend and she wanted him to keep it. She'd told him that someday it would be worth far more than the 60,000 dollars he was currently asking. Two women showing up out of nowhere and offering full price for it on the spur of the moment was an indication that Timothy would have no trouble selling it later if he wanted to.

As I held the phone receiver close to my ear trying to block out the truck noise from Highway 287, I struggled to find words that would convince Frank to call Timothy again, to say whatever he must to convince Timothy to sell his cabin to me. The fulfillment of a need—a deep longing I hadn't even known I had until I'd seen the canyon again, until I'd seen the little cabin on the river—was slipping away. I would not give it up easily.

Frank told me Timothy was resolute. He wasn't going to sell. He was taking his house off the market even though Frank had tried to convince him otherwise. They'd talked for a long time the night before, he said, and he didn't want to bother Timothy again so early on a Sunday morning. But I didn't care what time it was or what day or whether or not I bothered Timothy. I'd driven 70-plus miles from Denver to sign a contract on his house and I was not turning around and going back until I'd done everything I could to talk Timothy into selling me that house.

Almost unable to hold back my tears and fluctuating between grief and anger, I told Jacquelyn what had happened when I returned to the car. I said that, girlfriend or no girlfriend, I was going back up the canyon to talk Timothy into changing his mind. After all, I'd convinced fathers and mothers to change the way they treated their children and husbands and wives to give their marriages a second chance. Surely I could convince Timothy that he really *did* want to sell me his house on the river.

With Jacquelyn sitting silently but willingly beside me, I pulled out of Ted's Place and turned west toward Poudre Park. This time there wasn't much to see. The temperature had risen overnight and the road was socked in with fog. If Jacquelyn wondered whether I'd lost my mind to want to buy a house so far from anything in an area that seemed pretty desolate that morning, she didn't say. She also knew me well enough not to try to talk me out of a plan on which I'd set my mind.

When we arrived at Timothy's house, I immediately noticed that he had taken down the "for sale" sign. The entire adventure was beginning to seem surreal, as if I'd dreamt the whole thing. In the fog, the Poudre Park community now looked more dingy than charming.

Timothy answered the door in bathrobe and bare feet, a mug of coffee in his hand. He perked up a little when he saw elegant and beautiful Jacquelyn standing slightly behind me and waved us in. His sad look returned when I refused his offer of coffee, didn't return his smile, and told him I only wanted to talk about why he'd decided not to sell the cabin. Looking around at the cozy room, frightened it would never be mine, I felt as if someone I loved had just died.

Timothy went over the facts his girlfriend had laid out for him, nothing more than we'd already heard from Frank. As Jacquelyn stood quietly beside me, I offered him more money, thinking perhaps this was a maneuver on Timothy's part to get me to pay more for his house. Perhaps his girlfriend had convinced him that, based on how fast Mom and I were willing to pay full price for a place we'd seen briefly, he was asking too little. But apparently this was not the case. Timothy would not budge.

I hesitated to leave, to give up. I knew that the moment we walked out the door it would be over: Mom and I would not own this house. We would lose Poudre Canyon again and this time probably forever. So I continued to stand, unable to make myself move, staring at this man in his bathrobe. Timothy looked as if he might cry. I knew that if I didn't leave soon, I *would* cry. Finally, I handed him a card with my home address and phone number on it. "Call if you change your mind," I said as Jacquelyn and I walked out the door.

We were just about at the car when Timothy, still wearing his bath-robe and slippers, came out of the house and hurried towards us. "Wait," he called. "I have an idea."

We turned and looked at him.

"The house across the road." He pointed and we looked. "There's no sign, but it's for sale. It's not on the river and they're asking more for it. The owners aren't home right now, but I have a key. Do you want to take a look at it?"

Jacquelyn and I looked toward the house he was pointing at, then at Timothy, and then at each other. "Yes," Jacquelyn said. "Of course we do." She had picked up my excitement. We were of one mind now, as we'd often been before.

Timothy dressed as we waited by the car. I was trying not to get my hopes up again. The house we were about to look at wasn't on the river and that had been an important feature of Timothy's house for Mom and me. From the outside it wasn't as cute as Timothy's bungalow and it was more expensive. The house looked bigger and had a much larger yard. We certainly didn't need that.

As Timothy turned the key in its lock he said, "The owners are gone for the morning, but they'll be back soon. Let me know what you think."

We took a few steps inside and I knew immediately what I would do.

While Timothy's house was *all man*, this one had the definite and distinctive touch of a woman. I had been so intent on looking out the window at the river in Timothy's place, I'd barely noticed the interior of his house. But here, with the backyard blocked out by a privacy fence, I was able to concentrate on the inside of this one and it was darling. I felt myself relaxing into the comfort and rightness of it. The mouse-hole-sized front entrance hall had what looked like an original Navaho rug on the floor. A great spider plant with baby offshoots dangling from its pot hung from the ceiling in the window by a door that led into a sitting room so small there was room for only an antique twig chair and tiny square table. Another Navaho rug covered the floor of the sitting room. A bank of old windows that had to have been in the house since it was built decades before was located along the entrance hall's left wall. The windows continued into the sitting room and curved around to the back. They looked out onto a patio and garden area now quiet and still with winter, but one that I imagined would bloom abundantly come spring.

The owner had furnished the large front room to the right of the entrance with antiques. An aspen-wood ladder leaned against the wall and ascended into a tiny loft above. Everything seemed quaint, as charming as a doll's house. It was a house for tea parties or reading Victorian novels while curled up by the fire. Lovingly attended plants were everywhere. They hung in baskets, sat on tables and were grouped in sunny pools on the floor. Whoever lived here loved to nourish living things. And I felt that nourishment washing over and into me.

There was only one big main room with French doors opening onto the back patio. The kitchen, painted an inviting yellow, was separated from the main room by a counter that had two stools pushed up against it. A round rag rug lay on the wood floor in front of the kitchen sink. A window over the sink looked out onto Poudre River Road and across it to Timothy's house and the river beyond. Directly off the kitchen there was a bedroom painted light blue, with a comfortable, cushioned window seat in front of three large bay windows opening onto the back garden. I imagined myself waking up in that bedroom to birdsong and the gurgle of a river swelled from spring run-off. A second bedroom and the only bathroom were beyond the kitchen and off a back laundry room. The bathroom had a deep tub, perfect for long soapy and fragrant soaks.

I fell in love.

Even though the house wasn't next to the river, it had more of the spirit of my grandmother's old house. Its back windows looked out onto Grandmother's mountain, the one from which *her* deer had descended on their way to the river. It had a wooden porch that I could pretend was like my grandmother's stone porch, the one on which we'd spread out food for skunk families. This was my house. This was the reason Timothy had changed his mind. I wasn't supposed to have *that* house. I was supposed to have *this* one. This was the grandmother house, the healing house.

Jacquelyn and I barely looked into the back rooms. By the time we'd even noticed them, I'd made up my mind. The health of the plants and the warmth of such details as the deep green flannel throw over a rocking chair in the front room convinced me. The house itself beckoned me to stop, to sink in, to rest. I could hardly contain my excitement or my need. I wanted this house. I *needed* this house.

I'd call Frank on our way through Fort Collins and change the bid. This time the owners wouldn't change their minds. I was sure of it. The pieces had come together. The little bungalow at 179 Poudre River Road would soon belong to me and my mother. I knew it as surely as if the little mailbox across the road already had my name engraved on it. The details of the offer and sale were a mere formality.

T W O

Cowboys and Ladies, Seashells and Skunks

My grandmother Mildred first discovered the Poudre Canyon with her second husband, Jack. I heard bits and pieces of their story from my mother and then after Mom died, my Uncle Gerald, Mom's only surviving brother, told me what he remembered.

Grandmother came to this part of Colorado from Iowa in the early 1920s with her first husband, George, my grandfather. They started a beet farm just north of Fort Collins. According to Mom, Grandfather was a difficult man. She told me about arguments between her parents that were so frightening she and Gerald would hide in their beds and pull the covers over their heads in a futile attempt to drown out the angry words. I never learned the cause of the fights.

One day in 1922, when my grandmother was perhaps most unhappy, a tall, thin, quiet man with a gentle smile and hat in hand came to the back door to see if there might be an odd job or two around the farm. He was willing to do anything for room in the barn and simple board. My grandfather gave him a job. When Jack arrived at the farm, Mom was only three years old, Gerald was a couple of years older, and the youngest sibling, Bob, had not yet been born.

My imagination conjures up scenes of angry night-time fights between my grandmother and grandfather and mornings after where Jack comes in from the barn for breakfast and notices the uncomfortable silence between George and Mildred in the otherwise homey and warm kitchen. He might see a tear roll down my grandmother's cheek as she turns pancakes on the grill or pours him a second cup of coffee, ducking her head to hide her pain. At some point, perhaps, Jack finds himself close to the house when Grandfather is away. Jack takes a chance. He locates Grandmother and shyly says a word or two of comfort to her in a very proper sort of way. These encounters continue between them and eventually grow longer and more intimate. He seeks her out more often and she finds herself longing for his kind and gentle company on the lonely mornings after fights with Grandfather. I imagine that she's guilt-stricken and ashamed of her growing feelings for Jack. But she can't help herself. She needs his smiles and assurances that she's still worthy of attention, that a man still finds her appealing and important.

It's hard to imagine my grandmother making a first move toward any man, especially when she is married to another. And from what I've heard about Jack, I don't think he was one to go after another man's wife. But something obviously happened between the two of them in the cozy kitchen on the little beet farm. Perhaps Jack made his move when they were alone on the farm with the children at school or napping. As she stands at the kitchen sink, I imagine, he puts his arms around her. Desperate for his strength and kindness, she leans back into him and lets him turn her and kiss her and start something neither one of them can stop.

I imagine that at some point they decide their love is worth all risk and they revel in it every chance they get: when they're alone on the farm; when the children are sleeping; when they can find corners away from the eyes of others. I envision Grandmother eventually slipping into the narrow cot in Jack's little room in the barn where he holds her and soothes her fears about the future. They consummate their love within the warm and safe embrace of fragrant hay and lowing cows.

Even before the Crash of 1929, my grandparents' beet farm buckled under the weight of my grandfather's poor financial management. And their marriage, already on very shaky ground, collapsed along with the farm. Uncle Gerald told me that he and my mother awoke one morning to find their father gone. I don't know how much Jack had to do with the final breakup of the marriage, but I assume his growing relationship with Grandmother had something to do with it. Perhaps, with Jack's love and support, she finally found the courage and the strength to stand up to Grandfather during one of his abusive tirades. Perhaps she told him to leave. Or Grandfather discovered Jack and Grandmother together one day, confronted them and she confessed. Grandmother might have told Grandfather she couldn't continue to live with him when she was in love with another man. Or Grandfather gave the final ultimatum—insisting that she choose between them—and she chose Jack. Whatever the case, my grandfather left his wife and children suddenly and Jack stayed in the picture.

For a couple of months, Grandmother, Mom, Gerald and the new baby, Bobby, lived with Jack in a small rental house in Fort Collins. One day, Grandmother told the children they were moving to Grinnell, Iowa, to live with her parents. Jack would stay in Colorado. According to my mother, Grandmother had agreed to return to her hometown because she and Jack were not able to support three children during the Depression. Grandmother's father, a well-to-do Grinnell insurance man, had agreed to support Grandmother financially and pay the children's expenses until all three of the children had graduated from college. The only requirement was that Grandmother had to leave Jack behind. My great-grandfather was a very religious man with high standards and he must have been appalled that Grandmother was living in what he most certainly considered sin. Grandmother decided she had no choice. She couldn't raise three children on her own in depressed Colorado and Jack, moving from ranch to ranch making what little money he could, was in no position to take on a wife and three young stepchildren. Grandmother left Colorado and Jack and returned to her parents in Iowa.

Although 900 miles separated Jack and my grandmother for more than ten years, the bond between them stayed strong. Through letters and the occasional trip back to Colorado, they kept in touch.

Then in 1941, when all three children had their college degrees and Mom was newly married to Dad, Grandmother returned to Colorado and to Jack. He finally had a stable job and residence on the Roberts Ranch in Livermore, Colorado, just a few miles north of Poudre Canyon.

Grandmother and Jack married and lived for a while on the ranch in the little white house set aside for hired hands. Mom spent the second year there with them while Dad served overseas in the Navy during World War II. Mom later told me that her year on the ranch was one of the happiest times of her life, even though she was far away from Dad and war was making the future uncertain for everyone. But on the ranch, the war seemed very far away. Grandmother, Jack, Mom, Catherine and Evan worked and played hard together while surrounded by the beauty and grandeur of the still unspoiled American West.

The Roberts Ranch is an enormous cattle ranch that has belonged to the Roberts family since the 1870s. At first, the ranch consisted of only 120 acres. Another 160 acres were added soon after and for many years that was all the owned land on the Roberts Ranch.

In the early days of cattle ranching in Northern Colorado, as in other parts of the western United States, ranch families didn't need to own the land on which they grazed their cattle, nor did they believe that doing so was particularly wise. They let their cattle roam and mix with other herds. When the time came to sell or wean or brand the cattle, the neighboring ranchers worked together to round up and sort out the herds. This system worked well until sheepherders moved into the area and wanted to graze their flocks on the open rangeland. The ranchers feared the sheep would ruin the land for cattle grazing. The Roberts decided that in order to protect the land they needed for their cattle they'd have to own and fence it. In 1900 they began to buy land from the Union Pacific Railroad until they were able to cobble together, over the years and piece by piece, close to 18,000 acres.

In 1980, the Roberts Ranch was given a Centennial Designation, a recognition that goes to ranches owned by the same family for at least one hundred years. The Roberts have always believed, like the Native Americans who lived on the land before them, that land is never *owned* but is instead *loaned* by Spirit or God and must be kept as natural as possible for subsequent generations. Due to Evan and Catherine's foresight, the entire acreage of the Roberts Ranch has changed little since the West was settled. And in 2006, Catherine Roberts entered into an agreement with the Nature Conservancy, a private non-profit organization dedicated to protecting undeveloped land, to legally protect the entire historic Roberts Ranch from future development.

The Roberts Ranch is part of the magic of the west for me. That magic most likely played a role in my desire and decision to have a home of my own in Colorado.

For as long as I can remember, my brother Paul and I were enamored with everything western. To have parents who actually had a personal involvement with this otherworldly place was almost beyond our belief.

When Paul and I were toddlers, we traveled to Colorado a few times to visit Grandmother. Mom usually took us while Dad stayed behind in Hawaii or traveled around the mainland on business. This might be why Dad never developed the love for Colorado that Mom felt and inspired in me. During our visits to Grandmother's house in Poudre Canyon, we'd spend time on the Roberts Ranch with Catherine and Evan. Paul and I were too little to remember those visits, but stories about them were handed down. Adults loved to tell us about the time Paul, thought to be taking a nap in Catherine and Evan's bedroom, toddled out to the living room—he was probably no more than two or three years old—carrying the loaded pistol he'd found in the drawer of the bedside table. The firearm was quickly confiscated before Paul had the opportunity to take a shot or two, as he liked to do with his toy guns.

Until the summer Mom, Paul and I lived with Grandmother in Poudre Park—when I was eight and Paul was six—all I knew about the West, the Roberts and their ranch was through stories told to me by others. But that summer the West truly came alive for me and it has lived on in my memory and imagination ever since. That summer Evan enchanted us with stories about pioneers who crossed the land—the land that would one day become the Roberts Ranch—on their way from the East to California or Oregon. As we stared round-eyed at the ground that hadn't changed in thousands of years, Evan pointed out deep ruts in the soil left by the pioneers' wagon wheels. He took us to the bottom of a hog-back cliff, pointed to the top, and described how Indians once drove herds of buffalo up to that very place and forced them over the edge to their deaths. He told us that the Indians made use of every bit of the buffalo—the meat, the fur, the bones, the fat—unlike the *white men* who killed buffalo mainly for sport or for the damage it would do to the Indian tribes they wanted off the land. Though Evan spoke quietly and with little dramatic intonation, Paul and I could hear the thundering hooves and taste the dust in our mouths as he told the story. We could see the buffalo falling and dying at our feet in great heaps.

The landscape of the Roberts Ranch was right out of the movies. As far as our eyes could see there was nothing but sagebrush, scruffy patches of cottonwood trees, red-rock cliffs and deep blue sky. It was as different from the lush tropics of the Hawaiian Islands where Paul and I had lived since birth as one could imagine. Even the air felt different. Horses, herds of cattle and cowboys with ten-gallon hats and spurs on their boots fired up our imaginations.

The Roberts lived in a house with a rocky creek not far from their front door. A chestnut mare, saddled and ready for a quick getaway Paul and I supposed, grazed under a nearby cottonwood tree.

To Paul and me, Catherine and Evan were mythical characters. Evan would have looked at home with Roy Rogers or on *Wagon Train* with his string tie, big cowboy hat and spit-shined leather boots. But unlike the cowboys on television and in the movies he was quiet and proper, always standing when a woman entered the room. He spoke almost in a whisper. Years later, when I mentioned this to Mom, she told me that *real* cowboys are always quiet so as not to frighten the cows.

My first memory of Catherine Roberts is from that summer when I was eight. She was standing on the front stoop of her house giving Mom a hug and holding open the door for me and Paul. I remember looking up at her, thinking how tall she was. Her beauty awed me into a shy silence. Later, when I was grown and came back to visit Catherine and the ranch, I realized she wasn't tall at all. In fact she was quite small and round and there was little sign of the beauty I'd seen in her when I was eight. But when I was a child, Catherine, like Evan and the ranch and the entire western landscape, was larger than life to me.

Catherine had curves where Mom was mostly straight and silky hair of a deep rich mahogany. She pulled her hair to the back of her head in a simple but elegant bun. Even though she lived in the dusty West, her clothes and hair were flawless. Her face, always absent any make-up other than lipstick, was as fresh as a young girl's. She could have easily played the starring woman's role in one of the westerns Paul and I liked.

During that first visit I sat close to Mom on the couch in Catherine's living room and listened as the adults talked. Everything was very quiet. I'd expected more noise, I think—perhaps the sound of men on horseback, gun fire, at least the rush and tumble of the river. But there was none of that. Catherine served tea out of a silver tea set instead of coffee in tin cups. She used good china dishes and passed around small cakes on a cut-glass dish. Nothing was as I expected and that added to the allure of the ranch, the attraction I felt for Catherine. The effect she had on me stayed with me though I didn't see her again after that summer until I was grown.

My mother had many stories about her own early years on the ranch. And all those stories added to my sense of Colorado as a magical place. This was a place where dreams really did come true, where great loves were found, where people were free to do what they wanted. During most of my life I looked at the West as a place where there were few rules or expectations.

My grandmother and Jack didn't have much time together considering how long they were apart. Their marriage lasted only twelve years, but in those years they made up for lost time. When the war ended, all the members of my family moved off the Roberts Ranch. My mother reunited with my father in Hawaii and Grandmother and Jack bought houses of their own, a main residence in Fort Collins and later a weekend place in the Poudre Canyon. While Jack worked for the water district, Grandmother involved herself with the life of the small but growing Fort Collins community. And at every opportunity she and Jack enjoyed each other's company in the canyon. Jack loved breakfasts down by the river and on the spur of the moment they'd pack up the picnic gear and the bacon and eggs and toast and head to their favorite riverside spots. They'd make a fire at the edge of the water, boil a pot of coffee, cook the eggs and bacon and watch deer as they came to the water to drink.

One morning at their house in town, Jack went to the basement to check on something. When he didn't return after a few minutes, Grandmother went down to check on *him*. She found him sprawled face down on the cement floor, dead of a massive heart attack. Catherine Roberts told me not too long ago that she was afraid for my Grandmother's sanity after Jack died. But Grandmother didn't fall apart. Instead, and against everyone's advice, she sold the two houses she and Jack owned and bought another one farther up the canyon, the house in Poudre Park. Like a wounded animal that slinks off into the brush to either heal or die from its wounds, and as I would do some 40 years later, my grandmother took herself away. Like me she needed nature and, particularly, the canyon. She needed a different house, a place to be that didn't remind her so much of what she'd lost and how, perhaps, she'd failed. And just like me, she was guided by something whole and strong and healthy within to do what she needed to do. She followed that little inner voice even when it meant going against the well-meaning advice of everyone close to her. She packed up her things and moved into the canyon to heal.

When I was a little girl I loved my grandmother more than anyone and I was overjoyed to spend a whole summer with her the year I turned eight. What I remember most about Grandmother is the quiet that seemed, not only to surround her, but to emanate from her. Whether she was at her home in Colorado or later in Illinois, the quiet was with her. She brought it along wherever she went. Being with my grandmother was like taking a deep sigh or sinking into a soft bed or a warm bath. Grandmother's quiet was most apparent when she was watching her world, the world made up of the grandeur of the Rocky Mountains and the animals that lived in their shadows. Each night, Grandmother fed a family of skunks who lived beneath her porch and one of her greatest joys was watching the mother skunk and her babies cautiously waddle onto the porch, sniff the air for any sign of danger and tentatively—at first—sample the dinner leftovers Grandmother had laid out on a dented tin plate. Grandmother didn't need to remind Paul and me to be quiet as we crouched by the window to watch the skunks eat their dinner. Without her needing to say a word to us, Paul and I, usually a bit antsy and unable to sit still, absorbed Grandmother's awe and knelt in silence with her at the window until the skunks had finished their meal and returned to their nest under the porch.

As far as I can remember, I never heard Grandmother preach about how someone should act or live their life. She taught through her actions and we absorbed the lessons, just like we learned how to sit still and appreciate the natural world and its inhabitants by watching her and imitating her actions and demeanor.

Grandmother never paid much attention to how she dressed, wearing mostly cotton house dresses she made herself and hand-smocked. She wore support hose and sensible shoes. And she smiled a lot, but I don't remember ever hearing her laugh out loud. Hearing laughter coming from my grandmother would have sounded wrong, jarring. But a smile from her was right. It started in the corners of her mouth and extended to her eyes and made you know that the very best thing that had happened to her that day was seeing you.

No one, except perhaps Jack, would have called Grandmother pretty when she was older. Her nose was a bit too big for her square face and her eyes were a watery, nondescript blue. Still, she drew people to her as if they hungered for whatever it was she offered. Even though her house was more messy than homey, with its balls of string and saved tin cans—labels carefully removed, smoothed out and piled on the little table in the kitchen for some reason that no one but Grandmother ever understood—people came to visit and relax in the calm that surrounded her and to enjoy a piece of her freshly made angel food cake or chocolate meringue pie. She made those desserts only for her guests and for us, because her diabetes prevented her from eating any of it.

My grandmother collected things. She collected small china figurines and sea shells and buttons. She had a large collection of Hummels, the porcelain figurines based on the drawings of an early 20th-century German nun, and several child tea sets. She had collections of tiny forest animals: squirrels, rabbits, raccoons, bears, deer. Grandmother kept these items in several china cabinets squeezed into her very cluttered Poudre Park cabin. While she displayed her large sea shells on window sills, bookcases and end tables, she attached all the small shells to sheets of cardboard and labeled each one. On her manual Royal typewriter, Grandmother typed in rows the common name for each shell—egg yolk moon snail, Polynesian harp, prickly winkle—and then carefully and symmetrically cut the words apart and glued the names beneath the correct shell. She also included on each label, information about where the shell had been found or the name of the person who had sent it to her. Grandmother did the same thing with buttons, but instead of gluing them onto the cardboard she sewed them on and then labeled them in the same way she had the shells: carved bone from the Philippines sent by Dwight during the war; coconut shank button from Betty in Hawaii; ebony wood button from Bob in Aruba; four-hole classic anchor button from Mabel. She kept the cards of buttons and shells in boxes and brought them out for Paul and me to look at in the evenings that summer we lived with her in Colorado. She also let us play with her little china figurines. We took them out of their cabinets, arranged them on the floor and made up stories and games with them.

Every morning that summer, Paul and I raced each other out of our beds, excited to find out what new adventures Mom and Grandmother had planned for us. Sometimes it was a walk in the fields by Grandmother's house through waist-high brush, where we screamed with delight as grasshoppers jumped and whirred and bumped into our legs and arms. Sometimes it was a car trip up the road to picnic at a quiet bend in the river, where Paul and I would sail our homemade boats or pretend we were Indian children living 100 years before on that very spot, our tee-pee located out of sight behind us. Sometimes Mom and Grandmother took us on all-day excursions out of the canyon and north to the Roberts Ranch where, if we were lucky, Evan would let us accompany him while he checked on the new calves. If we'd been very good, he'd lift us onto one of his gentle mares and lead us around the pasture so we could pretend we were real cowboys.

And at the end of each day, tired and filled with new adventures to dream about, I crawled into the bed I shared with Grandmother and waited for her with heavy eyelids as she sat in the dim light of her vanity table lamp. I watched as she released her long grey hair from the thin braids that she always wore wrapped around the top of her head and tried not to fall asleep as she brushed her hair exactly one hundred strokes. Then she'd climb into bed and turn on her side away from me and I'd gently caress that long, silky hair as we whispered about the activities of the day until we both drifted off to sleep.

THREE

A Questionable Paradise

My parents married in 1942 in Norfolk, Virginia, where my father was based during his naval training. When it was rumored that Dad would soon be shipping out for such places as Puerto Rico and beyond, Mom traveled from Iowa to Virginia so she could marry him and live with him for at least a little while. When Dad was eventually sent to Puerto Rico for duty, Mom returned to Colorado and joined Jack and Grandmother on the Roberts' ranch.

By the end of the war, Dad was stationed in Honolulu, Hawaii. When he was released from the service in 1946 and while still in Honolulu, he called Mom and asked her over the party line if she'd like to live in Hawaii. Hawaii's lush tropical forests, its unusual and colorful birds and plants, its beaches and its balmy weather charmed Dad, a poor boy from Iowa, and he must have waited anxiously as Mom took a few moments to collect her thoughts. Before she could answer him and to the surprise of them both, the telephone operator exclaimed, "Betty, if you don't accept that man's offer, I will!"

While Mom made her preparations to close one chapter of her life in Colorado and open another in Hawaii, Dad was hired as a clerk in an insurance firm with promises of pay increases and promotions in the near future. Because of his experience in the insurance business before the war and his bachelor's degree from Grinnell College, Dad was assured that he would have a solid and lucrative position in the company for as long as he wanted to remain with the firm. Dad believed this job would give him the security he wanted so that he and Mom could start a family.

Dad worked hard at the company and, as time went on, he was given more and more responsibility for overseeing the internal affairs of the office. Mike, his friend and colleague, was another young man new to the Islands and to the firm. Mike and Dad broadened the client base to include professional associations. This was a new concept in the insurance business and the pair made a lot of money for the company.

Mom and Dad developed and maintained a strong, close-knit group of friends in the years they lived in Hawaii. One of those friends was a fun-loving physician, the son of Dad's boss. He was apparently quite taken with Mom and often asked her to attend parties with him, obviously unconcerned that she was another man's wife. Wealthy, attractive and single, Bill was invited to *a lot* of parties.

"Get your old man to take care of the kids tonight and come with me to the AMA bash," he'd say. "It'll be boring as hell without you." When she hesitated or asked something like *won't it cramp your style,* Bill always answered, "I want it cramped. I'm tired of every woman I meet thinking she should be the one to end my bachelorhood."

Mom would then ask Dad if she could attend such-and-such party with Bill and Dad always told her to go. He made excuses about how tired he was anyway and that he preferred to stay home with us kids. He always assured her that she deserved a night out after taking care of us all day. "Go," he'd say. "Have fun."

I don't know how deeply Mom felt about Bill. I do know that she talked about him off and on for the rest of her life, mentioning tidbits here and there, innocuous asides, even up until just a few days before her death. It was Bill she called when Dad died suddenly on a beach in Barbados and it was Bill who reassured her he hadn't suffered, that Dad had been dead even before he'd hit the sand. Once, when she was in and out of lucidity after the serious lung surgery she had in her late seventies, Mom tried to confess to George something she had done that was, she said, *very, very bad.* George didn't want to hear whatever it was she wanted to confess and quickly changed the subject, but I've always wondered if it might have had something to do with Bill.

Mom told me once that Dad was jealous of her friendship with Bill. Long after they'd returned to the mainland to live, Dad finally admitted to her how he'd hated those nights when she'd gone off with Bill. Dad had never tolerated conflict well and perhaps he thought it was easier, strange as it sounds, to send her out with another man than risk an argument.

He also told Mom, long after the incident, that he was particularly upset once when he saw Mom and Bill step off a plane together. Mom was returning from a visit with her mother in Colorado and Bill was returning from a medical conference in California, he said. Apparently, it was coincidental that they found themselves on the same returning flight. Dad, however, thought it was odd that Bill and Mom, close friends as they were, wouldn't know *before* they boarded that they would be returning to Hawaii on the same flight. Back then there weren't many flights to Hawaii so perhaps it *was* merely a coincidence and they *were* surprised to find each other on the same plane. Still, it must have been hard for Dad to avoid the conclusion that Bill and Mom were more than just friends. Perhaps he kept quiet because it was easier to trust them than it would have been to discover that yes, his wife was having an affair with his boss's son. The fallout from that knowledge would be painful and widespread.

Sometimes I've wondered whether Mom did have regrets that she married Dad instead of waiting for someone like Bill, someone raised in privilege and capable of commanding such admiration and approval. Did she regret even a little that she wasn't the one who ended Bill's bachelorhood? Bill appeared forceful and in charge, while Dad was often tentative and afraid, especially when he was younger.

Dad's childhood was difficult. He was born in Longmont, Colorado—an interesting coincidence as he and Mom spent their early childhoods only 40 miles apart in the same state but didn't meet until much later in Iowa. His parents and older brother moved out west from Iowa, because his dad had tuberculosis. Like many TB sufferers then, they hoped the dry air and high altitude of this mountain state would cure Granddad and it did help for a time. He might have lived if the family had stayed in Colorado, but Granddad's parents, my father's paternal grandparents, pressured them into returning to Iowa so they could help out on the family farm. Not long after they returned, Dad's father died, leaving his mother to raise him and his two brothers alone. My father and his older brother were young teenagers when they lost their father and were therefore old enough to help out by working. Dad's little brother did what he could around the house and his mother took in laundry and ironing to do her part to support the family.

Dad met Mom through my mother's grandfather, John Evans, the man who years before had taken in Mom, her mother and her brothers. He hired Dad to work in his insurance agency when Dad graduated from Grinnell College. I could imagine Mom with her bubbly and friendly personality attracting Dad the moment he first saw her, perhaps on a day when she stopped by the insurance agency to say hello to her grandfather.

Dad's financially insecure childhood and the mentoring of my great-grandfather, a man he respected and admired, probably led to Dad's lifelong belief that to be an insurance man was as high or even a higher calling than medicine or the ministry. People needed tangible safety nets and providing a safety net for the unexpected was, to my father's thinking, what the insurance business was all about. And Dad was driven to succeed at it so his wife and children would never know the hardships he'd known.

My father was what you might call "high-strung" and like me he struggled with anxiety and panic attacks much of his life. He was a chicken-little sort of man with the sky always about to fall. I have early memories of times when Dad shook and struggled to catch his breath. It terrified me when he got like that, but Mom would sit him down and have him breathe long and slow and deep as she quietly assured him that everything would turn out fine. While I was scared by whatever was happening to my dad, Mom never appeared particularly disturbed by it. She merely spoke slowly and gently to him, as if she were comforting a child.

Still, Dad's tendency to suffer from panic attacks meant that Mom always had part of her focus on him when he was around and I think that prevented her from letting herself relax completely. In the summer of 1958, when my father was in Chicago and we were in Colorado, Mom was noticeably happier and easier to be around.

Dad was always greatly affected by what was going on in the world. He read at least one newspaper every day and, once we owned a television, watched the news every night. Mom didn't pay any attention to current events. Most of it she considered too depressing. It wasn't that she focused on the positive as much as it was that she didn't acknowledge that there was anything all that important to get upset about. And she didn't want Paul or me to bring unhappiness into our home either.

Like Grandmother, she rarely needed to spell out her preferences: she let us know her thoughts by how she acted. If Paul or I brought up current events such as the Viet Nam War or civil rights or any other topic that had the potential of turning a conversation heated or morose, she quickly changed the subject with a perky tilt of her head and a steely cheerfulness in her voice. "Let's talk about something happy, shall we? Mary, how was your Girl Scout meeting this afternoon?" She also refused to let Paul or me bother her or Dad with any personal problems we might have had, any issues that, in her mind, we should be able to handle ourselves or better yet not have at all.

As I grew closer to marriageable age, Mom casually tutored me in the delicate art of "how to handle a husband." In other words, she affirmed that outright lying was okay if necessary and at a minimum it was perfectly acceptable and probably even admirable to withhold information that might upset men. Wives did this for their husband's benefit. A wife was not to deceive him for her own selfish interests. Withheld information could be as minor as the cost of new wallpaper for the dining room or as big as a child's experimentation with drugs.

As the years passed and no official changes were made to the ownership of the company, Mike and Dad finally had to admit that perhaps the owners had no intention of ever making them partners in the business. First Mike and then Dad decided they should move on. Unfortunately, neither of them was able to secure a new position in Hawaii. They would have to leave the islands.

Mike moved his family to Chicago, a city which, because of its location in the middle of the country, was in the 1950s rapidly becoming a center of new mail order businesses. He wanted to establish a mail-order insurance brokerage. His company would broker between large insurance companies like Mutual of New York and group associations such as the American Psychiatric Association. He asked Dad to go with him as his partner, to handle the administrative side of the business while Mike did the selling. But Dad remembered cold winters in Iowa and perhaps even the death of his father from the harsh weather and wanted something different for his own family. He wanted to find another paradise. If it couldn't be Hawaii, perhaps California would do.

Even at seven years old I think I realized on some level that this move would be a huge change for us, that it would be particularly upsetting for Dad and even cause him to have more of the attacks that upset me so much. I think I also realized and feared that the move would take yet more of Mom's attention away from Paul and me. I would have to take care of myself and my little brother, too, as best I could.

We moved to San Mateo, California. At least the weather was good, warm year round. It wasn't Hawaii, but it was the next best thing, my parents thought. Surely, Dad would be able to find an insurance industry position in such a booming state. We spent a month in San Mateo living in a small apartment complex with a lot of other families who were also kind of down on their luck. Every morning, Dad left our little apartment to search out insurance agencies that might need a good administrator. Mike had some family money on which to rely while he started his business in Chicago, but Dad had no such thing. He needed to find an established firm to join. He understood that his gift was administering insurance plans, not selling them as Mike could. They'd nicely complemented each other when working together in Hawaii. Now Mike was gone and Dad would have to find a company to join that had other good salesmen. Dad was able to make a sales staff look good because he backed up their work with quality service; that's what he wanted to continue to do. While he searched, Mom stayed home and tried to provide some semblance of normality for all of us.

And Paul and I did try to make the best of things in this world that seemed—irrespective of how good the weather was—very, very strange indeed. Although there were many children around our age to play with at the apartment complex, they too were taking on the fears and frustrations of their parents and took it out on the newest members of the group: my brother and me. We took the brunt of their ridicule and pranks.

If being taunted by other children weren't bad enough, I also had to face daily swimming lessons at an indoor community pool in San Mateo. I'd learned to swim at the Pacific Club in Honolulu at about the same time I'd learned how to walk, but I had never taken a formal swimming class and my stroke was more of a desperate dog paddle than anything as elegant as the Australian crawl. Still, I'd managed to adequately maneuver around the pool at the Pacific Club and the shallow edge of the Pacific Ocean off Waikiki Beach. The dog paddle kept my head above water and me relatively safe in the water. But Mom and Dad thought that as long as we were in California, Paul and I should learn to swim the right way, so they signed us up for a class. I found out what it was to have a really bad teacher and the swimming class reinforced what I was discovering about myself on the playground. I didn't fit in: I was too skinny, too brown and too stupid to learn.

One day our instructor decided it was time for us to learn how to dive. The class lined up, one child behind the other, from the edge of the pool's deep end to the back wall of the cavernous building that housed the Olympic-sized pool. The diving instructor worked with us one at a time and each student before me dove happily and courageously into the pool. When it was my turn the teacher, a boy probably just out of high school, told me to stand at the edge and curl my toes over the side. Then he bent me over at the waist as I held my arms over my head. Screaming, splashing children swarmed through the murky pool water below me and pushed each other around. There was no way I wanted to jump into the midst of them and certainly not head first. Kids waiting their turn in line behind me hopped up and down and urged me to hurry up.

My teacher was impatient with my hesitance. He pinched me hard through the thin fabric of my old bathing suit and leaned down close to my face. He smelled of chlorine and cigarettes.

"Go," he ordered, and pushed me just as I dug my feet into the cement and stiffened. I pushed back against his hands and tried to stand up.

I wanted to tell him that I couldn't dive that day and that I hadn't understood his instructions, that I wanted him to explain over again exactly how I was supposed to do it. But before I could get the words out, he shoved me forward just as I was pushing back against his hands. I hit the water with a smack. The pain shooting up my back and down my legs was bad, but not nearly as dreadful as the humiliation of my public belly flop.

I didn't tell Mom or Dad what had happened at the pool. They were proud that even though Dad was out of work and our financial situation was somewhat precarious they could still send Paul and me to swimming lessons. I didn't want to hurt their feelings. But I did complain about the pain in my back even though it had pretty much disappeared as soon as I climbed out of the water. The pain was gone, but not the humiliation and there was no way I was returning to those classes. Mom and Dad agreed to let me quit the lessons. I failed to learn how to do the Australian crawl that year or how to dive, but I discovered that I could get out of doing things I didn't want to do if I was sick or hurt. Mom and Dad seemed a bit relieved that they didn't have to pay for me to go to swimming lessons so I also assumed that it was easier for them if I kept them in the dark about the genuinely bad things that happened to me. I decided they were happier with me when I figured out my own answers and I never changed my mind about that—not for the rest of my childhood nor beyond.

Dad was unable to find work in California. Only one option made sense: he would go to work with Mike in Chicago. Mike offered to make Dad his partner, not just his employee, and together they would build the future they'd hoped for in Honolulu. As much as Dad hated the idea of returning to the cold and damp winters of the Midwest and feared that owning a business with a friend would be the demise of that friendship, he decided for the sake of his family that he had no other choice. He would travel ahead of us to Chicago to find a place for us to live. Mom, Paul and I would spend the summer with Grandmother in Poudre Canyon.

FOUR

Brief Reprieve

T he summer of 1958 was a comma between two turbulent phrases in my family's life. With Grandmother in a little cabin in a tucked-away canyon, my brother, my mother and I enjoyed a brief reprieve.

Although I was too young to understand at the time, Mom needed the refuge of the canyon as much and perhaps more than Paul and I did. She had loved her life in Hawaii: the sun, the warmth, the good women friends. What great fun to be a young person in a tropical paradise just after the war when the country was optimistic again and the future looked bright. Mom also had to miss the very special relationship she'd developed with Bill. I think Bill made her feel witty and beautiful and special, three qualities Mom never would have applied to herself. Now she was leaving all of that to go to Chicago, a place that couldn't have been more different from Hawaii in character than another country would have been. In fact, Mom would have embraced the opportunity, relished the novelty, of living in a foreign country. Chicago, however, must have felt to her merely damp and colorless and cold.

But Mom wouldn't have complained about the move to anyone and especially not to Dad. She never would have undermined Dad's confidence or his new professional endeavors. So she pasted on a smile and promised Paul and me that we were in for a grand adventure in the dynamic city of Chicago. She reassured Dad in their weekly phone conversations that they'd made the right decision. Moving to Chicago would be fun and the new company most definitely would succeed.

The last time Mom had been in Colorado for any length of time was the year she'd stayed with Grandmother and Jack on the Roberts' ranch during the war. Now she could renew her friendship with Catherine and Evan as well as spend time with her mother. It was because of that summer with Grandmother that Mom and I retained fond memories of Poudre Park and Colorado.

Whenever we went anywhere that summer, Grandmother always drove. Grandmother careened around the curves of the canyon like, Mom said, "a bat out of hell." She admonished Grandmother over and over to slow down, that she'd kill us all or at the very least, make Paul and me sick. And we did get carsick. Still it didn't slow Grandmother down. She'd pull over to the side of the road, let us throw up in the bushes and then continue at the same speed as before. After we'd thrown up on almost every trip we made up or down the canyon, she let us in on a little trick she'd suddenly remembered. If she safety-pinned brown paper to the insides of our T-shirts, she said, we would not get carsick. *Anything*, Paul and I thought, *anything to keep from throwing up*. From that day on we wore the brown paper every time we got into the car with Grandmother; the paper covered our stomachs and chests and made crinkly noises whenever we moved. When we didn't throw up we thought the paper was working and when we did get sick we figured something had happened to over-ride the paper's power. Mom only laughed at all of this and shook her head. "Mother, you'll never change," she'd say.

And Grandmother would counter, "Why should I? I know this road like the back of my hand," and, "Children, you don't mind, do you?"

"Noooo," we'd answer as we clung to the arm rests in the back seat.

Sometimes Mom took the car and drove up to the Roberts Ranch to spend a day with Catherine alone. Even though Paul and I begged her to take us along, wanting every possible opportunity to play cowboys and Indians on the ranch, Mom would look at Grandmother in a way that conveyed how badly she needed time to herself and Grandmother would take Paul and me by the hand and lead us off to the river, saying something like, "We'll go to the ranch tomorrow, but today we've got some fishing to do."

During that summer, Mom spent most of her time reading or resting. Sometimes after lunch, especially if the day was rainy, she disappeared into the small guest bedroom she shared with Paul—I slept with Grandmother in Grandmother's double bed—and we wouldn't see her again until supper. Those were times when Grandmother played quiet games with us—gin rummy or hearts—or sat in a chair next to us as Paul and I spread Grandmother's shells or buttons over the rug and made up stories about them. If we talked too loudly she'd hush us, whispering that Mom needed her rest.

As the summer wore on Mom didn't ask for so much time away from us. She laughed more and napped less. And to Paul's and my delight, she often joined us for games of gin rummy or hearts or spread out on the floor with us and listened to the stories we concocted about the buttons and shells.

Mom had an easy relationship with the canyon that summer. She leaned into the mountains and evergreens and river, soaking up their exuberance and freshness and strength. She breathed deeply and smiled a lot.

But when we left the canyon and moved to Illinois, something in her changed. Though she was rested and ready to lead us into this new adventure she'd been promising us, once we got to Chicago she was also sadder and quieter than she'd been in either Hawaii or Colorado. And something between her and Grandmother changed too. In Colorado, they never picked at one another or fought, but they did later when Grandmother stayed with us each winter in Illinois. I thought it was my fault, because they mostly argued about me.

FIVE

I'm Fine, Thank You

We lived in the inner city of Chicago briefly until my parents could afford to buy a small bungalow in the northern suburbs. Because of the quality of its schools, they stretched themselves financially to buy a house on what is referred to as the North Shore. For my parents, a good education wasn't merely a priority, it was a necessity for children—another insurance policy against poverty and suffering.

On the outside, life looked pretty good for the Porter family. We had a house of our own, a bit more money to spend, Mike and Dad were making a go of their new business venture and Mom went back to school to be trained and certified as a first-grade teacher. But there were signs that all was not okay under the surface. Paul got into fist fights with neighborhood boys on a fairly regular basis and I had panic attacks whenever I tried to spend the night away from home. During the fourth and fifth grades, I could never get through an overnight without waking my friend's parents and asking if they'd please call my dad. I wanted to go home. Almost every weekend I'd try again, hoping that *this* time it would be different. It never was. I didn't feel safe away from my own bed or my own mother and father. Still, we assured ourselves and each other that all was *just fine*. We looked good on the outside and in those days, looking good mattered.

The year of 1962 was an especially bad year for my family and me; it became harder to pretend that everything was fine. Mom had just finished her training at National College and was ready to begin teaching again for the first time since before I was born. In June, she found a lump in her right breast and was scheduled for surgery two days later. When Mom and Dad sat Paul and me down and told us Mom might have breast cancer and would need surgery to find out for sure, a wave of panic far worse than any I'd ever experienced washed over me. I wanted them to reassure us that Mom would be okay, that she wouldn't die, that our lives would go on as before. I wanted to know the details, what the doctors were saying and what the risks were, but instead of having a discussion between the four of us that might have helped to alleviate my fears—and probably Paul's as well—they matter-of-factly pronounced that until we knew for sure whether Mom did or did not have cancer, there was no need to discuss it any further. We were to go on as usual, acting and thinking as if nothing had changed. "The discussion is closed," they said, before Paul or I could utter a word.

Dad retreated outside to do some yard work. Mom took off in the car to do the weekly grocery shopping and Paul, after tossing me a quizzical look, left to meet his best friend to do whatever it was the two of them did when they got together.

For a moment I sat by myself in the vacated living room, engulfed in barely contained terror and wondering what I could do to make the awful feelings go away. Then I remembered something. When Dad arrived home from work stressed or worried, Mom always offered him a drink. Dad liked vodka, and it worked for him. In fact, it worked very quickly. One or two drinks and he grew mellow, laughing with Mom about his day, teasing us kids. There must be magic in alcohol. Perhaps if it helped Dad it would make me feel better, too. But I had to act fast. Dad or Paul and his friend could walk through the door at any moment.

Mom and Dad kept the liquor in the linen closet off their bedroom. I grabbed a small brown paper lunch bag from a drawer in the kitchen, rushed down the short hall to the linen closet and stuck the smallest bottle I could find—a bottle of vodka—into the bag. I lifted up my T-shirt and stuck the bag into the waistband of my shorts. Then I went to the back door and called out to Dad that I was going for a walk. Without turning from the hedge he was clipping, he waved his right arm in agreement and I was off.

The school that I'd attended from third through fifth grade, Crow Island Elementary, was only three blocks southeast of our house. Holding my hand against the bottle under my T-shirt so it wouldn't slip out and taking long determined strides, I walked to the school. I went directly to the large swing set on the far side of the building and, looking around, made sure I was alone. Even though I no longer attended Crow Island, I returned to the school often on weekend days or after school when there were few kids around. Unlike the junior high that I now attended that was closed in by residences on every side, Crow Island was surrounded by open fields and wooded areas. I liked to sit on the swings by myself and think. So, on this day, with bottle in hand, I sat on a swing, steadied myself with my feet and without taking the bottle from its paper bag, unscrewed the top. I had a feeling that vodka wouldn't taste very good by itself. I remembered Dad liked to drink what he called *vodka tonics*. For an instant, I wished I'd brought a bottle of tonic with me, but I hadn't so I screwed up my nerve, held my breath and took a quick swig. At first it burned my mouth and throat, but surprisingly left quite a pleasant after-taste and a warm feeling in my stomach. *Not bad*, I thought. I took another sip. And another. After a few more sips, waiting several seconds in between each one as I kicked at the ground and swayed back and forth on the swing's canvas seat, the warmth in my stomach spread to my arms and legs, neck and head. Standing up a little unsteadily, I recapped the bottle and stuck it back into my waistband. I had to admit Mom and Dad were onto something. I felt amazingly better than when I left the house. Calm had replaced panic. In fact, as I reviewed what Mom and Dad had told us just an hour or so before, I had a strange sense that all would work out okay. Could alcohol actually do this for someone? As I walked home, I felt surprisingly happy. I'd found a solution—one I was pretty sure I'd turn to again.

Back then doctors never wasted any time getting women with lumps in their breasts into surgery. Once the patient was on the operating table and under anesthesia, the mass was removed and sent immediately to the lab while everyone waited and the patient remained unconscious. If the lump was malignant, the surgeon removed the breast, the tissue around it and the corresponding lymph nodes. This was what happened to Mom. She awoke to a lopsided chest and I became aware that my parents were not immortal and that my mother might die.

I sat in the hospital waiting room with a very nervous father for what seemed like hours, waiting for Mom to get out of surgery and to find out whether she had cancer. Finally, the surgeon appeared and said Mom was back in her room and we could see her briefly. He also told us that Mom did have cancer and that he had removed her right breast and the lymph nodes under her right arm. His words didn't prepare me for the shock of seeing my mother lying flat on her back in a metal-sided hospital bed, her face gray, eyes closed, a reddish substance staining her neck and one side of her chest flat. Black spots appeared before my eyes and I had a growing sense that the room was tipping. I grabbed at Dad's arm and started to pull him from the room. "I think I'm going to faint," I said.

Dad handed me off to a woman in white who'd been standing just inside the door to Mom's room. The nurse led me to a little room where she sat me down and directed me, not unkindly, to put my head between my legs. It was the first time I'd come close to fainting and the feeling of losing control over myself frightened me almost as much as seeing my mother lying so still and gray.

After spending much of the summer recovering from surgery, Mom began her teaching job in September as planned. I was used to having a stay-at-home mother, but now, when I wanted her constant presence in order to be reassured that she was okay, she was almost never available. I called her at school so often that she finally forbade me to call her at all. I was bereft, left with a sense that there was no longer any security in my life. I felt I'd lost my mother when I needed her more than ever.

Later that same year during a Christmas concert at my junior high, someone in front of me fainted, slumping into a body next to her. Then another girl passed out. And a boy. It was like a game of human dominoes. When I saw those kids fainting I started to faint too. I stopped singing, inadvertently held my breath and—as I had in the hospital—saw black spots before my eyes. Visions of Mom unconscious in her hospital bed flooded my mind. No matter how hard I tried, how much I concentrated on the words I was supposed to be singing, I couldn't make the vision of Mom lying so still in that bed go away. I managed to get off the stage before actually passing out, but the experience left me convinced that I had no more control over my own body than I had over my mother's body. Suddenly life seemed very precarious. None of us had control over our bodies. They could become sick or act involuntarily when we were least prepared for it. Our bodies could cause us pain or fear or embarrassment.

Shortly after the school concert, our family flew to Mexico for a Christmas vacation. It was my first time out of the country. We stayed at what was for us an exotic resort on the beach in Acapulco, took a bus ride up narrow, winding roads to the tiny mountain town of Taxco and on Christmas Day watched Mexican men, women and children walk on their knees to a large cathedral just outside Mexico City. Children younger than me begged in the streets at night and there were overcrowded tent cities and dusty, dirty, poverty-stricken villages. On the trip to Taxco, my brother and I suffered motion sickness and instead of brown paper bags lovingly pinned beneath our shirts, hypodermic needles were shoved into our skinny arms by an American doctor on the bus who, unfortunately for us, happened to have his black medical bag with him. In Acapulco I developed a gut-wrenching case of Montezuma's revenge from—my parents thought—eating fresh lobster cooked on a fish-peddler's portable grill.

When we returned from Mexico shortly after New Year's Day, 1963, Mom went back to teaching her first-grade class. She looked strong and healthy every morning when she left for school. I, on the other hand, was too sick to return to my classes. Even though Mom was the one diagnosed with cancer, I was the one who felt sick all the time.

One day when I was still home from school, a friend phoned to tell me that one of our classmates had suffered a *grand mal* seizure in the lunchroom in front of the entire Skokie Junior High student body. I slid the rest of the way into mental collapse. Cancer had attacked Mom with no warning or permission; I, and many of my fellow vocalists, had fainted on stage in front of an audience; a family vacation that was supposed to be energizing and relaxing and fun had made me sick. And now a classmate's body had betrayed him in the most horrific way, too. How would he ever live down such a mortifying experience? How would *I* ever live it down if something like that happened to *me*? And it could. Nothing was under our control, not even our own bodies.

Illness allowed me to remain in the safety of my room and my bed. I didn't feel capable of doing anything: school, homework, connecting with friends, participating in activities, helping Mom and Dad around the house. Whenever I tried to get up, to move about, to go outside, a sense of helplessness invaded me, black spots appeared before my eyes and the world spun. Though I lived with constant guilt that I was making life much more difficult for my already worried parents, I couldn't help myself. I wanted to stay in my room, preferably in my bed, forever if possible. I didn't want to be sick, but I did want to be safe. I figured my bed was the safest place to be. I couldn't fall down if I was lying down and I had no faith my body would hold me up.

Luckily for me, my Poudre Canyon grandmother had just arrived for her yearly winter visit. I didn't have to be strong anymore. I could let down physically, mentally and emotionally. She'd take care of me and I figured that, unlike Mom or Dad, Grandmother wouldn't force me to do anything I didn't think I could do. I was right. The first action she took was to tell my mother in no uncertain terms that I wouldn't be returning to school until I was good and well, which clearly I was not. Mom was dubious as I no longer had a fever, inflamed throat or bad headache. Mom thought my complaints of weakness and dizziness were more a ruse to stay home from school than actual illness, but she was too busy and concerned about her own health to argue. She deferred to Grandmother and turned my care over to her.

While I thought lying in bed for the rest of my life was a satisfactory option, Grandmother didn't agree. She wanted me to get well mentally as well as physically. After about a month of her gentle attention, I did feel better. With the return of my physical health, Grandmother devised a plan to recover my emotional health as well.

Like a formally trained behavior modification counselor, she used reinforcement to change my behavior. Because it was close to Valentine's Day and they were readily available, Grandmother chose the heart-shaped, pink, white and yellow candies—the ones with sayings on them like *4Ever* or *Love Me* or *Be Mine*—as the reward.

The first time Grandmother gave me a candy heart, she was trying to get me to sit up and swing my legs over the side of the bed without help. Even getting up to go to the bathroom or take a bath was an ordeal that required a family member for me to lean against. "Come on, Mary," she urged quietly. "Just try. You don't have to do anything but sit on the edge of the bed for a few minutes."

"I can't, Grandma. I'm too weak. Let me wait until tomorrow. I'll feel better then."

"Mary, you say the same thing every day. Today's the day. I have something here that will give you a little extra strength." She pulled a pink cardboard box from her pocket and flipped open the lid. I turned to see what she had for me.

When I realized that all she had in the palm of her hand were a couple of small candy hearts, I turned away. "Those aren't going to help. It's just candy."

"Yes, it's just candy, but sugar will give you a little jolt of energy. Just like it's impossible for me to go into a diabetic coma when I have a bit of sugar, it will be impossible for you to faint if you have some."

I thought she might be pulling my leg, but as far as I knew she'd never lied to me and her reasoning made a little sense. I ate the candy hearts and hesitantly swung my legs over the side of the bed. I sat there for a moment, both hands gripping the edge of the mattress, waiting for the familiar black spots and dizziness. Nothing happened. Just as she said, the candy worked.

Soon I depended on the *magic* in those little energy pills like I'd depended on the brown paper pinned to my T-shirt to keep me from throwing up that summer in Colorado. Eventually, I moved from sitting on the side of the bed to walking around the room and to reaching the bathroom down the hall by myself. I once again ate meals with the family and sat with them in the evenings to watch television.

Grandmother continued to use the candies to give me the little boost of energy I thought I needed to keep from feeling faint. Sometimes she waved a small vial of smelling salts under my nose, because I was as much afraid of the sensations that preceded a fainting episode as I was of actually blacking out. The smelling salts made those initial feelings go away.

As early spring broke into the cold Illinois winter and the memories of what had happened to my classmate in the school lunchroom faded, Grandmother often lured me out of the house with the assurance that candy hearts and smelling salts were always at hand. Eventually, I could get into the car, at first lying down on the back seat and later sitting up in the front. After I became comfortable in all the rooms of the house and the family car, Grandmother took me to church. After a few aborted trial runs, I was able to sit through hour-long church services with her. Soon after that, I was strong enough to return to school just in time to participate in my eighth-grade graduation and also, reluctantly, to say goodbye to Grandmother when she flew back to Colorado for the summer.

When I was fourteen and before she had the opportunity to visit us again, Grandmother had a serious stroke. In an instant she went from living independently in her rustic mountain home to needing full-time nursing care in a Fort Collins residential facility. Mom and Dad decided that Paul and I could not see her again. It would be too difficult for us and for her, they said. Let her be remembered by her grandchildren for who she'd been, not for who she is now, they insisted. Go on with your lives, enjoy yourselves, Mom told us, because that's what Grandmother would want us to do.

That time of my life is pretty much a blur to me now. I wish I could remember more clearly an experience as big as being told that my beloved grandmother had suffered a stroke, was incapacitated and living in a nursing home. I should be able to remember wanting to see her and comfort her and do everything for her as she'd done for me, but I don't. I only remember that part of me shut down and I felt an almost physical stiffening, as if I was bodily forcing myself to release my grandmother and resolving to go through whatever I'd have to go through from then on without her. But beneath my resolve, buried so deep within me it was as if it didn't exist at all, was not only grief but guilt—massive, excruciating, staggering guilt—because not only would I be going on without *her*, I was agreeing to let her go on without *me*.

I think that when Mom and Dad made the pronouncement that we would no longer be seeing her, I simply shut a door on Grandmother and her situation and never opened it again. I buried it so well and so deeply that when my grandmother finally did die seven or so years after her stroke, I hardly thought about it. I didn't grieve her death, nor did I attend the simple memorial service held for her in Fort Collins by Catherine and Evan Roberts and Mom and her two brothers. By that time I was in college and my mother told me not to bother to come. I didn't argue with her. I merely went on with my life as if nothing had changed.

And nothing *had* changed, not at her death at least. The changes and the damage had occurred seven years earlier when she suffered the stroke and I was prevented from seeing her. When Mom, Uncle Gerald and Uncle Bob decided to sell Grandmother's house in the canyon a couple of years after her stroke, my last link to her was cut.

When I lost my grandmother, I projected some of the good feelings I'd had about her onto nature. Despite periods when I was afraid to leave my house, it wasn't the out-of-doors, the natural world that frightened me. I never felt any *thing* in the environment would hurt me or couldn't be trusted. What I couldn't trust was what I might do around the other humans that inhabited the earth. What if I inadvertently did or said something that embarrassed or shamed me? But when I was outside and alone, I could stop worrying about that and focus instead on the beauty around me.

Spending much of the first eight years of my life outdoors in untamed, tropical Hawaii initiated my sense that the whole of the world—plants and trees and rocks and dirt, even bugs and bees and birds—was as safe and familiar as the four walls of the bedroom I shared with my little brother. This belief was strengthened in the lull between the sorrow of leaving Hawaii and the shock of arriving in downtown Chicago—the summer we spent with Grandmother in Poudre Park. After Hawaii and California and before Chicago there was Grandmother and the canyon: calm and stable, beautiful and safe. And ever since that time, my feelings for Grandmother and my feelings for the natural world have blended together like a long-simmering pot of vegetable stew.

Somehow I got the sense that if Grandmother could comfort me when I needed comforting or heal me when I needed healing, then so could nature if Grandmother wasn't around. Perhaps because I'd attended church with Grandmother and found some sort of healing there, God was also present in the grandmother/nature mix. Whenever I was in beautiful, natural surroundings I sensed I wasn't alone: a nurturing presence—whether Grandmother or God or both—was always with me.

I went on to high school the autumn after Grandmother's stroke.

New Trier East was a huge high school—over 4,000 students—and well known as one of the best in the country. It was highly competitive and many of the 99 per cent of its students who went on to college attended top-rated, Ivy League institutions. But for me, the school was often intolerable. The noise, the kids, the narrow hallways with their long rows of gray lockers stacked one on top of the other made me want to run away, to get outside so I could breathe deeply again. I needed a wild and free place where I could feel the air going in and out of my lungs. I'd cut class and walk the several blocks to Lake Michigan where I'd descend the winding path from the top of the cliff down through the shaded woods and out onto the secluded beach. From there, I'd climb the steps to the pier and walk out to the end where I'd stand looking over the choppy water with its little white caps and breathe in and out, in and out, as I squeezed the cold metal bars of the railing.

I looked for similar connections with nature in places like the Forest Preserve that bordered Winnetka and at Boot Shay Resort in Wisconsin where my family and I spent our summers and on the farms of Iowa during my college years. When George and I moved from suburban Illinois to Iowa, I was the one who made the decision to live in the country outside the city limits of Cedar Rapids. I reached out to the natural world for healing and comfort like others would reach out to a person and like I had once reached out to Grandmother. But its reach back to me always felt halfway and puny. The connection was never quite there, not really—not until I discovered the Poudre Canyon again.

S I X

Coping Skills

The natural world and alcohol became my two very best friends the summer after Grandmother had her stroke. Whenever I was leaving for one of my frequent solitary bike rides to the forest preserve or the beach, I'd take one of the small bottles of vodka or gin or whiskey from the liquor cabinet and stick it into my book bag. After that first day on the playground, I'd include a can of cola or ginger ale to cut the bitterness of the booze, then I'd put the book bag into the wire basket attached to the handlebars of my bicycle and ride off in the direction of my destination for that day. Knowing I had the bottle with me gave me a little twinge of guilt, but a stronger sense of anticipation. I knew that once I was able to have a sip or two of the forbidden drink that Mom and Dad used to ease *their* stress, I'd feel better, too.

Once I arrived at the beach or the forest preserve, I'd lean my bike against a tree or wall, find a secluded spot away from the prying eyes of lifeguards or visitors, spread out a towel if I was at the beach or sit on top of a picnic table if I was at the forest preserve and take out my stash.

I'd drink about one-quarter of the soft drink and then I'd surreptitiously pour some of the stolen alcohol into the can. I'd swirl it around carefully so as not to spill any and sip the drink as I looked out over the water. As it had the first time I'd drunk it, the alcohol always produced a warmth that spread from the center of my body outward to my extremities and head and led quickly to an overall general feeling of well-being. All was right with my world. Or so it seemed.

Of course, nothing was really right with my world. My favorite grandmother was seriously ill and I was forbidden to see her; I was intimidated by most of the kids at school; I was terrified my mother was dying of cancer and they weren't telling me so and I was hurt and confused by the clear pulling away from me that Mom had done since my illness and Grandmother's visit. Whenever I tried to talk to her, tell her about my day at school and ask about hers, she looked impatient, as if she wanted me to hurry up, say what I wanted to say and leave her alone. I'd hear her on the phone with her friends, laughing and talking as if she had all the time in the world, but when it came to talking with me she never had the time. It was as if I bored her. On the rare occasions when Mom and I did talk, she quickly directed the subject away from me and instead wanted to tell me about what her friends' daughters were up to. She mostly liked to talk about the Kent girls. According to my mother, Gail and Alice Kent were beautiful and smart and accomplished. Sometimes I think Mom talked about them as a way to get rid of me because whenever she did, it was only a matter of minutes before I'd leave the room.

Paul was pulling away from me, too. Whenever I tried to start a conversation with him he'd brush me off quickly, making it very clear that he wanted nothing to do with me. One day when Mom and Dad were gone, I discovered Paul and a couple of his friends in the kitchen roasting banana peels. When I asked what they were doing, they wouldn't look at me and Paul told me to mind my own business and forcefully ordered me out of the kitchen. The unfamiliar look in his eyes scared me, so I did what I was told—I left the kitchen. I knew I wouldn't tell on him to Mom or Dad. I was too loyal and loved him too much. It never occurred to me that he was merely trying to deal with all the confusing changes in our lives just as I was. I used alcohol, he experimented with drugs. But at the time, I didn't understand his behavior and was worried and hurt.

Almost since birth, I'd considered Paul my best friend and favorite playmate. I didn't miss having lots of other friends because I always had my brother. We never tired of playing hundreds of games of what we called "little men" on his bedroom floor or racing each other up the stairs to drop our stuffed animals down the laundry chute and down again to "rescue" them from the clothes basket in the basement. When the winter sidewalks were icy, we roller-skated on the basement's cement floor. On family car trips, we huddled in the back of the station wagon with comic books and bags of candy.

Perhaps because Paul and I had been so close for so long, I recognized the change in him sooner than Mom and Dad did. When he was thirteen and I was fifteen, I realized that my gentle and playful brother had been replaced by a distant, insolent and sometimes even violent boy. One time, as I passed him on the stairs, Paul pushed me and I almost lost my balance. I didn't confront him again after that and spent more and more time either in my room or away from the house.

I populated my world with made-up friends and an imaginary family, people who loved me and wouldn't hurt me, people I could depend on to be there for me when I needed them. The more Paul and Mom distanced themselves from me, the more I went into my imagination. Dad had never been particularly available to me. He was of the generation that believed his most important duty was to provide his family a financially stable life. And that's exactly what he worked hardest to do. Mom didn't want us to bother him with any of what she considered our inconsequential concerns and so we didn't. Before I realized exactly what I was doing, I had created an imaginary world that was more important to me than my real world. With alcohol and my fantasies, I felt I was coping just fine. I'd be okay, I told myself, even without my brother, grandmother, mom or dad.

When I was sick, Grandmother had taught me how to imaginatively leave behind the feelings I didn't like with such questions as, "We're going on a trip. Where should we go?" I'd think hard and come up with the name of a country I'd perhaps seen on television or read about in a book. Once I'd picked a place, Grandmother would ask another question: "So we're off to Paris. What shall we pack in our suitcases?" And we'd come up with an entire list of items we'd need on our trip. In her little room in the basement or in my pink-and-white room at the top of the house, we plotted our travels and made up our adventures. I'd forget how lousy I felt or how worried I was and before we knew it, Mom was calling us to dinner.

By teaching me how to use my imagination to escape painful and difficult situations, Grandmother gave me a method of dealing with adversity that would serve me for better or worse much of my life.

When Grandmother left in the spring of 1963 and had the stroke that would end our relationship, I continued to make up stories. At first, the stories I made up were similar to the ones Grandmother and I had concocted: stories about trips or about how she was healthy and would be coming back in the winter as usual. Before I knew it, entire worlds were springing to life from my imagination. Suddenly I was the sought-after friend, the popular and very bendable cheerleader, the honor roll student beloved by all the teachers. When the couple of friends I did have started to date but no boy asked me out, I simply made up a boyfriend.

I found a photo of a particularly good-looking male cousin, named him John Decker and told my friends I'd met him on summer vacation at Boot Shay Resort in Wisconsin. (It was true that we went to Boot Shay every summer.) I was pleasantly surprised that my made-up boyfriend not only fooled my girlfriends, but impressed them too. Making up stories for Leslie, Debbie and Karen about John Decker's nightly telephone calls and promises to visit me as soon as he could was as easy to pull off as planning imaginary trips with Grandmother. I became so good at telling John Decker stories that sometimes a thought would cross my mind such as *I wonder what John Decker is doing today* or, *I wonder if John misses me as much as I miss him.* It would take a minute or two before I'd realize there wasn't any real John. John wasn't doing anything today. And of course John didn't miss me—he didn't exist.

When Beatlemania hit the United States during my freshman year in high school, I easily transferred my fantasies about John Decker and me to fantasies about George Harrison and me. George was my favorite Beatle and I made up an entire love affair between us. I might not feel loved or appreciated or wanted by anyone else, but I was wanted and appreciated and loved, even desired, by George.

Instead of keeping my fantasies in my head as I always had, I started to write them down. I wrote them in an inexpensive, college-lined, spiral-bound notebook that I called my Beatle book. I ripped photos of George Harrison out of movie magazines and put them up all over my room. When Mom wasn't interested in hearing about my day, I'd tell myself, *Well, George will want to hear about it.* I'd take out my notebook and write down the words I imagined George and I would say to one another on the phone.

I wrote the love story of George Harrison and Mary Porter at every opportunity: during study halls and after school when I was supposed to be doing homework; in bed at night when Mom and Dad thought I was sleeping; and even sometimes in the bathtub during a long Sunday afternoon soak. In my fiction, I was sorting out my feelings and experimenting with what I thought adult love might be like. I was also learning how to develop characters, plot a story and write a scene. I was discovering how much I loved the process of writing itself and believing myself to be pretty good at it, I was also developing some self-esteem. I'd found a talent and a passion, I thought.

Deep in the throes of budding pubescent sexuality but having no *real* boyfriend, I *experimented* with George Harrison. I wrote about the other Beatles, too, and paired them up with my girlfriends. Expanding on what Grandmother had taught me, I made up an entire world inhabited by interesting people leading exciting lives and I wrote it all down. In my fictionalized world, no one, including me, suffered the consequences of their actions or had to do anything real, like go to school, deal with parents or work for a living. We hung out in their hotel suite between gigs, met with journalists and photographers for photo shoots and my friends and I even attended their rehearsals or watched from backstage during their concerts. Because of our special friendship with the Beatles, their entourage treated us like royalty and their fans envied us.

Writing the Beatle story seemed like a pretty harmless escape at the time. After all, I wasn't really in a Liverpool pub or a New York hotel suite with John, Paul, Ringo and George, or any man for that matter. Even though I later wrote steamy scenes about having sex with George Harrison, I wasn't *really* having sex with anyone. When I worked on the Beatle book, my real world with all its questions, concerns, fears and ineptitudes slipped away and I entered a fictional world of my own making. Because I was acting out on the page, I didn't have to act out in real life.

Writing about my escapades with the Beatles made me happy. I loved to make up scenes about George grabbing my hand and pulling me through crowds of screaming fans. Tucked within the crook of his shoulder, I was safe. As his favorite, I had something the other fans didn't have. On the page, I made myself feel special and the feeling sometimes carried over into my real life, too.

In the beginning, the sexual relationship between George and me was merely bits and pieces scattered throughout the story, but as I continued to write, it morphed into the focus. I made my story into what I assumed, given my age at the time and my naiveté, would be the perfect love affair.

I wrote feverishly, exploring the experiences and sensations I imagined occurred between men and women. When I'd look at a photograph of George Harrison in a magazine, one of those up-close photos of just his face, I'd run my fingers over the grainy image of his mouth and wonder what it would feel like to be kissed by those lips. Then I'd set up a scene in my book where that would happen. We'd be sitting on a couch in a room somewhere, side by side, and he'd be telling me about his latest fight with his real world girlfriend Patti and I'd reach up and stroke his cheek and he'd turn and look at me with those liquid brown eyes and stop what he was saying and dip his head and kiss me softly on the lips. I'd write it all down, what happened, how I felt. And I wouldn't stop there. I'd write about how he'd pull back with a shocked look on his face, how he was appalled that he had done something like that. He'd mumble something about my being too young and about how he was involved with Patti. But, as I also wrote, he couldn't help himself because I was too beautiful and kind and perfect.

As my body rounded and softened and my breasts became painfully sensitive, I wrote about those changes that I couldn't talk about with anyone. I wrote that I could talk to George about them and that he assured me that what I was going through was perfectly normal. I was growing up and that made him want me all the more. It was the fictional George Harrison who woke up my sexuality, who introduced me to the pleasures of touch between a man and a woman. Instead of just me being the one to stroke my arms and neck and face or touch my breasts and hair and the soft secret spot *down there*, I wrote detailed scenes in which George Harrison did the stroking and the touching. I wrote about how I thought he would look if he stood naked in front of me.

Even though I knew I wasn't ready to have real sex with a real boy, it somehow seemed okay to fantasize about it with a Beatle and write down my fantasies. I didn't feel guilty about what I was writing because I told myself it was just fiction, even if the sensations the words created in me were very real. Later, I did feel guilty about what I had written—really guilty. It took me years to realize there were benefits in the use of writing as a coping mechanism; that the Beatle book wasn't a sign of perversion or mental illness as I was later led to believe.

I never shared what I wrote in my Beatle book with anyone, not even my two *real* best friends, until I read it to Eileen Miller. I think I decided it was time to share it and I picked Eileen to read it to because I wanted real answers and feedback. I wanted to know if what I was writing had any truth to it, if couples who loved each other experienced the feelings that I wrote about when they made love. I think I wanted someone to assure me that my physical feelings and emotional longings were normal, understandable.

I decided that Eileen should be the first one to read my book because she was a young wife with a baby and was very different from my peers, who had no sexual experience, and from my parents who'd had sex at least twice but didn't seem sexual at all. I was pretty sure Eileen shared my interest in sex and that she might be willing to talk to me about it after she'd read the book. Yes, Eileen would be the perfect first reader of my novel.

But I'd have to read it to her, because Eileen was blind. My friend Leslie had introduced me to Eileen and her husband Robert when they moved into a small bungalow not far from my house. They often asked me to stay with their baby, Timmy, when they went out and before long I was in the habit of stopping by their house almost every day on my way home from school.

I looked up to Eileen because, even though she was smart, sophisticated and worldly—she'd studied French in Paris for a year—she was also kind and fair. I trusted her; she made me feel welcome and needed. Whenever I showed up at her house, she'd fling open the door, reach out her arms to me and quickly pull me in, as if there was no one she'd rather visit with at that moment than me. Perhaps if I read her the Beatle book, I thought, she'd give me some advice on writing or let me know whether she thought I had any talent.

I loved visiting Eileen at her little house on Elm Street. As I chattered away, she'd go about her housework, her lively and sensitive fingers never still. Every so often she'd throw back her head and laugh at something I'd said, as if she couldn't help herself. She enchanted me and I think I delighted her.

I hungered for the acceptance and understanding she provided. Eileen gave me what I needed most at the time: attention and the sense that I was okay just the way I was. I hoped that, in return, I helped Eileen smooth out some of the difficulties of being a visually impaired mother caring for her first and sighted child.

The day I read Eileen my Beatle book was a typical day shortly before the Christmas holidays in 1964. I stopped by her house as usual on my way home from school. Happy as always to see me, she told me to sit and tell her all about my day as she started potatoes for dinner. Timmy was sleeping in his crib down the hall; Robert was still at work. The late afternoon light slanted through the crisp white kitchen curtains and illuminated the spiral notebook with its somewhat battered red cover lying open in front of me on the yellow Formica table top.

Eileen agreed to listen to me read the story as she prepared the potatoes. I felt at home in her kitchen and safe in her presence. I had no premonition that I was about to make a huge mistake.

I glanced briefly at Eileen's slim back turned from me as she ran water into a pot and carried it over to the stove using both hands. She set it carefully onto a burner and turned a knob. A blue flame flashed beneath the pot. "Turn it to the left a little, Eileen," I suggested.

"Thanks." She returned to the sink and her potatoes. "I'm ready now. Let's hear it." She peeled and I read. The notebook contained over 200 pages of words written out in my round and swirly cursive. I didn't look up. I barely stopped even to breathe. As I read, page after page, I could feel more than see her movements slow. As my voice droned on, she stopped what she was doing at the sink and came to sit across from me at the table. I was afraid to look at her. I was beginning to sense I'd made a terrible mistake. The words I was reading sounded harsh and brittle as they reverberated off the pale yellow kitchen walls. I'd never read them out loud before. In fact, I'd never read them at all before. I'd been writing too furiously, moving from one scene to another. Now, as I read the book for the first time, aloud to someone else, it sounded disgusting, even sleazy to me.

I wanted to stop. I didn't want to hear my voice reading the Beatle book anymore. I felt it didn't belong in Eileen's pretty and spotless kitchen. My face felt hot, like the flame beneath the potatoes, but I couldn't make myself stop. I just kept on, reading one dreadful word after another, until Eileen reached for me across the table. Her palm landed on my wrist.

"Mary, don't. I can't listen to this any longer."

I stopped reading and looked down at the table, at her small hand with its long sensitive fingers resting on my thin wrist.

"You should not be writing this kind of thing, Mary," Eileen said, almost in a whisper.

My eyes blurred with tears. Horrified, I realized I was about to cry.

"Why did you write this?" Her words came out clipped and tight. She sounded more like my mother than Eileen. "Why would you assume you could read this to me?"

I stared down at my notebook and said nothing. I wanted to move my hand from beneath hers, but I couldn't make myself do it.

"What could you possibly think of me if you can write this and then read it to me? Do you think I'm the kind of woman who likes this stuff?"

I was confused. Why would Eileen say that? I was reading it to her so she'd understand *me*, so she would hear me like no one else seemed to be able to anymore.

"No …" I began, but couldn't continue. I didn't know what to say. Alarmed, I realized she was misjudging what I'd written. I had tried to portray the love and sex as something beautiful, but the words sounded dirty when I read them out loud. Horrified, I suddenly realized that she now thought I was implying that she was the type of woman who liked trashy novels. Shame washed over me. Not only had I embarrassed myself, but I had somehow hurt her, too. Clearly I'd misjudged her—she wasn't the worldly and sophisticated woman I'd thought she was. Maybe, as a woman raised in the thirties and forties in the Bible Belt of the United States, she didn't understand sex any better than I did. Maybe talk of sex embarrassed her or her marriage to Robert wasn't as sexual as I assumed it was. I saw them touching each other a lot, stroking each other's lips and eyes. I assumed they were fondling one another for the physical and emotional sensations it surely caused, but perhaps they were using their hands to *read* the mood of the other. Robert was blind like Eileen and deaf as well. They kissed and hugged often. Because I never saw my parents kiss or even hug, I figured Mom and Dad weren't sexual and Eileen and Robert were. But I must have misread that, too. They couldn't use sight, they had to use touch. Back then I didn't think any of that. All I knew was that I'd entangled us in a horrible mess and I didn't have the slightest idea how to get out of it.

As Eileen sat silently across the table from me, her hand still on my arm, heat rose from my chest to my throat and into my face. I couldn't look at her. I stared down at the page I'd been reading, the words blurring before my eyes. I watched as my tears fell onto the page in front of me, smearing the ink.

"Mary, your mother needs to know what you're writing about. I think you need some outside help. I can't get it for you, but your mother can. She's the one who should hear your story. Not me."

I tried to wrap my mind around what Eileen was saying. Was she thinking that I was sick, mentally ill? Was she actually suggesting I read this to Mom? Was she planning to call my mother or thinking that she could help me talk to her about this? Gradually it dawned on me that this was exactly what Eileen was saying. She wanted me to go to my mother and say I needed help. She was mumbling something now about how she would even help me do that. She was looking at me in a way I didn't want anyone ever to look at me, especially not Eileen. Certainly not my mother. Mom would hate my Beatle book. Suddenly I understood what a huge mistake I'd made by writing it in the first place. Now all I wanted was to get out of Eileen's sparkling clean home as fast as I could. I didn't want to see it or her ever again. But first I needed to make sure she wouldn't call my mom about what I'd written.

I stood up. "Eileen, I'll tell my mom… I promise. But now I've got to go. I didn't realize it was getting so late."

Eileen stared in my direction, but not seeing me, I realized, any more now than she ever had. "Wait," she said. "I'm sorry. I guess I've been a little rough. But Mary, something is very wrong with a girl who feels she needs to write this kind of stuff, a girl your age who even thinks about it. And then to be able to read it out loud…" Her words trailed off and she shook her head a little.

"I'm sorry, Eileen. I made a mistake. It's not about you. I'll tell my mom. You don't have to worry. I'll do it, I promise." I pulled myself together. I tried to make my voice sound normal. "I've got to go, Eileen. I've got homework. I'll see you tomorrow, maybe." Even as I spoke the words, I knew I wouldn't come back.

Timmy cried out from the back of the house and Eileen turned her head in that direction. "Are you sure you're okay?" she asked. "And you'll talk to your mother? It might be a good idea not to read her the... what did you call it... the Beatle book, but you've got to talk to her about sex, about what you're thinking, the questions you have." Eileen rose from the table and turned toward Timmy's room.

The moment she was out of the kitchen and with her son, comforting him and cooing to him like the loving mother she was, I was away from the table, notebook in hand and fleeing out the back door. On my way to the alley at the back of the house, I passed the Kinney's garbage can on the stoop. Without pausing to think about what I was doing, I yanked off the lid and dropped the notebook in. My Beatle book rested on a mound of decaying orange peels, broken egg shells and coffee grounds. With my hands I shoved it deeper into the muck, replaced the lid quietly so Eileen wouldn't hear and ran.

I was terrified Eileen would call my mother. But when Mom didn't say anything after a week or so, I stopped worrying and tried to go about my life as if nothing had happened, as if I'd never known Eileen or her family. I shoved them into the dark place at the back of my mind where I kept the people and events that were too painful for me to think about, like my grandmother's stroke and what it did to her or my mother's cancer. Sometimes, if thoughts of them or feelings of shame threatened to overcome me, I'd find a way to steal a small amount of vodka or gin from Mom and Dad's linen closet, mix it into ginger ale or Coke and take it up to my room or outside to drink in private.

Three months later I learned that, like my mother, Eileen had cancer. Unlike Mom, though, she was given only weeks to live. Finally, I got up the nerve to go over to see her. I don't know what I expected would happen—I guess I thought that Eileen might apologize, tell me she'd been wrong to say what she did. Perhaps I'd have the chance to apologize, too, and make things right between us. But it didn't happen that way. I called to see if I could come over and the woman who answered the phone told me that they'd be leaving for the hospital as soon as the taxi arrived. If I hurried, I could see her to say goodbye. They doubted she would be coming home again.

When I got to Eileen's house, I was shocked to see how sick she really was. Even right after surgery, Mom had never looked the way Eileen did as she sat slumped over in a wheelchair with a blanket over her lap. Her legs were like sticks beneath the blanket and her skin was pulled tight over the sharp angles and edges of her pale face. Pain and anguish dulled her normally bright eyes. She didn't look like she'd live long enough to make it to the hospital. The familiar feelings that precede a fainting episode washed over me and I reached for the door jamb to steady myself.

Eileen's husband, toddler, mother and best friend were gathered around her. Clearly there would be no opportunity for me to talk to Eileen about what had happened between us. This was not the time and there would never again be a time. I was the outsider to this little group surrounding Eileen. Once again, I felt unnecessary and that I didn't belong and was not wanted by anyone. I'd been wrong to come. If I'd wanted to settle anything between us I should have come earlier, as soon as I'd learned of her cancer. Now it was too late.

"We're on the way to the hospital, Mary. We've only got a few minutes before the taxi arrives," her mother said. She sounded brittle, as if at any moment she'd shatter.

I moved closer to Eileen's wheelchair. I felt as if I towered above her and that everyone was staring at me, waiting to hear what I would say, wanting me to make it quick so they could get Eileen to the hospital where doctors and nurses would make her feel better and perhaps even help her live a little longer. I leaned over and gave her a gentle little hug. I felt her bones beneath my arms. "I won't keep you, Eileen. I just came over to say hello," I whispered close to her ear. She nodded a little and tried to smile. I stood up and backed away as Eileen's mother started to wheel her towards the door. I knew this would be the last time I'd ever see her. I wanted to apologize, but I couldn't think of anything to say and

I doubted that she was thinking about our last time together or about my book. I watched as they carefully wheeled her down the front stoop and lifted her into the taxi. I watched as the taxi pulled away from the curb. I waved one last time and turned for home.

Eileen never made it out of the hospital. She died a week later. With the help of alcohol, I managed to convince myself I could put the whole situation behind me and move on. Alcohol helped me bury the Beatle book, the episode in Eileen's kitchen and her death. In a little over a year, I'd found out my mother had cancer; developed an emotional and physical illness and missed most of the end of eighth grade; started attending a massive, almost factory-like high school where I felt over my head and out of my element most of the time; and my Grandmother had suffered a serious stroke that would keep her away from me for good. A boy I'd known since grade school committed suicide and another child, one I'd babysat since his birth, drowned during a family vacation on the shores of a nearby lake. On a national scale, our country was reeling from President Kennedy's assassination. Both my big and little worlds were out of control and the only way I knew how to cope was to shove all the feelings and thoughts about anything painful deep within me, shut the door on them and, whenever the door flew open, drink enough alcohol to slam it shut again.

I didn't understand then that nothing is ever truly and permanently buried. I didn't understand that all those memories and feelings would be festering within me, doing damage and creating wreckage whether I acknowledged them or not.

I spent the spring and summer hanging out with friends, vacationing in Wisconsin with my family, flirting a little with boys and drinking when I had to numb any painful feelings or shut out unwanted thoughts. What I didn't do was write any more imaginary stories.

In fact, I wouldn't do that again for another 24 years.

SEVEN

A *Real* Boyfriend

Fantasizing got me into a lot of trouble when I started having actual relationships. Even when the boy or man was real, much of what I thought about him and our relationship was still a figment of my imagination. When a man let me down, I pretended he didn't. When he treated me badly, I either ignored it or convinced myself that it was my fault, not his. I'd tell myself that he was perfect so it *couldn't* be his fault. When he showed signs of not loving me or of using me, I merely pretended none of it was true or made up excuses for his behavior. Because I couldn't see, clearly and realistically, the person I was involved with, I set myself on a dangerous path. And I walked onto that path when I was only 15, a sophomore in high school.

During the fall of that year, my town opened a teen nightclub called the Rolling Stone. These were big back in the sixties. This hangout was just for kids between the ages of 13 and 17, served only non-alcoholic beverages and was located in downtown Winnetka within easy walking distance of my house. There was no need to have a date to go to the Rolling Stone, so groups of boys and groups of girls showed up every Friday and Saturday night. The club was an exciting place to be on weekends. Live bands played music by the Beatles, the Stones and the Animals. The popular high school kids didn't usually come to the Rolling Stone because they held their own house parties or had dates. Therefore, kids like me who rarely dated considered the Stone their own: a place to hang out, meet kids from other schools and dance. Boys came from all over the North Shore and sometimes from as far away as Chicago.

I met Jeff at the Stone. Within minutes of meeting him, I was spinning stories in my head about who he was, what he was like and about the relationship we'd soon have. There was no way Jeff could ever live up to my fantasy of him, nor could any real-life relationship be anything like the one I was creating in my mind. When there were signs even from the beginning that Jeff or our relationship was far from perfect and might even be dangerous given my age and naïveté, I ignored them and continued on in my make-believe world.

We met on a Friday night in October shortly after my 15th birthday. I was standing just outside the door of the Club with a Coke in one hand and a cigarette in the other. A guy wearing tight blue jeans, a button-down light-colored shirt and an olive-green army jacket walked over to me. He was obviously older than I was and I'd never seen him at school. He asked me if I'd like to dance. I waved my hand in a way that I hoped looked casual and said, "When I finish this," trying to sound cool even though the words caught in my throat. He gently removed the cigarette from between my fingers and dropped it to the sidewalk where he ground it out beneath his boot.

He smiled. "You've finished it," he said. In the lamplight beside the door, he looked a little dangerous. But instead of being frightened by that, I sort of liked it. The stories I'd made up about John Decker and George Harrison always had a bit of danger to them, too.

He took my hand and led me inside. I glanced around for my friend Debbie, found her and gave her a look as I nodded slightly toward the guy at my side. She nodded slightly back, indicating she understood I was pretty excited about this new state of affairs.

I wasn't sure yet, but it felt as if this might turn into something pretty big. Jeff was so different from any *real* boy I'd ever known. He fit my idea of what a serious love should be. For one thing, it looked like he'd come to the Stone alone and no one ever did that. No one had the nerve. The boys came in groups of boys and girls showed up with at least one or two other girls. And he was older than the rest of us. In fact, he looked too old to be legally in the Stone at all, unless of course he was an employee. He wasn't. Debbie's sister Ginny was, though, and she knew he didn't belong there. Ginny looked over at us often, as if she were trying to decide whether or not to throw him out. At one point, after Jeff and I had danced with no one but each other for an hour or so, Ginny walked over and whispered, "What's up?"

"I like him. He's nice," I whispered back, while trying to indicate through my facial expression that I didn't want her to say anything to him. She got it and walked away. She probably figured he wasn't hurting anything and liked the fact I looked happy.

I was happy—happier than I'd been in a long time. When he held me, I didn't think of anything but how good he felt, how spicy sweet he smelled. I didn't think of Mom or cancer or Grandmother or even how frightening the world could be. That night when Jeff held me, I felt safe and for the first time I also felt beautiful.

Jeff walked me home. I lived six or eight blocks west of the Rolling Stone and he lived about the same distance in the other direction. I was impressed that he was willing to walk me so far out of his way. The night was chilly and he casually draped his arm around my shoulders and pulled me in at his side. I liked looking down at our legs as we walked in step, the feel of our bodies touching. He didn't say much on the way to my house. He hadn't talked much in the Stone either, but I thought that was mostly because of the noise. Now it struck me that he might be a little shy and I decided I liked that about him.

We talked outside my door for a while. Neither of us wanted the evening to end. Finally, I said I had to go in and he asked for my phone number. I rattled it off: Hillcrest 6-6576. He gave me a brief kiss on the lips and I liked the way he tasted, like cinnamon and cigarettes. I'd only been kissed once before, outside Mrs. Woolson's dance class in seventh grade. But that kiss had been on a childish dare and this one, I knew, was very different. This was a grown-up kiss.

I walked into the house, shut the door behind me and leaned against it for a second. Mom and Dad were already in bed. Paul was out, probably spending the night with a friend as usual. I called out to my parents that I was home, waited for their sleepy response and floated up the steps to my room.

A week or so after meeting Jeff, I had convinced myself that I was in love with him. Based on what I knew from watching musical comedies and soap operas and reading the steamy novels I picked up at the newsstand in downtown Evanston, I was pretty sure that the feelings he and I had for each other were the real thing. In a literal sense, the world suddenly looked brighter. Every object I noticed appeared to be lit from within: maple and oak trees shimmered; Lake Michigan glowed with a luminosity that radiated up from its depths; a routine walk around the neighborhood turned magical. It was as if Jeff and I could see what no one else could see, as if we were in a world separated from others. I was positive that no one before us had loved one another the way we did.

Because I was seeing Jeff through the filter of fantasy (and he might very well have been seeing me the same way), I ignored the signs that Jeff was not the right boyfriend for me. He was almost four years older. He hadn't graduated from high school as I told my friends he had. He'd dropped out in his junior year, even though it meant he might be drafted and sent to fight in the Viet Nam War. He didn't have a job and wasn't trying to find one. He still lived at home with his parents and spent his days watching television, smoking, probably drinking a little and waiting for me to get out of school for the day. Without my asking him to, Jeff met me at the corner of Winnetka and Woodland Avenues as soon as school was out. I told my parents I walked home with Karen and Debbie, but as soon as my friends saw Jeff they'd hurry off, leaving me to walk home alone with him. Once we reached my house, he'd stay until we heard Mom turning into the alley. While she was parking the car in the carport and walking into the kitchen at the back of the house, Jeff exited the house quickly and quietly by the front door.

What I thought were signs of love from Jeff was actually an unhealthy obsession. He'd call me numerous times every night and it became increasingly difficult to get him to hang up the phone. When I tried to tell him that I needed to go to bed or do my homework, he'd plead with me to stay on just a little while longer or, when I did manage to hang up, call me over and over again. He also stayed away from my parents, but I was relieved that he didn't have any interest in getting to know them. This should have raised a red flag with me; why didn't he want to meet them and why was I so glad that he didn't? I often lied to Mom and Dad about where I was going and with whom, something I'd never done before.

I knew my friends were concerned about my relationship with Jeff, but instead of considering the possibility they might be right to be worried, I avoided them and spent my free time only with Jeff. I didn't want my friends to be right and I didn't want to give him up. What if no one ever loved me again? Silly as it sounds since I had not even had my 16th birthday, it was inconceivable to me that I might have another chance at love.

There were plenty of warning signs that Jeff had emotional issues, but at first I didn't realize the magnitude of them. And I didn't know that when I finally *did* want to end our relationship, Jeff would make it very difficult—even dangerous—to do so.

A month after we met, Jeff gave me the first gift I'd ever received from a boy. I saved the package to open on Christmas morning, but waited until Paul, Mom, Dad and I had finished opening our family presents. I didn't want to share my experience of learning what Jeff had bought for me with them. In fact, I hadn't told them he'd given me a present at all. While they were busy preparing the traditional Eggs Benedict breakfast, I took the gift-wrapped box into the downstairs bathroom where I would be alone and undisturbed. There in the tiny cramped space, sitting on the lowered lid of the toilet seat, I carefully removed the black and gold paper and discovered a small bottle of perfume—Chanel #5. It was in one of those tiny spray tubes, a little bigger than a lipstick but rectangular instead of round, the Chanel label black with a little gold accent. It fit perfectly into the palm of my hand and I rolled it back and forth and felt its smooth edges. It was so elegant and so completely *not* me. I loved Jeff all the more for choosing an item for the woman I wanted to be rather than for the gawky and inexperienced teenager I actually was. Jeff had played into my fantasy with his Christmas present.

In a skewed way, I thought that his grown-up gift of Chanel #5 perfume warranted an equally adult gift in return. When he held my hand or put his arm around me when we walked, when he kissed me and held me for a long time at the door after a date it felt good. I felt special and loved and beautiful. But after Christmas, I decided it was time for me to let him do more.

It was an ordinary Saturday night. As usual, we'd seen a movie and later stopped for hamburgers and fries. Jeff drove to the parking lot of the Sheridan Road Beach. At that time of night, it was dark and deserted. I knew we'd make out—we almost always did for a little while after our dates—but this time I was ready for it to be different. We got out of the car and walked down to the beach and out onto the pier. I loved the pier in winter. I loved the waves splashing up over the railings and how we'd have to yell a little to hear each other as we braced against the cold wind. I often came to this beach by myself to think. I always thought a little better when I was by the water. When Jeff told me that he also came to this beach to think, it made the place and Jeff even more special to me.

A full moon reflected off the ocean waves and turned the sky a silvery gray. I could see the intensity in Jeff's face. He didn't explain his intentions, but somehow I knew we were going to step over a line together. I'd not thought out the decision I'd made to let him make love to me, never considered what it might mean, that it would change our relationship and change me and might even result in a pregnancy. I never considered that it would take us past some indefinable point of no return. It never crossed my mind that I should talk to him first about birth control or ask if there was the slightest possibility he could have a sexually transmitted disease.

I never considered asking him any of those things or learning about them myself before taking such a huge step. If I did have such thoughts, I must have dismissed them immediately. Perhaps I was afraid such a clinical discussion with Jeff would ruin the romance.

When we returned to the car, he opened one of the back doors instead of the front passenger door as he usually did. I hesitated briefly, but climbed in. He got in beside me and locked the door. Jeff didn't have a car of his own. On our dates he drove his parents' old station wagon, a big rusty boat of a car. Though both of us were quite tall, there was room to lie down if we scrunched up our legs a bit.

Without saying anything, he pulled me close to him and reached behind my back to unhook my bra. He'd done that before. The first couple of times I'd resisted and tried to move his hands away. On other dates, he'd just persisted until I gave in. This time he didn't stop with the bra. He unzipped my jeans and in one smooth motion maneuvered my legs onto the seat as he pulled down my jeans and panties. I felt a pang of fear and hesitation. Maybe I wasn't ready. Still I didn't want him to stop. Making love was romantic and grown-up and the next natural step, I thought. I wanted to know what it was like to feel someone's hand on me that way. I felt a physical ache for him. It was real this time, not fiction, and I wanted him to continue doing what he was doing, even while my head was telling me that this was dangerous, that I wasn't ready, that I might be sorry later.

Jeff acted as if he knew what he was doing, like it wasn't his first time. I had a sense of pride and power knowing that. Whatever he had done with someone else, he was choosing to do it with me now. Though I was scared once I realized I was finally going to make love for real, I also felt surprisingly safe. I didn't know what he would do exactly, but I believed he'd take care of me and wouldn't hurt me. Jeff never removed his lips from mine as he grabbed my hand and put it inside his waistband. He shoved my hand in and pushed it lower so I'd be touching him. I sensed his urgency, the desire he had for me and I was excited by it. I was willing at that point to do anything he wanted. The wind was blowing outside the car and I could hear the waves crashing against the pier. The windows steamed up. He took off my top and removed my unhooked bra the rest of the way. He tossed it onto the floor of the back seat. He cupped my breasts in his hands and kissed my neck. Then he was on top of me and shoving me up against the door. I think I asked him about a condom and he mumbled something about how I didn't have to worry, that he'd pull out. That sounded risky, but I didn't want to stop him and didn't think I could anyway.

A few minutes later, I was pulling on my clothes and thinking that making love wasn't anything like I'd expected. It happened so fast—in seconds, actually. Jeff was hardly inside me before he was pulling out and my inner thighs were sticky and I was a little sore. Dressed again, I got out of the car. I needed to breathe in the cold fresh air coming off Lake Michigan. I'd been fantasizing about this moment for a couple of years, writing it into scenes in my Beatle book. Was this all there was to it? I felt let down, disappointed. Jeff walked up to me from behind and put his arms around me. He lowered his head to my shoulder. I could feel the wetness of his tears on my neck. "I'm sorry," he said. "I shouldn't have done that to you. You weren't ready. I won't ever do that to you again…"

I felt the need to comfort and reassure him at the same time I was wishing that it hadn't happened. I didn't want him to be upset or feel bad about what he'd done. I turned to him and hugged him and caressed his face. I assured him that I had wanted it too, that I *was* ready and it was okay and that I loved him. But I hadn't been ready and it wasn't okay and I wasn't sure at that moment that I did love him. I was trying to convince myself as much as him. I wanted both of us to think me older and more mature than I really was.

After that and despite what Jeff promised me, we had sex often. Our relationship switched from innocent dating with some heavy petting thrown in to an intense sexual relationship with a date once in a while to make things appear normal to everyone else.

Practically every time we were together, Jeff figured out a way for us to be alone long enough to manage it. I always consented even when I didn't want to, and looking back, I don't know why. Was it because it gave me a sense of power to know I could have that kind of effect on another human being? Was it because I needed to be touched and I was willing to pay the price of sex to be held and cuddled and caressed? Was it because I didn't know how to say no to someone I thought I loved? Or was it because it was easier to agree to have sex with Jeff than to constantly argue about it or worse, to hear him pitifully plead with me to make love?

I liked the cuddling and touching, but I never got any satisfaction from the sex. Mostly, I just felt scared we would be discovered or I would get pregnant. We took terrible risks: groping fully clothed as we leaned up against the kitchen counter with my parents sleeping down the hall; checking into rundown by-the-hour motels in dangerous sections of Evanston or North Chicago; having sex in his bedroom when his parents were ostensibly at work; and of course, making love in his parents' car, at the edge of the forest preserve or on a school playground after dark or in the parking lot of a shopping center closed for the night where anyone, including the police, could pass by. Jeff never used protection and there was no way I could get any. So I bit my lip and trusted him to pull out in time and prayed each month that I'd get my period. While other girls my age worried about what to wear to the prom or what college they'd be attending, I worried about periods and pregnancies. Even though I'd put on an elaborate show for Mom and Dad of choosing the right outfit to wear to whatever function we were supposedly attending, Jeff had stopped taking me to movies or parties or school dances. For him, it was now all about—only about—the sex.

I went from seeing Jeff as the perfect romantic partner to looking at him as someone I had to humor and obey so he wouldn't fall apart. I lost all sense of having a choice about what I would do with him or whether I would do anything at all.

Sometimes Jeff could look so tough in his black leather jacket and his boots. But that was deceptive: Jeff wasn't tough at all. He cried a lot, setting up situations where I was always calming him down, reassuring him. He cried about what he was doing to me and he cried about how he couldn't help himself. He cried because he was afraid he'd lose me and he cried because he thought he *should* lose me. "I don't deserve a girlfriend who's so good to me," he'd sob. I wanted to let him go but was afraid to try to break up with him. What would he do to himself? Sometimes he talked about dying and I took him seriously. He seemed miserable except when we were making love. I felt as if I had to hold him up, keep him together, but the job was too big and I didn't know what to do. I wanted to talk to someone, but couldn't think of one person who would be able to hear what I was trying to say without blaming me for bringing it on myself.

Mom and Dad made fun of Jeff. They laughed about the way he'd stand outside the house late at night, "pining" for me as they put it, and how my dad could only make him leave by driving him to the other side of town, like you'd take a trapped mouse to the far edge of your property, let it loose and hope it didn't return. They thought it was cute that I spent so much time on the phone with him, not realizing that most of the time I was trying to get him to hang up so I could either go to sleep or talk to a girlfriend for a change. They had no idea how humorless the situation was or how frightening it had become. But I couldn't imagine telling them what was really going on. My father was too fragile; my mother would not believe what I was saying, thinking I was making *a mountain out of a molehill* as she would most likely phrase it, or blame me for my part in the situation. I wasn't close enough to any of my teachers to tell them. I couldn't tell my friends because I thought they wouldn't understand why I continued to have sex with Jeff if I didn't want to. Besides, I was afraid they'd think I was a slut. I thought anyone I told would think that. Why wouldn't they? That's what I thought of myself.

By the time Jeff and I reached the point where all we did together was have sex, I was in my senior year of high school. I helped him study for his G.E.D. and he passed it. I hadn't become pregnant, although I'd had a few scares. Sometimes I thought Jeff was *trying* to get me pregnant, thinking that if I was carrying his baby I'd never leave him. There was a time early in our relationship when I imagined marrying Jeff, but those fantasies were long gone. Now all I wanted was a normal relationship with someone who didn't push me to have sex all the time, someone who just wanted to go to high school basketball games or swim meets or catch a matinee on a Saturday afternoon.

The times I did try to break up with him, he'd sob as if I was breaking his heart. I knew he'd had a painful and lonely childhood and I didn't want to add to the pain he'd already suffered. So I'd hold him and let him do whatever he wanted as I tamped down my growing hopelessness and helplessness.

I tried one more time to break up with Jeff in the autumn of 1966. I met him at his house after school. Jeff and his parents lived in a big ramshackle house in an area of homes that looked as if they'd seen more prosperous days. The front room and kitchen was a tangle of dusty, overgrown plants and I'd never seen the kitchen sink without its ever-present pile of dirty dishes. The house always had a slight odor of overripe fruit.

On this particular day, we went up to Jeff's room and I sat on the chair by his desk. I told him to sit down and he did, on the bed. I told him that we couldn't go on like this—that sooner or later we were going to get caught, either by my getting pregnant or by someone discovering us making love. I told him I was too young, that I planned to go to college and that my grades were slipping. I went on and on, throwing words at him, any argument I thought might help him understand. Without moving or responding, he sat on the bed looking down at his hands. He started to cry, but I steeled myself. This time I wouldn't let his tears work on me. I knew he expected me to get out of my chair, sit by him on the bed and while holding him, say I didn't mean it. I didn't move. Instead, I continued to sit silently, saying nothing and willing myself to be strong. I needed to follow through with my plan regardless of what he said or did. Unexpectedly, he stood up and, shoulders slumped, walked out of the room. I sat at the desk, holding my breath, waiting for him to return and wondering if I should just leave, walk the couple of miles home.

Before I'd made any decision, he was standing in the doorway to his room holding a shotgun. I looked at it and then at his face. I heard a car go by outside. Otherwise, there was no sound. I think I told him to put the gun down and I think he said he couldn't lose me. I don't know for sure. I do know that I suddenly realized I could no longer pretend I would be able to leave Jeff. I wouldn't be leaving him if I wanted him to stay alive or if *I* wanted to stay alive. At that moment, I was even afraid he might hurt my brother or my parents. As I looked from his face to the gun and back to his face, I grasped the full reality of my situation. I would not be breaking up with Jeff, not on this day, not ever. For the first time, I comprehended fully that I was his prisoner. I didn't have the strength or the power or the maturity to extricate myself from him.

So instead of leaving him alone with the gun, I did what I knew how to do. Once again, I reassured him I wouldn't leave. And finally, after sobbing and pleading with him to get rid of the gun, he left the room, came back in without it and sat down on the bed. He motioned me to come to him and while he cried and asked for my forgiveness, he raped me. Or maybe he didn't. Maybe I gave in to him so he wouldn't kill me. Or kill himself. Or both of us. I didn't know anymore.

EIGHT

The Senior Prom

After that day in Jeff's bedroom, life continued pretty much as it had before. Then he got the notice from the U.S. Government telling him to report for duty at Fort Campbell, Kentucky, on a specific day in November, 1966. He was now 20 years old and had managed to avoid the draft for two years while jobless, living at home with his parents and not attending school.

One night before he left for Fort Campbell and as we lay naked in bed after sex in a cheap motel room in Waukegan, he lifted my left hand off the grayish, threadbare bedcovers and stuck a diamond ring on my finger. I looked at the ring on my hand. The diamond was tiny and set into a plain white gold band much too big for my finger.

"I was afraid it wouldn't fit," Jeff said, somewhat apologetically. "But I didn't want to wait until the jeweler got around to fixing it. And I wasn't sure what size you'd need anyway. I borrowed the money from my brother to buy it." He pointed out a tiny flexible band within the circle of the ring.

"This will keep it from falling off until you can get it fixed," he said. "The guy at the store added that."

I shrugged. I knew I wouldn't be wearing it anyway. Mom and Dad were relieved that Jeff was going away. Now they could put pressure on me to get my grades up and find a college that would accept me even with a mediocre high school transcript. I could imagine the scene if I told my parents I was marrying Jeff instead of going to college.

Though I feared the inevitable scene with my parents and hated the way Jeff dominated me sexually and emotionally, a part of me was still excited about the ring. My friend Jacquelyn and I loved the idea of marriage in general and bought each new issue of *Bride* magazine the day it hit the newsstands. As crazy as it sounds now, the thought that I would be the first of my little group of friends to have a fiancé was intoxicating, even if it was only Jeff.

I lay beside him with the ring on my finger, captivated by the glitter of the diamond, and played out the fantasy. I enjoyed the idea of being engaged to a soldier, one who might actually go off to war. Commitment to Jeff meant I'd have the emotional benefits of engagement with rare contact; I'd only have to see him when he returned home on leave.

When Jeff dropped me off that night, I had the ring around my neck on the silver chain he'd given me for my 17th birthday, but it was hidden beneath my blouse. I told myself it wasn't all that bad. When Jeff was happy, usually after we'd had sex, he could be fun and kind. Once again I was denying the painful reality of my situation, pushing my fears and hopelessness down deep into a place where they wouldn't bother me. I was once again living in my fantasy world.

Healthy young women might wonder why I'd consider accepting an engagement ring from a man who treated me the way Jeff did. Even as I agreed to his proposal and felt some excitement about it, I knew it was wrong and perhaps sick for me to agree to marry him. And in the days that followed, I couldn't bring myself to tell even my closest friends about my engagement. Not talking about what was going on meant I didn't have to defend or explain my accepting the ring. I didn't have to reassure anyone that Jeff would treat me better when we were married. He would change, I told myself. I wore the ring when I could do so safely and pretended that all was good between us, that eventually I would be happily married to someone who would be good to me and love me and take care of me. The Jeff I planned to marry was a wholly imaginary person, as John Decker had been and my version of George Harrison.

I also think that, on some level, I thought marrying Jeff was my only option. No one had talked to me seriously about women having careers or told me that there would be many men in my future if I didn't marry the first one who came along. I wasn't secure enough or emotionally mature enough to believe I could leave my parents' house and make a home of my own without a man to help me do it. Jeff offered me a future—the only one I could envision—and the picture in my mind was not much different than what I imagined when I'd played house with my dolls as a kid.

I took Jeff to the train station in Chicago on a cold and brittle Saturday just after Thanksgiving. As I watched him board the train with all the other young men who would most likely be fighting in southeast Asia before summer, I felt a mixture of fear for the soft-cheeked, hope-filled soldiers and a sense of romantic drama at sending off a lover to war when I was only 17. I also felt the acute pain of losing a constant daily companion, someone who appeared to love me, even if the love often played out in twisted and risky scenarios. But I also felt relief in knowing I'd no longer have to shape my days around Jeff and his overwhelming emotional and physical needs.

After Jeff left, I was able to look more objectively at the insanity of our relationship. I could be grateful for my amazing luck in not getting pregnant or having my sexual conduct discovered by Mom and Dad. I had "dodged the bullet," so to speak, even managing to keep Jeff from falling apart and hurting either himself or me. But being grateful for what *hadn't* happened meant I continued to minimize the trauma of what I'd been going through for three years, the emotional issues I had that allowed it to go on and the long-term damage that would result. Because I told no one that I was being stalked and raped and emotionally controlled, he got away with it and I continued to believe I was totally and solely to blame.

Still, with Jeff several states away and his location and movement controlled by the Army, I was able to concentrate enough on school-work to rescue my grades, graduate along with the rest of my class and be accepted into a small private college in northeast Iowa. Without his constant presence and control and my inordinate focus on him and his needs, I relaxed a little and put the focus back on myself. By recognizing some positive qualities of my own, I thought perhaps I could have a future that didn't include Jeff.

And I met someone else. Even though my friend Debbie had moved with her parents and younger sister to Massachusetts, her older sister and brother still lived in a carriage house off the alley behind their parents' previous property. When I was lonely for Debbie, I'd visit Ginny and Tom who shared the small back house with their friend, Tuck. Tuck, a slight, soft-spoken man with dark brown eyes and hair, looked much younger than his 24 years, a fact that came in handy when I introduced him to my parents.

Tuck had mononucleosis when I met him and was on sick leave from his job at the post office. At first, we were never alone together and I didn't see much of him. But as his health improved, he sometimes joined the rest of us in the living room for conversation or a game of cards. I was drawn to his quiet attentiveness. I started to go over more often when I knew no one but Tuck would be home and he always seemed glad to see me. I liked his maturity and I felt safe with him. The fact he had a communicable disease allowed us to put off the decision about whether or not we should be intimately involved.

Tuck and I kissed for the first time as a joke. Earlier that morning, his doctor had given him a clean bill of health.

"No more mono," Tuck said.

"Let's give it the real test," I said. "Kiss me. If I don't get sick, we'll know you're cured."

Tuck walked over and hesitantly pulled me out of my chair. He kissed me on the lips once quickly and then again, longer. With those kisses something shifted inside me. I knew my relationship with Jeff was over. And something else was different, too. I wasn't spinning a story in my head about Tuck and me. I was just letting it be what it was for a change. No drama, no fantasy, no dream world.

Ten days later I had mono, too. Now it was Tuck who did the visiting, usually when Mom and Dad were at work and Paul was at school. Though we talked on the phone practically every night as I had with Jeff, it was different. I didn't feel the pressure or the intensity that had been such an integral part of my relationship with Jeff. Whenever I needed to get off the phone I'd merely say to Tuck, "Got to go now…" And he'd respond with an easy upbeat, "Sure. Later."

Tuck was the first person I told about my relationship with Jeff. I told him the truth—all of it—about the sex and about my inability to stop it and about Jeff threatening to kill himself if I broke up with him. Tuck didn't seem to think badly of me or hold any of it against me. He gently and quietly assured me that I wasn't to blame, that none of it was my fault, that Jeff had taken advantage of me. Tuck said out loud what I'd suspected but hadn't been able to admit: that Jeff was one sick dude and dangerous. He told me not to wait until Jeff came home on leave to break up with him in person—which I thought was the proper and kind thing to do—but instead to break up with him over the phone so I wouldn't have to see him again.

"No guy ever has the right to treat you or any girl that way," Tuck said. "You always have the right to say no to sex or anything else you think is wrong for you." Coming from Tuck, it seemed simple and right. Why hadn't I believed it before I heard him say it?

The more I shared about Jeff, the angrier Tuck got. "No guy ever gets to the point where he can't stop. You don't have to buy into that shit. It's just a game some men play to get you to do what they want you to do."

I wanted to believe him and I loved him for his attempts to reassure me. Still, I didn't fully believe it was true. Part of me thought that if Tuck knew the *real* me, he wouldn't like me as much as he appeared to. And I still felt at least partially to blame for what Jeff had done to me. Hadn't I wanted the sex, too? And led him on? And not been forceful enough in trying to stop him? At first I'd liked the feelings of having sex with Jeff. So, hadn't I set it all up? It was hard for me to believe Tuck when he said I wasn't at fault, that I owed Jeff nothing.

Soon I was having sex with Tuck. But he was a much different lover than Jeff. He wasn't demanding or pushy or manipulative. When we did make love, Tuck always used protection and he made sure I wanted to as much as he did.

Sex wasn't the focus of our relationship, though, and most of the time we didn't make love at all. We took drives in the country in his big white convertible. Unlike Jeff, he didn't take me for a drive in the country merely to look for a secluded dirt road on which to park and have sex. We went to movies. We talked. We laughed over stupid, silly jokes. We played endless rounds of board games, like Clue or Monopoly or card games like Gin Rummy or Go Fish or Hearts. Life felt normal with Tuck. With him I could believe I was an average teenage girl with an attentive boyfriend.

Jeff didn't know that I was dating someone else. He still thought I was waiting for him to return from the service. I couldn't bring myself to break up with him over the phone as Tuck urged me to do. Instead, whenever he called I played along with his illusion that someday we'd marry. I let him think I was wearing his engagement ring secretly on a chain around my neck. He didn't know I'd buried the ring at the bottom of my jewelry box and that, as far as I was concerned, our relationship was already over—that I was Tuck's girlfriend now. I convinced myself that it was cruel to tell Jeff the truth while he was in basic training and, when that training ended, I hesitated to break up with him while he waited for orders sending him to Viet Nam.

A couple of weeks before my senior prom, Jeff called and announced happily that he wasn't going to Viet Nam after all. Instead, he would be stationed in Germany for at least a year, a benefit of his surprising proficiency in the German language. And even better, he said, he was coming home to take me to the dance.

I already had my prom dress, a long, frothy, pink and white gown, the prettiest dress I'd ever owned. Tuck planned to be my date for the dance. In fact, he was as excited about it as I was and had rented a tux and made dinner reservations at a fancy local restaurant before the prom. We planned to make it a double date with Karen and her boyfriend. Of course, as far as Jeff knew I hadn't planned to attend at all. To him, his ability to come home meant that I would not miss the important dance.

I knew I was slipping back under Jeff's control, losing all sense of myself as an independent person able to make her own decisions and say no to what she didn't want. The fear and powerlessness I'd felt after the incident with the shotgun at Jeff's house and earlier came rushing back. Before I gave myself time to think it through, I had agreed to go to the prom with Jeff and even offered to rent his tuxedo. I'd been so sure I'd changed since I'd met Tuck, but now I realized with dismay that I hadn't changed at all. And, as if it weren't bad enough that now I had to go to the dance with Jeff, I'd have to disappoint Tuck. He might be so angry that he wouldn't want to see me again.

When I told Tuck that I had to let Jeff take me to the prom, he *was* angry and hurt, but he finally agreed that it was only one dance and then we'd have the rest of the summer together. I used sex to calm him down, just as I had with Jeff in the past. It made me feel bad about myself, but it worked. I hadn't yet learned any other way.

The night of the prom, Jeff came to the door carrying a corsage box. Once inside the house, he fumbled around trying to pin the gardenia onto the bodice of my strapless dress. He looked handsome and somber wearing the black tuxedo I'd rented for him and with his army-issue haircut. Dad took our picture standing in front of the fireplace. Everything looked very proper. I was cautiously optimistic. Perhaps the Army had changed Jeff. Perhaps he wouldn't expect to have sex since we were all dressed up and it was the night of my senior prom. We walked out to his father's old station wagon while Mom and Dad watched from the front stoop. Before getting in, I turned and gave them a little wave. Jeff opened the car door for me and helped me in, lifting the skirt of my long dress and tucking it gently around me before closing the passenger door. He walked around to his side of the car, got in, started the engine and drove slowly away. He wasn't normally a slow or careful driver and I knew he was putting on a show for my parents. As we drove off, I looked back to see Mom and Dad one last time, but they'd already gone inside the house.

When we reached Willow Road, Jeff needed to turn left toward the high school. He turned right. My heart sank. I knew where we were going and what was coming, but I didn't know how to stop it.

"Jeff, we have to get to the dance. Leslie and Karen will be there waiting for us. They want to hear all about the Army. They're looking forward to seeing you." It wasn't true: they were confused and angry that I'd canceled my plans with Tuck in order to go to the dance with Jeff. But I hoped my lie would work. It didn't.

Jeff took my hand and put it on his leg. "I haven"t seen you for months. I want to be alone with you. Just for a little while. Then we'll go."

I didn't know what to say. What could he do, anyway? He had on a rented tux and I was wearing an expensive new dress. He wouldn't mess us up before we even got to the dance. I tried not to think about the other times we'd had on nice clothes and how it hadn't stopped him from doing whatever he wanted to do. I tried to convince myself that he only wanted to talk for a little while, but when he turned onto a service road in the forest preserve east of town, my apprehension deepened.

Jeff pulled the car off the road onto a grassy knoll under a big willow tree and turned off the ignition. He turned to me. I could tell by the familiar look in his eyes what he wanted. As he moved toward me, he whined something about how badly he'd missed me and how hard and lonely it was in the Army.

"Jeff, don't," I said, trying to push him away. "We have to go."

Jeff, it came to me in a flash, hadn't changed at all. Nothing about him had changed except that he was stronger now after basic training. And apparently he was determined to pick up where we'd left off.

He shoved me against the passenger door and pulled me under him, pushing my dress up to my waist. He loomed above me and held me down with one arm as he removed his cummerbund and unzipped his pants.

He never stopped talking, telling me how much he loved and needed me. How he couldn't help himself.

I turned my head and bit my lip. "Please, Jeff, don't," was all I said. I knew, from so many times before, that whatever I said wouldn't matter.

"I need you so much," he whispered against my cheek. "It's okay. You know I won't hurt you."

He was hurting me—physically *and* emotionally. Again I lost all sense of who I was and what was in my power to control. I let my body go limp. I had no fight in me. "Just get it over with," I said and he shoved into me.

It hurt and I hated it, but I still put my arms around him. It wasn't as if I didn't know this man. I knew him intimately. I knew his fears and his failures and what had happened to him as a little boy. I knew his parents had called him Little Shit until he was old enough to understand what that meant. I knew his father had used a strap on him when he did nothing more than forget to put away his toys. My feelings about him were all mixed up. I didn't know if I loved him or felt sorry for him or merely didn't want to hurt him the way his parents had. I didn't know what to do with any of it.

As much as I hated him for controlling me for three years, for raping me and hurting me and for ruining my chance to go the dance that night, the only senior prom I'd ever have, I hated myself more for being powerless in the face of his need. I almost wished I was dead. I didn't know how I'd ever disentangle myself from Jeff otherwise. When I felt my dress tear as it caught between our bodies, something tore inside me, too. What Tuck had started to mend, I was again letting Jeff rip apart.

When Jeff finished, he continued to lay heavily on me. His face against my cheek was wet with tears. I pushed against him and he raised himself up on his hands. I tried to pull my dress down. "I'm so sorry, Mary," he said. "I shouldn't have done that."

I pulled myself up to a sitting position. I felt as dirty and ruined as my dress was. I leaned against the door and cried.

And then suddenly, unexpectedly, I got angry. "How could you do this to me?" I yelled. "Look at me." When he continued to stare straight ahead, I grabbed his chin and pulled his face around. "I said *look* at me. How could you do this to me again?" He pulled away and scrunched up against his door. "*Why?*" I asked him over and over.

And he, cowering and crying as usual, repeated that he didn't know why he did the things he did. It was just that he loved me so much and I looked so beautiful in my dress.

'I'm not so beautiful now, am I?' I said.

He went on and on, trying to justify his actions. I threatened to tell someone. He threatened to kill himself. I told him I didn't care.

My anger served only to heighten his desire and need and I knew from past experience that, if I didn't get out of the car quickly, he'd force me to have sex again. I had to get away from him.

I unlocked and shoved open my door. Shaking and unsteady, I stood up. I tried to smooth the white satin of my dress. I shivered in the cool night air. Jeff didn't get out; I heard him sniffling inside the car. Snatching my high heels off the floor below the front seat, I started walking toward the road in my nylons. I was about a mile from home. The hatred and rage I'd felt were suddenly gone, leaving me with only a deep sense of resignation and sadness. Jeff hadn't changed and neither had I. I felt ugly and used up and old.

With one shoe in each hand and my head down, I walked in the direction of Hibbard Road. I heard Jeff start the car and turn it around. As I walked along the parkway, he pulled up beside me, rolled down the window and pleaded with me to get back in the car. "I'll do anything to make this up to you. Please get in. We'll go to the dance."

"Oh sure," I shot back. "Looking like this? It's too late. I'm going home."

I didn't have a watch, but I figured we'd only been gone an hour or so. Mom and Dad went to bed early, but not this early. Though they'd obviously never suspected what was going on between Jeff and me in the past, I was pretty sure they'd figure it out now if I showed up looking the way I did. I kept walking. I'd come up with some sort of explanation before I got there. A flat tire maybe? Small pebbles dug into the bottom of my feet and I stubbed my toe.

Jeff slowly edged the car along beside me. "Get in the car, Mary. This is stupid."

When I reached Willow Road and saw the traffic going by in both directions, I knew I couldn't walk home in my fancy dress and bare feet, especially not with Jeff following in his father's car. Someone would stop or call the police. It was too early to go home, anyway. I stopped walking and when he pulled over, I got in. "We're going to have to go somewhere and wait this out," I said. "I can't go home yet. But I want to be where there are people, even though looking like this we'll have to stay in the car."

Jeff drove toward the business section of Winnetka and pulled into a parking space in front of the Sweet Shop. All the stores were closed for the night, but at least there were streetlights and I felt safer and more in control. Being with Jeff when I didn't want to be had happened so many times before, I knew what to expect and I would make the best of it until I could go home. We talked a little about the Army and school and Jeff intermittently tried to bring up our future. I nodded, although I finally understood that we had *never* had a future together. It had all been one big, shared fantasy. But I wouldn't say anything that might set him off again. I wanted the night to end. I wanted Jeff out of the state and I wanted to see Tuck.

When it was late enough for me to return home without looking suspicious, I spent another hour trying to convince Jeff to take me there. He didn't want to let me go until he made sure we were okay, that I forgave him for ruining my prom night. I pretended that I did, that everything was okay, that we'd go on as before. Finally, he backed the car out of the parking space and drove slowly toward my house. While he drove, I made him promise to go home and not to call me until the next day. He agreed to do as I asked as we pulled up to the curb in front of my house. Exhausted, I got out of the car and walked up to the front door, quietly letting myself in. Mom and Dad had left a small light on in the living room, but they'd gone to bed. As was usual for a Saturday night, Paul was out with friends.

Mom and Dad's bedroom was on the first floor of our Cape Cod bungalow. Paul and I each had our own bedroom on the second floor. I figured Mom would hear me come in or hear my wood floor creaking above her, but I knew she wouldn't come up to my room to find out how the night had gone. She wasn't that kind of mother. She had, however, left a dim light on in my room, turned down the covers on the bed and fluffed my pillows. It was a gentle, motherly thing to do. I so wanted to confide in her—to tell her what had been going on—but I knew I never would.

I stripped off my dress and hid it in the back of my closet; I'd deal with it later. I needed a shower and bed. I thought about Tuck. I wanted nothing more than to call him, to hear his voice, to assure him it was over with Jeff, but I couldn't bring myself to pick up the phone. I was afraid that Tuck would be able to tell I'd let it happen again.

I took a long, hot shower and put on a clean pair of cotton pajamas. Before crawling into bed, I took my phone off the hook in case Jeff went back on his word and tried to call me.

I didn't tell Tuck the details of prom night, but I didn't lie to him either. The week after my graduation from high school, he helped me write a letter to Jeff telling him it was over, that I didn't want to hear from him or see him again. Jeff, in his dramatic fashion, wrote back that he understood how much he'd hurt me and he'd "let me go." I never communicated with or saw him again.

NINE

Living the Lie

When I arrived at college—I attended a small private liberal arts school in northeastern Iowa—I quickly shut the door on my life in high school and even on my relationship with Tuck. Tuck had helped me make the break from Jeff and for that I was grateful, but it was time for both of us to move on. He knew I needed freedom to enjoy college without a long-distance boyfriend and I knew it was time for me to focus on guys my own age. We had an amicable break-up, but decided it would be easiest for both of us if we didn't see each other again, even as friends.

At college I reinvented myself. In high school I'd scoffed at cheer-leaders and jocks. Suddenly, in college, I was making friends with them *and* student leaders. In high school I wouldn't have been caught dead at a sporting event, but I went to every single one in college, even to pep rallies and out-of-town games. All three of our college's sororities asked me to pledge. Not that I saw myself as the cheerleader or sorority type: rather, I wanted to be—and feel—young and fresh and clean again. I told my new friends nothing about what had happened to me in high school and they probably assumed my previous experiences were pretty much the same as theirs. I *wanted* that to be true. I wanted to be one of the happy, confident young people who were in my classes and the sorority I chose to join in my sophomore year. So I pretended I was and I pretended, even to myself, that I was still a virgin. Once again, my habit of imagining I had the life I wanted instead of the life I had—or at least used to have—was in play.

Early in my freshman year I met Mike, a college football player, active in and later president of his fraternity and the man who would become my first husband. After Mike and I had sex for the first time, when I was 18 and he was 20 and we'd been dating for a few months, he said, "It seems like you know a lot about sex for being a virgin." I protested angrily that I didn't know anything: that I *was* a virgin. I must have acted angrily enough because he never mentioned it again, and strangely, I felt justified in getting mad. I had entered into my fantasy about myself so deeply that, on some level, it had become the truth for me. The problem was that, deep down, I knew I was living a lie and this incongruity was preventing me from developing a strong and healthy sense of self.

I also believed that I needed Mike in my life. I suspected my popularity was because I was dating him rather than who I was. I was afraid that when he graduated I'd lose my place, my popular position, at school. Because he was a year ahead of me, I dreaded the day he'd graduate and leave me alone. To make sure that didn't happen, I married him. It was the summer before my junior year in college and I had the *Bride* magazine wedding Jacquelyn and I had always wanted. Jacquelyn stood beside me as my maid of honor.

Mike and I found an apartment close to campus and, for the first year, nothing much changed for us. We partied with our friends, attended games and fraternity and sorority functions and continued to do well in our classes. When Mike graduated, I stayed on in Iowa so I could continue my education as my parents required before giving their blessing on our marriage. I moved back into the dorm and Mike returned to Illinois to live with his parents and work at a nearby insurance company. It was then I realized I hadn't needed Mike at all. Even with him gone, I was still popular—and now *trapped*. I couldn't date anyone else, couldn't do the things I would have done if I'd been single and free. I'd married Mike to continue having the life I wanted, only to discover that because I was married, I *couldn't* have the life I wanted.

It took a long time for me to realize I was trapped in a much deeper and more dangerous way: in a persona that wasn't my true self. During that second year of marriage to Mike, I stopped drinking for fun and drank to bury unhappy thoughts and feelings, as I had in high school. I went on drinking mainly for that reason, getting progressively worse, for the next 19 years.

The woman who married Mike on August 9, 1969, was not me so much as the woman I wanted to be. I thought I could be a proper house-wife and mother living in a suburb of Chicago, married to a man who wore a suit and worked a nine-to-five job, a man determined to climb the proverbial corporate ladder. I thought I was the kind of woman who could entertain my husband's business associates, keep an orderly home and raise children the way they'd been raised on the North Shore of Chicago for generations. But deep down—so far inside I didn't even know it most of the time—I realized something was wrong. It was as if another woman lived inside me, looked out through my eyes and asked herself who *was* this woman who lived in a well-to-do suburb of Chicago, was married to this man named Mike and was friends with upper-middle class fashionable and conservative women? Was this other woman—who peered through my eyes and asked these disturbing questions—the teenage girl in the ripped prom dress, the girl who'd been raped at gunpoint? Or was that girl gone, replaced, now only a wisp of a painful memory, the lingering of a hazy nightmare?

When I discovered my surprising popularity at college, I must have decided that anyone learning about *that* girl and her dirty, shameful secrets would not want to be friends with me. I'd surely be looked at in some different and devastating way. Because of *her* I would be shunned. But I was mistaken if I believed that not acknowledging her meant she wasn't a part of me and part of my history. She was, and during those early years of marriage and motherhood, she waited quietly for the right time to make her presence known.

After Mike and I divorced, I used to joke with friends that I didn't even know what kind of furniture I liked when I was 19, much less what kind of man I should marry. Most of all I didn't know myself, though sometimes I'd have small inklings or signs of who the *real* me might be. Perhaps, in the process of denying the girl in the ripped prom dress, I denied other parts of me, like the simple earth mother who wanted nothing more than to live in the country, plant a garden and raise a bunch of children. I never thought about why I felt so much more at home on a humble Iowa farm than I did in my own well-appointed suburban home. Why did I prefer walking a deserted winter beach by myself to joining friends at a luncheon where crab salad was served on crystal and silver? Why did I still think that if my friends knew my history—knew the real me, knew what my high school years had consisted of—they wouldn't like me very much? Why didn't that bother me more than it did? Most of the time, often with the help of alcohol, I shoved down the thoughts and feelings that bubbled to the surface because they brought up the possibility that I was living the wrong life with the wrong man. I couldn't let myself think that because I had no idea how to change it or how I would manage a different life.

When I accepted Mike's proposal, marrying him seemed a natural evolution of the relationship we'd developed in college, that when we were married we would simply continue our college lifestyle. I didn't understand until many years later that I was fantasizing our future much as I had my relationships with John Decker and George Harrison and the travel scenarios with Grandmother less than ten years before. I was fantasizing my relationship with Mike as I'd fantasized that my relationship with Jeff was better—could be better, much better—than it actually was. If I'd taken the time to sort things out before marrying Mike, I might have realized that my happiness in college was based on far more than my relationship with him. In college, I discovered how much I loved to learn about practically anything: history, literature and even science. It was in college that I discovered a deep affinity for the concerns and needs of others and had strengthened my passion for civil rights and learned about the serious problems that minorities and the poor still struggled with in the United States. And it was in college, through meeting Heloyce and Hugo—parents of a school friend—and spending time on their farm, that I realized how much I yearned for a simple rural life.

When Mike and I were first married and still in college, nothing much changed. But when I graduated and moved back to Illinois, where Mike had already entered the business world and where we tried to start a family, I somehow left those other interests behind and focused only on the life I'd acquired through marriage to Mike.

For the next seven years I tried to live that life and play out the fantasy. We upgraded our house to a nice neighborhood in a more upscale suburb. We had a child. We entertained. After Brad was born I quit my job and became a suburban housewife, leaving Brad with friends or Mom and Dad while I traveled with Mike to insurance company events in glamorous resorts on Caribbean islands and spas around the United States. I tried to keep up with the other wives by wearing the right clothes and an up-to-date hairstyle. I made friends with other women living the same way I lived. We joined each other for coffee in the mornings, babysat each other's children and chatted over cocktails before the men returned from the city on the evening commuter trains. We went to monthly luncheons where we drank more than we ate and attended dances at the town country club where we flirted with each other's husbands.

I had small crushes on some of those husbands and played around in my head with the idea of being in a relationship with someone other than Mike. I sometimes had the uncomfortable thought that perhaps women who were in love with their husbands didn't entertain secret fantasies about other men, but most of the time I rationalized it or pushed it to the back of my mind and went on with my life, staying busy so I wouldn't have to think about things too much.

Many of my friends seemed happy in their lives and with their husbands. They'd tell me that sometimes on a Saturday afternoon, in the middle of gardening or yard work, they'd look at one another over the rose bushes and need to hurry into the house to make love. Mike and I never looked at each other like that, never even thought of making love in the middle of an afternoon. Though we were still very young and supposedly in love, sex took place hurriedly in bed, in the dark, on Saturday nights only. After our quick love-making sessions ended, with Mike giving me a pat on my shoulder and turning away with his usual "Good night, Chief," I'd lie in the dark feeling lonely and sad and wondering if all women hated sex as much as I did. Sometimes Mike would broach the subject of what he called my "frigidity" and I wondered what was wrong with me. Those were the only times I'd let myself think back to my relationships with Jeff and Tuck and remember that I'd never felt satisfied with them either. Perhaps there really *was* something wrong with me—something physical and maybe even *mental*. It wasn't as if I couldn't be sexually aroused. I often was when thinking about sex or reading a particularly erotic passage in a novel. I'd even feel sexually aroused when Mike and I started to make love, just as I'd been with Jeff in the beginning and with Tuck. But at some point in the lovemaking I'd feel myself shutting down, feel myself desperately trying to hold onto the sexual feelings long enough to experience a climax; I never could. No matter who my partner was, I'd never been able to catch up to him and when he was finished sex was over. Any interest in me and my satisfaction disappeared. He'd turn away and go to sleep as I lay there feeling disappointed in myself and frightened that I wasn't like other women.

A therapist once pointed out to me that for a woman to reach sexual satisfaction with a man she needed to trust him. At that moment, she was most vulnerable to her partner and if she didn't trust him, her body would not cooperate even with her own apparent wishes. This therapist's hypothesis resonated with me when she said it, but it wasn't until many years later that I realized my feelings about sex and my inability to trust men originated in the unhealthy relationship Jeff and I began when I was only 15 years old.

I could talk big at that age. I could light up a cigarette and wave it around as I amused my friends with stories about the sexual encounters

I was dying to have, but the truth was I wasn't anywhere near ready for a sexual involvement when I had sex with Jeff for the first time. It wasn't sex I wanted: it was attention and gentle loving touch, something I was no longer getting from Mom and Dad when I probably needed it most. Through sex with me, Jeff used my need for touch and attention to try to heal his own brokenness. After I cooperated the first time, it was easier for him to get me to do what he wanted. And because I was used to having little or no control over what happened to me, it was easier for me merely to give in than try to stop him. If I had to have sex in order to be touched and held and given attention, then I'd have sex. But somewhere deep within my subconscious a part of me decided that even if I participated in the act, I wouldn't enjoy it—not completely. If I enjoyed it, then not only was Jeff winning by taking control of all of me, but I was *bad* for letting him do it.

In therapy I discovered that because I still believed myself to have so little control over my own life—a life seemingly driven mostly by the needs and wishes of others—I had unconsciously decided I would at least control the physical responses of my own body. And I'd be damned if I'd let a man override that decision with his touch even if the man was my husband. My therapist said that, because of my unhealthy and too early sexual involvement with Jeff, I believed sex was a way for a man to control a woman. I suspected I'd also learned sex was a way for a woman to control a man. She could use it to keep him from being angry or sad, to get him to leave her alone at least for a little while. And a woman didn't have to lose control, have an orgasm, in order to do that. She merely had to give him her body while she kept her mind for herself.

I entered my first marriage believing that sex hurt and was dirty and had to be hidden. Some of those beliefs stemmed from my involvement with Jeff, of course, but even before I'd met him, Eileen—by her scandalized reaction to my Beatle book—had taught me that desire was something to regret, to be ashamed of feeling. When I married Mike I discovered that a wedding ring on my finger wasn't enough to change any of those beliefs. As I thought about all I'd learned from my therapist, I wondered if my involvement with Jeff and Eileen's response to the erotic fictions depicted in my Beatle book had damaged me so deeply that I would never feel safe enough or in control enough to have a healthy relationship with any partner.

As the years went on, I learned that one way to maintain the illusion that Mike and I were happy, that I was fulfilled, was by comparing my life to the lives of others. I was very good at getting women friends to confide in me and when they did I discovered most of my friends weren't any happier than I was. Because I never shared with them what was going on with me, everyone else thought my marriage was perfect and I was in a good position to listen and even give advice. It wasn't until I joined a 12-step program years later, long after my divorce from Mike, that I learned how to share honestly about myself with friends and how to take a good hard look at what was truly going on in me at any given moment.

Several years into our marriage and after our son Brad was born, Mike applied for a sales position with an insurance company located in Fort Collins, Colorado. The imminent opportunity to take over as head of the office once the current manager retired intrigued Mike and I loved the idea of living close to where Grandmother had lived even though she'd died a few years earlier. Mike and I flew to Colorado and while he had his interview, a real estate agent drove me around to look at houses in the area. I tried to tell her I wanted to look at houses in Poudre Canyon where my grandmother had lived, but instead she drove me around Horsetooth Reservoir without explanation. Up there the view over Fort Collins was breathtaking, but the treeless, brown landscape dotted with modern houses built haphazardly into the cliffs was nothing like the Colorado I remembered from my childhood. I wasn't at all impressed with downtown Fort Collins either, and I wondered why I'd been so in love with Colorado as a kid.

When we returned home, Dad offered and Mike quickly accepted a lucrative position in Dad's company. I think all of us were relieved that we wouldn't be moving so far away from our families. Perhaps Mike and I also suspected that our marriage wasn't strong enough to withstand the changes of beginning again in an area where we knew no one. I sometimes wonder how my life would have played out if I'd moved to Fort Collins with Mike rather than with George, my second husband, many years later.

TEN

Wrong *and* Right?

In 1978, my carefully constructed make-believe world, maintained with the help of alcohol and a focus on the problems of others, finally collapsed when I fell in love with another man. George was a lawyer who looked on the outside no different than the rest of us. But I could see beneath his persona the same way he could see beneath mine. He was a hard-drinking, dune-buggy driving, motorcycle-riding guy who could hold a child like he was handling a newly hatched baby bird. He had sensitivity and a keen intelligence, as well as an edge not noticeable in any of the other men I knew. I could talk to him at length and felt he heard and saw and understood the *me* beneath the façade. Like me, he was more comfortable away from the crowd and the life we were all living back in those days in Lake Bluff, Illinois. Like me, I think he drank to help him manage his life and do what was expected of him.

George and I were close friends for a couple of years before we realized we felt more for each other than just friendship. He had moved to Lake Bluff from Washington, D.C., in 1976 with his wife and small son. They socialized with the same tight-knit group of young families in the community as Mike and I, and I saw them practically every weekend.

A couple of years after we'd met, at a party at my house, I felt unusually uncomfortable when I saw George spending a lot of time talking with a particular woman. She and her husband weren't regular members of our group. Slightly tipsy and clearly upset with her husband about something, this particularly attractive gal hung onto George and listened intently as he leaned in to talk quietly to her. Finally, I couldn't take it anymore and approached them.

"Can I talk to you for a moment?" I asked George.

"Sure." He followed me into another room.

When we were out of hearing range, I confronted him. "I don't like what seems to be going on between you and that woman." My words clearly surprised George and surprised me even more. *Where did that come from?*

George grabbed my arm. "Come with me," he said. "We have to talk."

He pulled me through the kitchen toward the basement stairs. Mike gave us a strange look as we passed. "Where are you going?" he asked.

"To get ice," George said and swept the ice bucket off the kitchen counter on our way by.

Standing beside the freezer in the basement, George scooped ice into the bucket and then turned to me. "What did you mean when you said you didn't like what you saw?"

"I don't know," I answered. But I knew that wasn't true. I was jealous of her for getting his attention and, strangely, I'd also felt a bit proprietary. As if he belonged to me. It was crazy. I had no claim on him. But I told George the truth about what I'd felt. "I think I was jealous."

George just stared at me.

"Yeah, it's crazy. Stupid, isn't it?" I shrugged.

George set the bucket down on top of the freezer and came over to me. He grabbed my shoulders and said, "No. It's not crazy. I'd be jealous if the situation were reversed. I love you."

I stood there, open-mouthed, wide-eyed, speechless. Finally I said, "We'd better get back upstairs."

George nodded. "I'll call you."

We returned to the party, both clearly shaken by what had just transpired.

After that, George and I talked on the phone almost every day. He was the only attorney in a small office and had a private line. He'd call me from work and sometimes we'd talk for several hours. We began to see each other secretly once or twice a week. He'd leave for work in the morning on the southbound train with the rest of the husbands and, as soon as the train arrived at the Chicago Northwestern Station in the Loop, he'd turn around and immediately board a returning northbound train. He'd get off several stops before Lake Bluff where I'd be waiting for him in my car. Then we'd drive to a deserted beach where we walked and drank Asti Spumante out of paper cups and wondered what we really felt for each other. Was it just that we were unhappy in our marriages and looking for a respite or was this something real and worth pursuing? After a couple of hours of trying to sort it out, I'd return George to the station so he could pick up a train back to downtown Chicago and I'd go home feeling lost, empty, confused *and* strangely happy.

Although George constantly assured me that he loved me, I wasn't sure what I felt about him. I didn't know whether I loved George or loved his loving me and his attention. I couldn't break up my family and try to make a life with George if my motives were wrong. Even if my motives were right, I doubted I could do something as drastic—and what I considered to be immoral and irresponsible—as admitting I was in love with one man when married to another.

Then one day George said, "Knowing I can feel this way makes it impossible to stay in the situation I'm in. I don't want you to leave your marriage *for me.* I don't want you to leave if you want to stay in it, but you've got to know that I can't stay in mine. I'm going to ask Janet for a divorce."

After they'd talked about divorcing, Janet took their son to Pennsylvania to visit her parents for several weeks. For a couple of days while Janet was gone, Mike needed to be out of town on business. George asked me to spend that time with him. He could make arrangements for us to stay at Blackhawk Ridge, a small rustic resort just over the Illinois/Wisconsin border. Everything fell into place, making it possible for us to be alone together for more than a couple of hours. I understood the magnitude of the step I was taking. It scared me to realize that spending a night with George might make it impossible for me to stay in my marriage. But I very much wanted this time with him; I wanted to know whether the feelings I thought I had for him were real.

I asked my mother to take Brad, telling her I needed to get away on my own for a while. Mom wanted to know why and Dad teased her about asking too many questions. Several times I'd talked to Dad about being unhappy in my marriage, but I'd never told my mother that. I believe now that my father suspected I was going to meet someone during my little time away, but he said nothing and agreed to watch Brad for me.

"Just bring old clothes," George said when we were making our plans to go to Blackhawk. "I'll take care of everything else."

We had two days and two nights to be alone with no phone, no television and no newspaper. We had only each other, a hardwood forest, a treed ridge overlooking the lush Wisconsin Valley and a tiny one-room log shack with nothing more than one bunk bed and a rough-hewn, slightly tilted table beneath a small dirt-streaked window. I was surprised at how comfortable and at home I felt in the one-room shack with George—more at home than I felt with Mike in our Lake Bluff house.

Although I didn't understand at the time, I see now that what happened at Blackhawk Ridge was a shedding, of sorts, of the person I'd pretended to be for over 11 years. It looked like George understood this about me. Perhaps he needed to leave his life behind for a little while, too. Surrounded by the fragrance of pine, with no sounds but birdsong and the wind rustling in the evergreens, with the feel of packed earth beneath my feet, all my reservations and confusion fell away. I understood then that I was deeply, completely, helplessly and hopelessly in love with George.

On our first day at Blackhawk Ridge, we sat on top of the picnic table in front of what we now called *our* shack and took an I.Q. test we'd found in a magazine I'd brought along. We were amazed at how close our scores were. Somewhat immaturely, I took that as a sign that we were meant to be together. But the similarity in our intelligence quotients, judged with unlikely reliability by a popular woman's magazine, was not as significant as our ability to laugh together or talk endlessly about anything and everything, from whether or not children should go to kindergarten to the current popularity of the Bee Gees or the presidency of Jimmy Carter. The sweet-smelling breeze cooling our backs as we hunched over the magazine and read silly articles together, the fragrant woods enveloping us all added to the feeling that, no matter what happened when we returned home, our being together now in this place was not bad or immoral or even irresponsible. It was as it should be. It was right.

After spending an easy and intimate day together and eating the bags of food George had brought for dinner, it seemed only natural to crawl into the cabin's narrow lower bunk together. For a long time, as the world darkened around us, we lay on our backs, held hands and continued to talk. George stroked my hair and my cheek and finally turned to me and said he wanted to make love with me. The word he used—*with* instead of *to*—surprised me for a minute. I'd never heard 'making love' described exactly that way before. I didn't respond. I only reached out as he turned to me. I encircled him with my arms and pulled him close. I was scared but I wanted him, wanted to know what it would be like to make love *with* a man I felt I knew so well and loved so much.

And the love-making was a mutual act, more than any love-making I'd ever done with anyone. Clearly George was as concerned about my pleasure as his own. And the safety I felt with him allowed me to understand for the first time why everyone thought sex was so great. It *was* great. More than great. It was the exquisite act of complete union of two people deeply in love, deeply lost in the essence of each other. Later, as we cuddled in the tiny bed together and listened to the night sounds beyond the walls of the small building, I had my answer about what I needed to do. There was no going back to the life I'd been attempting to live. In every sense of the word, George was my lover, my life partner now, and I would not, *could not*, go back to living a life with another man.

Because neither Mike nor I had confided in friends or family members about our problems, everyone was stunned by our announcement that we were divorcing. When I told my mother, the intensity of her anger shocked me. "How could you?" she asked, her words more of an assault than a question. "Don't you understand what this will do to your father and your son?" By this time Mike was a vice-president in Dad's company and the two of them worked very closely together. Mike was in line to become a partner in Dad's firm and probably even take it over when Dad retired.

"Your dad can't run that company on his own," Mom continued, her voice shaking as she held herself rigid. "He's already had one heart attack. Do you want to kill him? You will, you know. And you'll destroy your son, too."

Her words were like a slap across my face. It had never been Mom's style to be so loud and upfront about her feelings and I was devastated, not only by her words, but because I'd had no idea that my divorce—or for that matter *any* of my actions—could cause her so much pain. Had anything I'd ever done mattered that much to her? After what she'd said, how could I even consider doing something that would hurt her so much and destroy two of the people I loved more than anyone else in the world: my son and my father. But how could I stay in a marriage when I loved someone else as deeply and as completely as I loved George? Stay in a life that wouldn't include him? That would surely destroy me.

Before my mother could see the full effect of her words, I grabbed my coat and headed for the door. Rain and my tears made it difficult to see the tree-lined road before me and the thought crossed my mind that everyone would be better off if I drove fast into one of the big oak trees at the side of the road. I knew I couldn't continue in my marriage to Mike, but I couldn't be the one to destroy my son and my father either. I never thought to question the truth of my mother's words or her motives. I kept the car on the road and as soon as I arrived home I called the therapist I'd been seeing for several years. She assured me no one would be destroyed and that everyone would eventually get used to the idea of the divorce. She said perhaps it was time for me to pull away from my mother with her angry opinions while I did what I needed to do.

My divorce from Mike was final when Brad was four. Mike didn't leave my father's business and Dad didn't have another heart attack. Brad saw his dad and grandparents often and was the happy little boy he'd always been. Mom decided to go into therapy to deal with her strong feelings around my actions and I continued to see my own therapist. As she had predicted, no one was destroyed by the divorce, but my relationship with Mom was strained throughout the following year.

A year after the divorce I was married again, this time not because I believed I couldn't make it on my own—in the year between marriages I'd bought a condo, returned to school and was holding a good position with a large corporation—but because I was deeply in love. For the first time, I felt I was making a decision to be with someone for all the right reasons.

My mother reacted to my announcement that I was marrying George almost as violently as she had to my announcement that I was divorcing Mike.

"George is divorced and already has a child of his own," she needlessly pointed out. "He'll leave you someday," she warned. "Just like he did his other wife." But she also offered her house for our small wedding on a Thursday in May 1979 and prepared a wedding lunch of my favorite foods for our guests. Perhaps she made the offer because she thought it was the proper thing to do, but it was a nod towards healing our relationship and I welcomed it.

It would be many years before I understood that my mother reacted so strongly to my decision to divorce Mike because she hadn't completely accepted her parents' divorce. She was only ten when that happened and was perhaps projecting onto Brad what she'd felt when her father was no longer in her life. I learned later that there were times when she'd thought about leaving Dad but made the decision to stay. She expected me to do the same.

ELEVEN

Unexpected Change
of Plans

By the summer of 1981 George, Brad, and I were living in Alburnett, Iowa, in a house in the country with cows across the road and blackbirds on the fence posts. Mike had remarried and so had Janet. Mike stayed in the Chicago area with his new wife and her two children from a previous marriage and for a while—despite Mom's earlier fears—continued to work at Dad's company. Janet moved with her new husband and George's only son, Jon, to South Carolina. There, she had two more children with her second husband.

I was pregnant again the year after George and I married, but that turned out to be an ectopic pregnancy. Emergency surgery saved my life, but we lost the baby. The surgeon performed an intricate reconstruction of my fallopian tube during the life-saving operation, so that I'd have a better chance of becoming pregnant again. Pregnancies had always been difficult for me: I had miscarried several times when married to Mike.

Now George and I were expecting again and I considered myself blessed. I was awaiting the birth of another child and living in rural Iowa, an area I'd always loved; George had a good job with a large international corporation; Brad was doing well in the second grade; and I had, in a manner of speaking, "found God."

After George accepted the position with the company but a couple of months before he began the job, Mom and I had headed off on a road trip to Iowa. We were to visit her father, a widower living in Newton; look for a place for George, Brad and I to live near Cedar Rapids; and continue to work on healing our relationship. After visiting with Granddad we headed north to Cedar Rapids and kept going. I didn't want to live within city limits again.

Together, we found a house for George and me to rent just as she and I would rediscover Poudre Canyon in Colorado many years later. The house we found was about 15 miles north of Cedar Rapids. I should have thought about schools for Brad or George's drive into work every day, but all I could think about after living in a condo in a suburb outside Chicago was that I wanted fresh air and space to plant a garden, and I wanted to look at fields and birds and cows. I didn't want close neighbors. I wanted to hear nothing at night but the sound of crickets.

The house was on a corner. A paved country road ran in front of the house and intersected with a dirt road to the north of the property. When the owner, Darrell, showed it to my mother and me, he called it "the old home place" which sounded romantic to us. It was the original house on the family farm and had belonged first to his great-grandparents and then to his parents. When he married and took over the farm, Darrell told us, he and his new wife preferred to live in a bright modern tract home: they built one about two miles down the road.

The old home place *was* a mess. The grayish paint on the clapboard siding was peeling off in large curling sheets. The front porch looked as if it were about to fall off and the house listed a little to the side. Still, there were poppies blooming in the ditches beside the roads, red-wing blackbirds sitting on each fence post and a herd of cows nuzzling each other in a nearby field. I was delighted with the house and glad to learn that there was an elementary school for Brad about 15 minutes away by bus. The paved road in front of the house was a direct link to George's new office. And the price was right: $200 a month.

I had learned of the ectopic pregnancy just a couple of weeks before we were to leave Illinois. So on the day we arrived at our new Iowa home, I was still sore and weak from the surgery that had repaired the fallopian tube where the embryo had been growing. The pregnancy couldn't be saved and I was still grieving the loss. I needed country space and time to heal.

We arrived there late one afternoon in August. The moving van was coming the next day and this was the first time George had seen the house; I thought he'd be as pleased with it as I was.

Darrell was waiting for us in the driveway. We parked the car and met him at the back door. I was disappointed to see that the house looked a tad shabbier than it had when my mother and I discovered it. More paint had peeled off its exterior and no one had mowed or watered the lawn recently. Weeds had replaced the poppies in the ditch beside the road and no cows lowed peacefully in the neighboring field. Darrell must have noticed my questioning look and said, "I'm in the process of stripping it." He pointed to the side of the house. "I'll have it looking good as new in no time."

As George and I walked up the back steps behind Darrell and Brad hurried off to explore, George gave me a dirty look. I whispered to him to be patient. He would *love* the inside, I told him quietly.

We followed Darrell into the kitchen and I felt myself brighten. George *would* love the house. The kitchen walls were now a lovely sunshine yellow—not the nauseous green they'd been before.

"I just finished painting it," Darrell announced, standing a bit straighter. He nodded in the direction of the kitchen ceiling. "Since you were here, Mary, the bathtub fell through from above and I had to repair the ceiling. The wife figured it'd be just as well if we went ahead and painted the whole kitchen for you." Darrell said this as if a bathtub falling through the ceiling was an everyday occurrence in his world.

George gave me "the look," but didn't say anything as Darrell led us through the living room—*it* hadn't been painted and looked every bit as dingy as the exterior of the house—and up the stairs. As Darrell walked ahead of us, he attempted to stomp on the jumping crickets that were thick in the worn carpet on each stair.

"They're good luck," I whispered to George.

"I'm not spending one night in this house," he whispered back.

But George and I did spend that night in the house. We spent the next three years there. George stopped complaining except to use the house as the butt of his jokes and all of us had wonderful times. Darrell never did paint the outside and George refused to on principle. But I made curtains for the windows out of brightly colored bed sheets I bought at K-Mart and we painted some of the interior walls. Mostly we spent our time outdoors, snowmobiling in the winter and gardening in the summer, or leaving altogether to visit our cabin in Galena or camp in nearby state parks. We made friends with families on the road who had children close to Brad's age. We stayed in Alburnett until my long drive to graduate school in Iowa City provoked a move to Cedar Rapids, where I could be closer to school and George could be more available to Brad when I was away. Except for the loss of another baby and the continued ups and downs of managing our blended family, life in Alburnett was good.

When George and I lost our first baby due to an ectopic pregnancy, I developed the uncomfortable belief that I was being punished. I discussed my feelings with one of my new Iowa friends Julie because I had noticed that she talked about Jesus in an offhand sort of way—as if He was not only Jesus, the son of God, but also a personal friend of hers. Despite having always longed for a spiritual connection, I had been estranged from the church since my divorce and I had not grown up in a church that was on such familiar terms with Jesus. Several members of the church Mike and I attended when we lived in Lake Bluff blamed me for the breakup and warned of eternal damnation if I went through with the divorce. After the loss of one baby and my difficulty conceiving again, I wondered if perhaps they were right and the damnation had already begun.

I confided my fears to Julie and she told me about a time when she had felt guilty, too. But there was an answer, she said. She knew a minister who could help me.

I was willing to do *anything* to feel better, so I made an appointment with the minister Julie recommended. Instead of being in a church, his office was located in a modern office building in downtown Cedar Rapids. And what I thought was going to be a counseling session was actually an informal discussion in which, quite unexpectedly, I was asked if I wanted to accept Jesus Christ as my lord and savior. Because I wanted desperately to feel better and because I didn't want to disappoint this very nice and helpful man, I said that, yes, I did.

The minister said a prayer or two and asked a few questions. Then I bowed my head and he put his hand on top of it and asked me if I wanted to be forgiven for my sins and I said yes I most certainly did and then I accepted Christ. The minister, whose name I can't for the life of me remember, declared me new and clean in Christ, our lord and savior, and directed me to go forth and sin no more. I was, he said, born again.

I walked out of his office and felt as if life really *had* changed in that instant. I felt lighter, happier and in love with this Christ I now thought I'd never really known before. And right then, I believed what the minister had told me was true: that because I had honestly asked for forgiveness *and* accepted Jesus Christ, life would be about as perfect as any human life could be. *The next time I get pregnant*, I assured myself, *I'll carry the baby to term and it will be healthy. George and I will finally have the child together we want so much.*

Soon I *was* pregnant again. This time I believed that because my sins had been wiped clean and Jesus was now in charge of everything that had to do with my life, nothing bad would happen to this baby. But within a matter of days after my pregnancy was confirmed, I started bleeding and having a familiar pain in my side. I couldn't, *wouldn't* believe that this embryo was also growing in one of my fallopian tubes, the same one that had been fixed before. But my obstetrician didn't share my faith. She said, "Mary, it isn't unusual to have another ectopic pregnancy after having one, especially in the repaired tube. We need to do a test to see if you're bleeding internally. If you are, your life is in danger."

"Could the test you want to do abort the baby?" I asked.

"Yes it could," she said. "I'm not going to lie to you. But we need to do the test anyway."

"If there is a chance that a healthy baby is in my uterus and not in my tube, and having the test could cause it to abort, then I'm not having the test.'

George sat beside me with a stricken look on his face. "Mary..." he started to say.

"No. I'm going home. I believe this baby is fine. We will both be fine."

As soon as I got home, I called the friends I'd recently made in my new church. They were all born-again Christians and followers of the belief that what you claim in Jesus' name has already come to pass. I called Julie, too. She and my new friends told me what I wanted to hear. All I had to do was pray for the health of the baby and the baby would be fine.

So I went to bed and prayed. I claimed the baby in Jesus' name. I skimmed books by believers such as Fr. McNutt, a Catholic priest who insisted that we could be healed by faith alone. I searched for the words I wanted to hear and read them over and over. I, too, affirmed that my faith in Christ's power would protect my baby.

Every night I said the same prayer over and over like a mantra, repeating the words so automatically and constantly that I soon stopped hearing myself say them at all. *I claim the health and the life of this baby in Jesus' name. Amen.*

Then one night, something strange happened. As usual, George and Brad were downstairs in the living room watching television. I was in bed alone, propped up with the Bible open to the psalms on my lap, saying my prayer over and over. Suddenly the light in the room changed. It flickered like the bulb in the lamp was about to burn out. I whispered my prayer again: *I claim the health and the life of this baby in Jesus' name. Amen.*

I must have dozed off while repeating my prayer because later in the night I was awakened by a sound. Though I hadn't heard George come to bed, he was now asleep beside me. The light in the room was off, my Bible was on the bedside table to my right and George was on my left with his back to me. Without thinking, I did what I always did whenever I woke up in the night those days—I said my prayer. I said it several times in a row, again, not thinking much about the words.

Then I heard a voice. I turned to see if George had said something to me, but his back was still turned and his breathing was the slow rhythmic breathing of sleep. I heard the voice again, emanating from within my body and outside of it at the same time. The voice sounded deep and masculine and very clear. And it said, "Mary, you are praying the wrong prayer. You are praying for *your* will to be done, not mine." On one level I knew the voice wasn't really there, but on another level I believed it was and that it spoke the truth. Very gently, almost soothingly, the voice said, "Pray for *my* will."

I let go. I felt my body relax into the mattress. I felt all the fight and will and desire and need and resolve go out of me. I knew, body and soul, that the voice was speaking the truth. I had been praying for the wrong thing. Now I whispered, "God, I pray for *your* will, whatever that might be. If it is *your* will that I don't have this baby, then I accept that." And I knew that I was speaking the truth. I knew I would and could accept whatever it was that God willed for me.

The next morning the pain was gone and I was sure God had answered my prayer, that the baby was fine and the test, if I chose to have it, would not cause me to abort. I sensed that God was leading me to let the doctor do what she wanted to do. George took me into the hospital to have the test on his way to work. I didn't even ask him to stay with me. I felt certain that I and our baby would be fine.

But we weren't. I was bleeding internally: it was another ectopic pregnancy. While I waited and prayed in my bed at home all those days, the embryo had grown large enough to burst the fallopian tube to which it had been attached. When the tube burst, the pressure was relieved and the pain stopped. If I hadn't heard what I thought was the voice of God and listened, if I had once again chosen to stay home alone that day, I would have bled to death before the bus had dropped Brad off after school.

Later, my doctor told us that it was too risky for me ever to get pregnant again. One tube was gone and the chance of another embryo getting stuck in my other tube was high. Next time I might not be so *blessed*. Another tubal pregnancy could kill me.

I had surgery to tie my last remaining tube, cutting off the possibility of another pregnancy for good. I was paralyzed with grief. Even though I had a ten-year-old son, I could hardly look at him, much less do the mothering he so desperately needed. I didn't want George near me, sexually or otherwise, especially after he told me he wouldn't consider adoption. I hated him for that.

Then one day as I lay in bed, wondering if I was hungry enough to make the effort to get up and find something to eat, George came in and sat down on the side of our bed. He touched me on the leg. "You need to get up," he said. "You need to get up and find something to do. Go get a job or find a volunteer position. You've felt sorry for yourself long enough." I scowled at him. I thought I had plenty of reasons to feel sorry for myself and a couple of months didn't seem nearly long enough to grieve for all the children I'd never have.

But there was something in his voice: a firmness, a resolve. He went on to say that he needed me and Brad needed me and I needed to find a way to get over the grief and move on. He didn't think my staying alone all day in the house while Brad was at school and he was at work was the answer. He told me to find a job and to find one fast.

I don't know why or how I found myself down at the Department of Human Services in Cedar Rapids but I did. I walked in one Monday morning after dropping Brad off at school and asked to see the director of volunteers. I told her I wanted to work with children. "I'll do anything," I said, "as long as it's not in administration. As long as it's hands-on work with children."

I worked for a year with a program called Kinship. Kinship was similar to Big Brothers/Big Sisters, except that the Kinship children who were matched with mentors all had troubled parents who'd come to the attention of Social Services in one way or another. I did eventually take on administrative duties when I was elected president of the board, but mostly I worked with the children. Instead of overseeing just one child as the other mentors did, however, I supervised the adults and in that way connected with all the children, the mentors, the Board, and with Sylvia, the woman who hired me.

Sometimes George and Brad joined me and the Kinship kids and mentors for picnics or other outings. One year around Halloween, George had the idea that we make our basement, which was already pretty scary, into a haunted house. By then we had moved to Cedar Rapids and were living in a rambling old house. The inside was cavernous and drafty and almost as rundown as the Alburnett rental, but it had a beautiful park-like sloping lawn, a circular driveway, a wrap-around porch, a back staircase between the boys' room and the kitchen, and fireplaces in the living room, bedroom and dining room. George said we should invite all the Kinship families over for the Halloween party. There was plenty of room for a big adult gathering upstairs and he and Brad could run the haunted house in the basement. I happily agreed.

Brad and George hung cobwebby stuff all over the basement and piped in scary noises and created different spots where the kids could put their hands into buckets or barrels and touch fake eyeballs and spiders and other ghoulish sorts of substances. At one point in the evening, I looked around with satisfaction. My home was filled with children—laughing, playing, happy children. I only had one of my own, but in some ways I had many. That night it clicked. I suddenly understood that there are many ways to have children and the God I believed in had led me to one way. As I watched the laughing Kinship kids and their parents maneuver through our makeshift haunted house, I gratefully saw that George and Brad were helping me realize my lifelong dream to have a great big, happy family.

One day, Sylvia suggested I go back to school for a graduate degree in social work. At the time George, Brad and I were still living in Alburnett; we had not yet moved to the big house in Cedar Rapids. "You're a natural," Sylvia said. "You should get paid for doing this work."

So again without thinking much about it, I meekly followed another's suggestion, as I had when George told me to stop feeling sorry for myself over the loss of our baby and find something to do. As Sylvia suggested, I went back to school and obtained a degree in social work. I decided to specialize in the treatment of abused and neglected children.

Because of my work, I've been fortunate to have many children in my life. There was David, who was abandoned by his parents at the age of two-and-a-half when he was thrown from a car and left a paraplegic. There was Cynthia, who had been sexually molested by her father over a period of years and had stopped talking until the day she started talking again to me. There was Jamie and her baby, Little Jamie. Jamie was an unwed teenager who lived with us on and off for a year. There have been numerous young girls in 12-step programs and in jails, and young mothers who didn't know how to diaper or feed or comfort their newborns and wanted me to help them. There were young MSW students I supervised and my son's friends. Each young person meant something special to me. I could say that each one occupied a special place in my heart like the babies I'd lost.

One of those exasperating questions that loops in and out of my mind periodically is "what does God want from me?" It came to me recently that perhaps one of my purposes was to be sort of "mom" to these young people—every single one of them. And if I'd birthed all the children I'd wanted, I wouldn't have volunteered to work with children at the Department of Human Services, nor would I have returned to school to study the treatment of high-risk minors. Most likely, I would not have opened myself so completely to all those children and young people I've had the honor to know.

Not long ago a friend of mine asked whether I think I'll ever see my lost babies again. She was talking about meeting them after my own death. I told her I didn't have to wait that long. "I've already seen them," I said.

TWELVE

Opportunity for Growth

At the beginning of 1986, George announced unexpectedly that he had accepted a promotion from the company and was moving to Southern California, with or without me. If I'd rather, I could divorce him and stay put, he said. He didn't much care one way or the other. We still lived in Cedar Rapids and I was finishing my graduate degree at the University of Iowa. Brad was just a few months shy of completing sixth grade. George and I weren't getting along at all. Neither of us remembered what we'd loved so much about the other when we first got together; instead, we were concentrating on the difficulties between us, of which there were many. We each tried to live up to our self-imposed expectations of ourselves as partners and parents while juggling over-extended schedules. We flung the "divorce" word at each other quite freely.

I was also drinking too much. Looking back, I think I used alcohol in a futile attempt to bury my belief that I'd failed at so many of life's basic tasks, like marriage and motherhood. Even something as natural as conceiving and carrying to term another baby had eluded me. I worked with parents who often hadn't wanted the children they had and certainly needed help in caring for them adequately. But instead of dealing in a healthy way with the resentment and grief their situations brought up in me, I tried to bury all of it with alcohol. And George seemed angry at me or disappointed in me much of the time, too, which also fed my belief that I had failed again. He was unhappy with his work situation and our geographical distance from his son and I felt that nothing I did or said made up for his own feelings of loss and disappointment. I stopped trying to fix the problems between us and turned to the people I was meeting at graduate school for friendship and comfort. Because of the deep love George and I once had for one another, I naively believed our marriage could withstand anything. Now, like our first marriages, it was in imminent danger of dissolving.

Drinking played a role in our marriage from its beginning and it was my medication of choice for years. From the time George and I had first lived together in Illinois, I'd been drinking to manage my fear that I wasn't good enough for him and that sooner or later he'd figure that out and leave me. And before that I was drinking in high school, college and when I was married to Mike. For years, alcohol had helped me cope with whatever was going on in my life, whatever fear I happened to have at the time.

Now George was saying that he wasn't sure he wanted me with him in California and all my fears were on the brink of coming true. Even if George had wanted me with him, I wasn't sure I wanted to live in California anyway. I had nothing but bad memories from when I'd lived there briefly as a child and when I'd visited a couple of times with Mike. Once, Brad had almost drowned in the Disneyland Hotel pool while I read a book and drank a Mai Tai. Brad, barely three years old, was in the water and edging himself around the side of the pool when he lost his grip. I looked up just in time to see him frantically paddling his little arms and legs, his bright blue eyes growing bigger and rounder as he tried to keep his mouth and nose above the surface of the water.

Moving from Iowa to California meant I would be leaving my world of interesting and progressive thinkers and Iowa's deep blue sky and gently rolling farmlands, for cement and smog and shameful memories and John Birch Society types. I had to think about it. What if we moved out there and our marriage failed? I'd be away from my family and friends and a guaranteed job. Though I'd left my volunteer position at Kinship when I was halfway through graduate school, Sylvia and Dan and others I'd met through the program were still good friends. I had friends at the University and I was active in social programs around the community. The small non-profit agency where I was currently an intern had promised me a paid position after graduation. I'd be giving up a life I loved and felt comfortable in for a life I was certain I wouldn't like at all. But I'd taken my son away from one father already and I couldn't bring myself to take him away from another, especially since I didn't think he had much of a mother in me. Regardless of the difficulties between George and me, Brad loved and needed him. And I loved and needed George, too, even if sometimes it was hard to remember that or to understand why. I still hoped he felt the same way about me. Perhaps if we moved to California together, I thought, we'd discover once again the love I knew we still had for each other.

So just days after Brad finished sixth grade and I graduated from the University of Iowa's Social Work School, we made our move. George's corporation paid for a moving company to take our belongings to California, so we only had to worry about ourselves and the plants and animals. With Brad and a fun-loving friend of his who, at the last minute, decided to accompany us to California for a quick vacation, belted into the backseat of our brown mini-van and our ride-loving cocker spaniel tucked in between them, we made one last attempt to capture the member of our family who hated to ride: a very stubborn tiger cat named Lucky. We were about ready to leave her behind with neighbors when the feline tranquilizer we'd given her that morning took effect. She wobbled a couple of times and crumpled to the ground. We handed her to the boys and were finally on our way, heading south to pick up I-80 West. When Lucky finally came to, she spent the remainder of the several-day-long trip on the dashboard, looking warily out at the road ahead and complaining loudly about the indignity of it all. I could relate. I felt the same way about the move as she did, but with slightly less complaining. She was leaving wide-open outdoor spaces for life as a suburban tract-home cat; I was leaving my friends and relatives and a job I loved for an unknown future with a husband I wasn't sure loved me anymore. Everyone had said it would take me at least two years to find a social work position in California because I didn't speak fluent Spanish. I couldn't let that happen. If I needed to brush up on my college Spanish, I would. We needed the money and I needed a job just to keep myself from going insane.

George and I had bought a relatively new home in Yorba Linda, the town next to the one where his office was located. He had traveled back and forth between California and Iowa for almost six months while Brad and I finished up our last semesters at school. The house was a typical California subdivision home, very different from the two houses we'd occupied in Iowa. The California house was on a cul-de-sac and had a triangle of dirt that was the backyard and a concrete slab for a patio. I knew we could change that and I was entranced with our view of the hills just to the east of us and the yipping of coyotes at night. When we moved in, the hills were covered in pine, pinion and scrub oak. When we left 11 years later, row upon row of look-alike mini-mansions had replaced the beautiful foliage on the hills.

Despite all the warnings, I found a job within two months of moving to California. It was in Riverside, a 30-minute drive east on the 91 freeway. I worked for the Riverside County Child Dependency Unit as an investigator. After a first responder from the Child Protective Service Unit removed a minor from an allegedly dangerous home, the case was transferred to our department and one of us was charged with investigating it within the three-week period required by law. We would then make a recommendation at a court hearing about whether the child should be kept out of the home or sent back. If we thought further investigation was needed, we had to make a case for keeping the child away from his parents long enough for discovery and for treatment recommendations to be made. The cases were assigned on a rotational basis, and because I began with an empty docket, my cases came rapidly at first. I had to learn how to do the job by doing it. And I had to learn without making serious mistakes. A mistake could mean life or death for a child: if I overlooked something or didn't file the necessary papers on time, the whole case could be thrown out of court and a child returned to a dangerous home. My stress level shot up when I was suddenly immersed in the challenges and emergencies of the position, a position for which graduate school had done little to prepare me.

In every other job I'd held, no one's life actually depended on what I did. Not so with this job. When I worked with abused and neglected children in Iowa, it was difficult and often heartbreaking, but it didn't seem particularly overwhelming. In Iowa, I wasn't taking children away from parents; I was helping parents get their children back. And in Iowa, I worked in close conjunction with a team or partner or supervisor. But in California, I felt as if I were working alone in a war zone. We all had too many cases to be holding each other's hands or paying much attention to what our co-workers were doing. But just before court, and after I'd completed all the footwork on the case, I was required to discuss and defend my decision with a supervisor who then could, and often would, change my recommendation. Having worked so hard to come up with what I believed was just the right plan for a particular child and family only to have it superseded by a tired and jaded supervisor was crushing. I grieved for parents who loved their children but were incapable of holding onto them without court-ordered assistance. Worse were the cases where parents couldn't hold onto their children at all, the cases in which termination of parental rights would surely occur sooner or later.

One case in particular broke my heart. We rightfully removed the two-year-old son of a mother who was arrested and jailed for using heroin. She was also dating a long-time user and dealer who had hooked her on the drug. She'd not been using long and clearly wanted to clean herself up, dump the boyfriend and get her baby back. With a glass wall of the jail between us and clutching our phone receivers against our ears, we stared into each other's eyes as I tried to assess if she was telling me the truth and she tried to figure out if I were willing to help her. After numerous hours spent talking to her and interviewing her family members, I came to the conclusion that, with assistance, she was motivated and strong enough to turn her life around; she also had strong family support. So I recommended that her son be temporarily placed with his grandparents. I also recommended that we design a plan that included possible return of the son to his mother if she rigorously followed our protocol once she was out of jail. My supervisor didn't agree and, without visiting either the mother or the grandparents, rewrote my recommendation to the court. She recommended that we start the process to terminate parental rights immediately so the child could be put up for adoption; all contact between the child and his natural family would end forever. I was unusually and perhaps unprofessionally distraught over the circumstances of this particular case. I didn't realize that I was affected by *my* old issues as well as by what was happening to this mother and child. Instead of understanding why I reacted so strongly, I viewed my supervisor as overly punishing and vengeful. I judged the other investigators in my unit as out-of-step with my social work values. I felt misunderstood and undervalued as I struggled to do my job.

And there were other cases, horrible cases, where children would be returned to dangerous home situations if we didn't convince the court to safeguard the children in foster care until the parents either changed—often highly unlikely—or until we could initiate the process of terminating parental rights. Some of these children had been so brutalized or neglected—often left to fend for themselves while their parents and other caretakers spent days in drug-induced stupors—that we had to work almost around the clock to make sure our case reports and timing were impeccable, so that no slip-up on our part could cause the case to be thrown out of court.

I interviewed people in jails, crack houses and on their hospital deathbeds. Sometimes I had to call for police back-up. Often I'd find myself in my car in the dark, wandering around the Riverside County high desert, trying to find the road that would lead me back to my own clean, warm, safe home. Drugs were taking their toll in Riverside County in the late 1980s. I started to think—wrongfully, of course—that everyone I saw on a street in my territory was an addict or a child molester. One late afternoon at dusk, I broke my foot stepping off a poorly lit porch and walked around in almost unbearable pain for a couple of days, afraid to tell my supervisor. I believed I couldn't afford to be away from my post even for a little while: too much was at stake. The safety of too many children depended on my doing my job.

Driving home at night, I'd sometimes have a panic attack like the ones I used to have in junior high and high school. Going west on the 91 Freeway towards home after work, I'd find myself claustrophobic, with semis closing in on either side of me. I'd pray that I wouldn't faint as I frantically searched for an opening in the traffic so I could pull off to the side and sit for a while until my breathing slowed and my shaking stopped.

I suffered from recurring nightmares, too. A child was screaming and I was trying to get to her in some mansion with many closed and bolted doors. Once I'd manage to unbolt the door and swing it open, I'd discover a horrifying scene of some sort, but no screaming child. I'd continue to search as the screaming went on.

I quickly figured out that if I drank enough wine before bed I didn't have the nightmares: I could pass out to a dreamless sleep. But by self-medicating, I was creating other problems not so noticeable at first, problems that chipped away at the foundation of my family and home. I was neglecting George and Brad and often even emotionally abusing them at the same time I was trying to rescue the abused and neglected children of others. I left my husband and son to fend for themselves and sometimes even raged at them, while I suffered from almost inestimable fears and insecurities of my own. Brad was in his first year of high school and the school was big and confusing for him. George now had more responsibility than he'd had in the Cedar Rapids position and the pressures on him were also great. Both he and Brad had their own fears and insecurities, but I didn't let that be my concern. All I could think about were those other children screaming for me behind countless closed doors.

Desperate for help, I talked to my internist, Dr. O. Perhaps he had a pill he could give me, an anti-anxiety drug, so I wouldn't have to change, but could feel better. Instead of immediately prescribing something for me as I wanted him to do, he asked me a series of questions. One question was, "How many alcoholic drinks do you have in a day?" I didn't know doctors asked those sorts of questions. But I answered him honestly. That surprised me, because I wasn't being particularly honest about anything in those days with anyone, including myself.

"I only drink wine," I said a little defensively. "But I drink enough of that to put me to sleep every night."

"How much is that, Mary?" he asked gently.

The kindness in his voice helped me to continue. "I don't know. We have one of those wine boxes. You know, the kind you put in the refrigerator, the kind with the spigot?"

"How many glasses, then?" He wasn't letting me off the hook.

"Two or three, I guess."

"Wine glasses?"

"No. Water glasses." I didn't have to fill them as often.

For a few minutes he didn't say anything. I could hear people laughing and talking at the nurses' station beyond the closed door. The clock on the examining room wall ticked loudly. I looked at my bare legs hanging over the side of the examining table. My paper gown crackled when I moved.

Finally, Dr. O came around to the side of the table and gently lifted my chin with his hand so I'd look at him. I sensed his caring and wanted to cry.

"Mary, I think you have a drinking problem. It's understandable given the work you do and your sensitive nature. But it can't go on without causing real physical and emotional damage to you. I want you to get help and the best help out there for people with a drinking problem is a 12-step program: Alcoholics Anonymous."

He walked away from me and put a card down next to my purse. "This is the number for AA. Call them. They'll tell you where the meetings are located. Please go right away. You can't mess around with this."

I looked at that number for days. I played games with myself. I prom-

with me following, screaming at him to answer my questions. Without looking at me or responding, he picked up his wallet and car keys and left the house. Shaking and crying, I poured a drink to calm myself. When he returned hours later, he found me asleep on our bed, curled up in a fetal position. One more time, Brad had been left to fix his own dinner and wonder what the hell was going on with his parents.

I still hadn't called the number for Alcoholics Anonymous that Dr. O had given me.

Shortly after Christmas that year, 1986, a friend from Iowa arrived for a week-long visit. Callie was a woman I'd met at graduate school. She was a few years younger than I was and unmarried; we'd become close friends in Iowa and stayed in touch after I moved to California. Callie was very aware of the ups and downs of my marriage. Several times during graduate school, I drove the 30 miles or so between my house and hers to fling myself into her arms and sob about a fight George and I'd just had. She always listened, but never gave advice until the day I drove her to the Orange County airport after her visit. Then, she finally spoke her mind.

"Mary, let me tell you what will happen after you drop me off at the airport."

I looked at her. I could hardly hold in the tears. My marriage was deteriorating and my work was terrorizing me. I had no friends in California, no one I felt I could talk to the way I could to Callie. And now she sounded angry. Glancing at her as I maneuvered through the freeway traffic, I tried to make sense of what she was saying.

"As soon as you get home, you'll go to the kitchen and pour yourself a drink," she continued. "It will only be early afternoon, but that won't make any difference to you. After you've had two or three glasses of wine, you'll go to George who will be sitting on a couch somewhere looking angry and you'll apologize. You'll apologize for everything bad you've ever done. You will say you're sorry for causing this last fight."

George and I had fought that morning as Callie was in the downstairs guest room packing to leave. I didn't think she'd noticed. I thought I'd been really good the whole week at keeping the problems between George and me to myself. I'd shown Callie around the Orange County area; we'd gone out to eat and to Disneyland; we'd talked about work, hers and mine. I tried not to dwell on the problems of my marriage, my fears about life in Southern California without my Iowa friends. But she'd seen through it all.

When I was sober and at least somewhat rational, I knew that I wasn't the only problem in our marriage, that George had serious anger issues he didn't know how to deal with and that I was often the focus of that anger. A very tiny part of me knew Callie was speaking the truth: that when I drank and George didn't, when George sat there on the couch looking furious, but also in a way holy and perfect and above me, I would wonder how he could stay with me and I would apologize. I would grovel, as Callie said. And eventually he would forgive me and give me some attention until it happened all over again. Although on some level I knew I wasn't always the one at fault, that sometimes I deserved an apology from George, I couldn't stand the tension our fights caused between us, so I'd give in and apologize.

It was not until much later, when I had been in recovery from alcoholism for a few years, that I realized George hadn't wanted my apologies. He'd wanted me to change my behavior and, until I got sober, I couldn't. Callie didn't see all of this in the short time she was with us. What she thought she saw was her friend being treated badly for no good reason and her friend doing everything she could to get her husband to stop his bad behavior. Just like my therapist before her, I think Callie thought I was making a fool of myself with George by constantly apologizing and begging him to give me the opportunity to improve.

"Mary, you've got to listen to me and you've got to do as I say. You need to call Alcoholics Anonymous. Today."

I didn't say a word. It was the second time someone had told me I needed AA. I kept my eyes on the road and tried not to cry.

When I returned home, I looked up AA in the telephone book. Shaking, I called the number. I wanted to drink, but I held off; I'd act the professional on the phone. I told myself to be the woman who could fake things—pretend to be calling on behalf of a client.

THIRTEEN

Hitting Bottom

The next day I pulled into the parking lot behind a nondescript beige building decorated with graffiti and litter. A tight group of what I took to be homeless men hovered around the back door. It was a beautiful, sunny Southern California day with a cool breeze. I sat in the car for a few minutes gathering my courage, trying to put on my professional demeanor, the one I'd used so many times before when I needed to enter frightening places to do my job. Finally, I stepped out of my car, walked confidently—I thought—across the parking lot, nodded to the men around the door, squeezed through them and entered the dim smoky building as if I knew exactly what I was doing. In my red blazer and matching pleated skirt, I couldn't have been more conspicuous.

The room I entered was a kitchen with several large coffee pots set in a row on a chipped counter. Beyond the kitchen was a large room with no windows and high ceilings. There must have been at least 50 people, mostly men, in the room. Some were sitting in the middle at long tables that had been pushed together; the rest slumped in chairs, legs crossed or spread out in front of them, around the perimeter. Several people leaned against the walls. I was late and the meeting had already started. The leader looked up from what he was reading to the group, hesitated, glanced around the room and motioned me to an empty chair against the wall to his right. I couldn't bring myself to walk down the long row of people to the chair he indicated so I shook my head, trying to appear nonchalant, and stayed where I was in the door between the kitchen and the main room. I leaned against the doorjamb. He shrugged and went on reading.

Thinking I'd made a huge mistake, I was just about ready to turn and run out the back door. Callie and Dr. O were wrong: I was *not* an alcoholic. I didn't fit in with these people. These people were from the streets, they couldn't have jobs or families or only drink wine at night or on weekends the way I did. Many didn't even look sober and if they were, they hadn't been for long. Some were mumbling to themselves or each other. Only a few were paying attention to what the man was reading. The room was stuffy and smelled bad. There was no way I could stay, no way I could return to work without going home first for a shower. I turned to leave and felt a hand on my arm. I looked up to see a tall, white-haired man smiling down at me. He was clean-shaven and smelled good.

"Come with me," he said. He led me through the kitchen to a small room off the back. He turned on a light and pulled two folding chairs into the center of the room. "Sit."

I did and he proceeded to do something that I would later learn was called "12-stepping." He gave me my own private AA meeting in that little room behind the kitchen. He said he'd seen many women like me walk through the doors of AA over the years, women who looked good on the outside but felt like they were dying on the inside. He told me that women looking like me didn't walk into AA meetings unless we belonged there, whether we knew it yet or not, and he was pretty sure that if he let me leave it would be quite some time and further down the ladder for me before I found AA again. The nice-smelling man with the kind eyes told me there were lots of different kinds of AA meetings and even though all alcoholics had one thing in common—the need to drink and lots of pain and devastation because of it—they could be very different from each other, too. This meeting, he said, had a lot of street people in it because of where it was located.

He touched my arm gently and smiled with such understanding I was sure that if I listened to him talk much longer I'd fall hopelessly in love with this man.

"Someday," he said, "you'll be comfortable in any kind of AA meeting anywhere in the world, but you need to begin in one with people you can relate to. Otherwise, honey, you ain't never going to stay around long enough to experience the miracle."

Even though much of what he said didn't make a lot of sense to me, I could relate to him when he told me his story. He talked about incomprehensible demoralization and about being powerless over alcohol. He mentioned the unmanageability of his life when he was drinking. I, too, felt incomprehensible demoralization when I thought about many of my actions over the last several years. And I knew I was powerless over alcohol. I drank even when I had no intention of drinking. Even when I wanted to stop drinking—or limit it to only one or two drinks—I couldn't. And my life was certainly unmanageable: all anyone had to do was look at my marriage to see that.

The white-haired man gave me a blue book (euphemistically called The Big Book) and suggested I first read chapters three and five and some of the stories in the back. He asked me what town I lived in and then pointed to the listing of a morning meeting in Anaheim Hills on a typed schedule. "This one will be more your style," he said.

We finished talking and walked back through the kitchen to the main room. The meeting was over, but small groups of men and women still hung around, laughing and talking. They looked a little bit more normal, a little less scary than they had before. I thanked the man for talking to me and, with my new book in hand, I went back to work.

That night I didn't apologize to George and we didn't talk. Familiar feelings of abandonment and loneliness welled up inside me, but I didn't drink. For the first time in a long time, I got through an evening without alcohol. And the next morning I went to another AA meeting, this time the one in Anaheim Hills. I could more easily relate to the people there, just as the man had said I would. Like me, most of these people were dressed for work in jackets and ties, dresses and suits. There were at least as many women as men. The meeting, like the one the day before, was big, but this meeting was a non-smoking one. It was in a sunny, plant-filled conference room in a bank building. There were two large tables pushed together in the center and folding chairs around the periphery, like at the other meeting. I stayed right through this time, sitting in one of the chairs along the wall. We went around the room and introduced ourselves. I noticed that everyone only said their first name and announced, quite proudly sometimes, that they were an alcoholic. Sometimes they said, surprisingly, that they were a *grateful* alcoholic. I wondered how anyone could be grateful for such a thing. When they got to me, I said, "I'm Mary and I'm an alcoholic." I'd never said that before and even though I stumbled over the word, when I said it, I felt what I can only describe as the tiniest sensation of peace.

But the sensation didn't last. For a few days I didn't drink and I didn't apologize to George. If he noticed I wasn't drinking or hadn't apologized, he didn't say anything. And then, even without an apology from either of us, George and I started talking again. For a few mornings in a row I woke up, dressed and left the house early enough to attend the Anaheim Hills meeting before work. George never asked what I was doing and at first I didn't tell him. When I felt the time was right and I had a couple of weeks of sobriety, I told both George and Brad I'd been to some AA meetings. I told them I recognized now that I had a problem with alcohol—that in fact I was an alcoholic, someone who couldn't keep from drinking even when she wanted to.

Brad was 13 years old. He put his arms around me and said, "I'm so proud of you, Mom."

George looked at me as if I'd grown a second head and said, "Why do you have to think you're an alcoholic? That's crazy."

Within a few days, I was choosing to believe that George knew what he was talking about: it was crazy to think I was an alcoholic. I stopped going to meetings and started drinking again, proving how cunning and powerful is the disease of alcoholism. Soon we were right back to where we were before: fighting violently and me apologizing in tears afterwards. I tried not to notice the pain in Brad's eyes.

I was in and out of meetings for the next six months, alternating between knowing I was an alcoholic who couldn't control her drinking or her life and thinking that, if I just read the right book or figured out a way to make George treat me differently or if I cut back on how hard I worked, I'd be able to participate in some controlled drinking.

I had managed to put together about a month of sober days by attending the Anaheim Hills meeting every morning and pretty much white-knuckling it for the rest of the day and evening, when on Saturday, July 4, 1987, several people at the meeting got into an upsetting argument about who should or shouldn't be allowed to speak at meetings. Looking for any excuse to quit the program, I grabbed this one. *Well,* I said to myself, *if sober AA members can't get along, why bother?* Later I learned that I was making a common and dangerous mistake—putting personalities before principles, it's called. I left the meeting and when I arrived home I picked a fight with George.

George and I had plans to attend a party that afternoon with the boys, Brad and Jon, George's son, who was visiting us for the summer. The alcohol would flow freely and no one at the party other than my family would think anything of it if I drank some of it. That afternoon, when I was asked what I wanted to drink, I didn't hesitate before I answered, "Vodka tonic, please."

I hit my bottom, as they say in AA, that day. I hit it when no matter how much I drank I couldn't make the pain go away. I hit it when I saw the look of fear and pain in the eyes of our boys. I hit it when I looked into George's eyes and saw only disgust. And I hit it when he turned from me at the party and focused his attention on a beautiful and kind woman who appeared to have her life together, who was my friend and whom, at that moment, I hated with every fiber of my being.

The next day I went to the morning meeting in Anaheim Hills, admitted I'd "slipped"—the too-gentle word we use when someone drinks again—was welcomed back with love and understanding and started the long climb out of the pit.

When I got sober, I hoped that *working* a program and doing serious work as a therapy client myself would cure me of my jealousy. It didn't. As far as I was concerned, now I was even less lovable than before: an admitted alcoholic, barely managing a career, unable to bear more children—who *would* want someone like me? And especially why would someone like George, who appeared to have it all together and was good looking and accomplished, want someone like me? I couldn't talk about it with anyone, not with my AA sponsor or with Dr. A, the therapist I had started to see. I was too ashamed. But I no longer could use a substance to numb my pain, so when my fear that George would leave me for another woman got to the point I couldn't stand it anymore, I brought it up with Dr. A during one of our sessions. Almost in a whisper, I mumbled my confession as I stared down at my hands tearing apart a soggy tissue in my lap. Dr. A didn't say anything and I looked up, expecting to see his horror or disgust. All I saw in his face was compassion. "How terribly difficult that must be for you," he said.

Dr. A's words helped me see my actions differently. He helped me understand that what I felt was more of a burden for me than for anyone else, even though it looked as if the only one who could possibly suffer from it was George. He also helped me understand that my actions were a result of old and unresolved traumas. He assured me that once those traumas were addressed, I would stop feeling so badly and reacting the way I did. Still, Dr. A's words and the numerous therapy sessions I had with him, the hypnosis and the EMDR technique he led me through—none of it cured me of this insanity. Because I was no longer drinking I could manage it a bit better, but it never went away. Not completely. Not until George and I moved to the Poudre Canyon in Colorado.

FOURTEEN

Breaking Down and Building Up

The constant refrain that ran through my head during the last years I lived in California, in the months right before I bought the cabin in Colorado, was, "I'm tired." My journals are full of that sentence. And I *was* tired, but perhaps more than that, I was overwhelmed. I was overwhelmed by what I thought were the expectations and the seemingly relentless neediness of others. I had no boundaries. I didn't know how to say no.

AA's philosophy is that you help yourself stay sober by helping others to do the same. It is strongly suggested that as a member of AA you agree to do anything that's requested of you by another AA member or by potential members. AA old-timers in particular want program newcomers to be involved. So I got involved. I went to at least one meeting a day and out to coffee to socialize with other recovering alcoholics, even when I probably should have been at home with my son and husband. I chaired meetings; I accompanied members with more sobriety than I had on 12-step calls, in-home or in-hospital visits where we talked to drunks and encouraged them to use the program to get and stay sober. I did all this in addition to trying to raise a junior high-age son and be a good wife to George, both roles that I thought were way too difficult for me. I worked full time as a therapist at a non-profit agency and refrained from drinking no matter what. I sponsored a few newly sober women with all kinds of problems who needed far more assistance than I could give them. I wasn't very good at keeping my roles as AA sponsor and social worker separate. I wanted to help them and believed that, with my training, I could be of service.

But I was in no condition to help anyone, not even myself. I was too emotionally depleted and I was physically ill with a chronic disease that had not yet been diagnosed.

For a long time, alcohol had helped me tamp down unwanted emotions and memories. When I stopped drinking and before I learned how to automatically pick up the compensatory tools offered by 12-step programs, I didn't have any way to separate myself emotionally from my work as a therapist. Situations often arose that hooked old wounds and I wasn't capable yet of seeing the connection.

I ran a program for unwed pregnant women and new mothers who lived in small, private apartments in a converted convent maintained by a private, non-profit Catholic organization. These women were either in the last trimester of their pregnancies or in the first three months of new motherhood. They were only a few years older than Brad, young enough to be my own daughters.

Although I didn't know it at the time, I hadn't adequately dealt with my feelings about my own lost pregnancies, my inability to conceive again or George's unilateral decision that we would not adopt a child. Working with pregnant women unprepared to raise children, and with so many emotional problems of their own to overcome, fed my need to be a *good* parent. Somehow I must have believed that if I couldn't have more babies of my own, working with women who were having babies was the next best thing. Instead of putting forth the effort to strengthen the family I already had with George, Brad and Jon, I focused my efforts on making these newly forming dyads of mother and infant my new family—my fantasy family. I was once again living in a make-believe world.

I dedicated most of my attention to two of the women at the home. One of them, Rhonda, was particularly hard to work with. I thought the only reason she was keeping her child was to prove that she could, not out of any instinctive love for her new little boy. She didn't take to mothering easily; she was more concerned with dispatching her baby's needs as quickly as possible so she could get on with the life of a pretty and popular teenager. We tried to convince her that letting her child be adopted by a stable and loving couple might be the best route, but we weren't having any luck. The staff and I were concerned that if she didn't bond with her little boy he'd eventually end up in the system one way or another.

Often, Rhonda called me at the last minute to ask me to watch the baby so she could go out. It would have been better for both me and Rhonda if I'd refused her requests so she could learn quickly that having a child was a 24-hour commitment. But I couldn't turn down the opportunity to play mother to a newborn and I was concerned that if I didn't give Rhonda the reprieve she asked for, she might hurt or neglect her baby. Once, I brought Rhonda's baby home and lay him between George and me on our bed. For a little while I pretended he was ours.

The other young woman I felt closest to was a plump little blonde named Jamie, who'd named her baby boy, Little Jamie. The father was in the picture briefly, but Jamie had enough strength to break off her unhealthy relationship with him. She knew what it was like not to have a family of her own: she'd spent her childhood separated from her siblings as they all made the rounds of one foster family after another. She wanted to be the kind of mother who never lost her baby to the system and I decided I'd do whatever I could to help her accomplish that goal.

I stayed in contact with Jamie and Little Jamie until the baby was two. I helped them move into apartments, bought them food and stayed with the baby when necessary. For a while, they even lived in our home. But I couldn't keep Jamie from making mistakes with regard to men. She finally hooked up with a mentally unstable older man, who convinced her that I was a bad influence on her and Little Jamie. The last time I saw Jamie and her son, we met at a restaurant. Jamie told me she was leaving the state with the man. I tried to talk her out of it. She wouldn't change her mind.

In the restaurant, Little Jamie was happy, talking in his baby-talk way that was difficult to understand, climbing onto my lap and wrapping his fat soft arms around my neck and planting wet sticky kisses on my cheek. But when we hugged in the parking lot and said our goodbyes, Little Jamie looked at me with confusion in his eyes. It dawned on me that he'd been under the impression he would be going home with me. When finally we broke apart and Jamie turned to walk to her car, carrying Little Jamie over her shoulder, he screamed and reached his arms out to me, his eyes pleading. Between his sobs, he begged to be with Mama Mary. Jamie continued to walk away, holding Little Jamie tighter as he tried to wrestle himself out of her arms. I wanted to make her stop, but I had no rights or power. I'd said and done everything I could, but hadn't been able to change Jamie's mind. I'd lost the woman I'd let into my heart as a daughter and the baby I felt as close to as I would a grandchild. As I watched Little Jamie scream and reach for me, I wondered if I'd done them more harm than good with my inability to establish healthy boundaries early. I'd never know. Choking on my own sobs, I turned away and walked to my car.

I heard from Jamie one last time. She called about a year later, just before she and Little Jamie and the man, who was now her husband, crossed the border into Canada. I wasn't home to receive the call. George told me she sounded frightened and confused. I waited weeks for her to call again, but she never did.

Besides running the unwed mothers' program, I saw clients in my office at the agency. Donna, one of my clients, had strange and inexplicable behaviors and fears. She flipped rapidly and without noticeable cause between what could perhaps be called sub-personalities. These personalities included, among others, a very young child and a very angry and abusive man.

For months I worked with Donna, an adult woman who had suffered a brutal infancy and childhood. She'd been repeatedly sexually abused by her father and received no protection, although her mother probably had a pretty good idea of what was happening to Donna. Sometimes Donna was able to handle the sudden and painful memories by numbing out, the coping mechanism she'd used as a child. But the reason she was in therapy now was that the numbing out was not working as it had in the past. Now, stressful situations sent her into post-traumatic stress reactions such as severe panic attacks, flashbacks and bouts of piercing but psychosomatic pain in various parts of her body, including her genitals. I believed Donna was suffering from a severe dissociative disorder that was out of my area of expertise. I wanted to refer her to someone more qualified, but my supervisor/boss thought we'd cause Donna more harm if we transferred her because, by the time I was able to make a definitive diagnosis, she'd bonded with me. I kept Donna as a client and put myself through a crash course on dissociative disorders. I attended conferences and consulted experts. Every expert I contacted advised me *not* to refer Donna to someone else, assuring me that the relationship between therapist and client in these particular cases was more important than how knowledgeable I was about the disorder. They assured me, as did my supervisor, that I could develop my knowledge base faster than Donna could learn to trust another therapist. Everyone urged me to give her a great deal of time, even seeing her daily if necessary.

Donna could have been my only client and still created a full-time job for me. I saw her most days and received numerous phone calls from her when we weren't together. I worked with her frequently and intensely and tried to keep up on the current research on dissociative diseases. I was also barely holding together my personal life. Though I was sober, I still fought the compulsion to drink and needed daily meetings and frequent contact with other recovering alcoholics. Brad was having difficulty in school, George was often stressed and angry, and my boss was expecting me to do what I could to raise money for the agency in addition to my work with clients. I was trying to do way too much and doing none of it very well.

I was often ill, running unexplained fevers off and on. Dr. O, the doctor who first recognized my alcoholism, couldn't find any explanation for the fevers. I decided the answer was to stop working for someone else where I had little control over my time, and open a private practice where I thought, mistakenly, I would have more control.

My boss at the agency told me that Donna was too attached to me to transfer her to another therapist at the center and said that I had no choice but to take her with me into my private practice. I sensed that this would not be a good idea, but I ignored my intuition and did it anyway. Donna had a power over me no other client had ever had. I didn't recognize it at the time, but she, too, was hooking into the deep unresolved pain in me, pain that had to do with the long emotional and physical abuse I'd suffered from Jeff, as well as pain from too much responsibility and too little attention afforded me as a very young child. Donna coaxed longer and more sessions out of me. Telling me she was afraid to visit me in my office, she pleaded with me to meet her at parks, restaurants and even at my house. Against my better judgment, I usually conceded. As Jeff had over 20 years before, Donna was calling all the shots.

I wanted to be able to help Donna, to free her from the flashbacks that ravaged her mind and body. In our sessions together, she'd often flip into the four-year-old who'd been forced by her father to perform almost daily sexual acts. Talking about her experiences was part of the psychiatric community's preferred treatment at the time. This was thought to be important because it disrupted the programming she'd received from her father to keep her abuse secret. Although I thought I was managing to keep a semblance of objectivity, I was not in the least detached as I listened to her stories and watched the physical and emotional contortions she'd go through when re-living her childhood horrors.

In fact, I was so sympathetic to what she was experiencing that her pain became my pain, her fear became my fear. The boundaries between us blurred. In a very real sense, I found it difficult during our sessions to know where Donna ended and I began. Her stories tapped into my stories and, while her flashbacks were out in the open for both of us to see, mine were far below the surface of my mind, still causing invisible but very real damage.

Donna didn't appear to be getting any better, although she assured me that she was, and I was getting worse. Both of us were now suffering the same post-traumatic stress symptoms. The panic attacks I'd had when I worked for Riverside County Child Protective Services returned, as did the recurring nightmares. But this time, instead of hearing a screaming child, an unseen attacker stabbed me over and over in the back. I'd feel the pain, know I was dreaming, but be unable to wake myself up. George would shake me awake, explaining that I was whimpering and moaning in my sleep.

Finally, I took my concern over my lack of control with Donna and my increasing symptoms to my therapist, Dr. A. With his help, I saw that Donna tapped into the place in me where I'd buried all my past experiences of powerlessness. Dr. A explained that when Donna talked to me or looked at me in a certain subtly threatening way, it subconsciously reminded me of other times when I'd been subtly threatened or controlled. Gently, Dr. A probed my old experiences, bringing them one by one to the surface, where I could see them for what they'd been and the damage they'd caused and then let them go. The one set of memories I would not let Dr. A touch, however, were my memories of Jeff. I mentioned the rapes briefly, but assured him they no longer affected me and I had no intention of revisiting those experiences again. He raised an eyebrow and temporarily dropped the subject.

Dr. A also suggested I think about transferring Donna to another therapist. He was the first professional I'd talked to who didn't seem to think Donna would be damaged by my doing so. I was surprised, but also relieved. I'd felt the weight of believing I'd have to keep Donna as a client for as long as she wanted to be one and suddenly, someone I admired and respected as a clinician was telling me this wasn't so.

I started to discuss the possibility with Donna and as I expected, her neurotic behavior escalated. She'd call me many times during the day and evening, complaining of panic and fears and physical pain. She'd refuse to get off the phone. She'd demand extra appointments. She'd threaten to kill herself if I wouldn't see her, if I transferred her to another therapist. If I stood my ground she'd either flip into her younger personality and sob, or into her angry personality and threaten that I'd live to regret it. When I tried to take a weekend off, she'd berate the person on call for me and demand they get me to call her back immediately. She'd show up at my house or wait on my street until I came home. She'd arrive at The Children's Place, where I supervised MSW students, and demand the receptionists let me know she was waiting for me. When we did have our scheduled sessions, she'd slide into the younger personality and whine, suck her thumb and want me to hold her on my lap. When I wouldn't, she'd turn from pouting to raging and I'd turn into a frightened and ineffective participant in her drama.

When I first met Donna, one of her sub-personalities was a very reasonable and capable woman and it was this personality that I dealt with most at first. This capable and mature part of Donna was the reason she had an advanced degree and held down a well-paying job. But eventually, the capable personality faded into the background and was taken over, at least in my presence, by the little boy and the angry, raging man.

Dr. A told me that no matter how much Donna acted out or threatened or challenged my authority, I needed to continue to impress on her that it was time for her to see a new therapist. He also told me that until she was transferred I needed to be firm with her about holding our meetings in my office, meeting at prearranged times only and keeping phone calls to a minimum. But I couldn't do any of that consistently. I was so ashamed of my inability to be the *therapist* with Donna that I began to lie to Dr. A about what I was and wasn't doing with her. He thought I was making progress when, in reality, I was slipping mentally and physically into a very dangerous place.

Because I couldn't be honest with Dr. A about what Donna was doing and how I was giving in, her power over me grew. She had a terrifying hold on me that I couldn't understand. I'd been sober for several years, but I was tempted to drink when I thought about the temporary numbness and fearlessness alcohol might give me. I talked to my sponsor and George about it and both were afraid of what would happen to me if I wasn't able to transfer Donna to another therapist. The career I loved was rapidly becoming a source of dread. All I wanted now was to get out of it as fast and as completely as possible.

I couldn't admit to anyone that Donna was often coming to my home for sessions. She'd talked me into it when her behavior in my office became so uncontrollable I didn't know what else to do. She was also now asking for hugs before she would agree to end a session. I hated it and knew it was wrong, but I couldn't stop myself. The only way I could get her out of the room was to give her a hug or to hold her on the couch for a little while as she sucked her thumb. When I gave in to her, I felt as if I'd been there before, giving in to someone else when I didn't want to. I didn't connect the feelings I had with Donna to the ones I'd felt when I was with my high school boyfriend, Jeff.

One day, Donna and I were standing in the hallway inside my back door; I had just told her that she could no longer come to my house and from then on we would meet in my office. As she stood in the doorway saying her long drawn-out goodbyes, I reminded her of our appointment *in my office* the following week. Her face crumbled.

"But I can't come to your office," she said in her small whiny voice, indicating she was in the "little boy" persona that came out when she wanted to be comforted. "It's so scary there and bad things happen to me in that room."

Donna didn't know how to ask for what she wanted or needed the way an adult would ask and it was futile to attempt to discuss an issue, one adult to another, when she'd taken on her child personality. Still, I didn't want to support her childish behavior, any more than I would want to support it if it were Brad being difficult.

"Nothing bad has happened to you in my office, Donna. You've had some memories there, but you've also had them here in my home. I know they're unpleasant, but because they are just memories they can't hurt you."

She reached out her arms and tried to pull me to her. I stepped back and she dropped her arms to her sides. "You don't love me," she whimpered, her chin lowered almost to her chest.

I tried to be strong, but I felt a shift inside. I was weakening. I didn't yet understand the reason why and I hated myself for it. "This has nothing to do with love, Donna," I said. "This has to do with what's best for you, for your treatment and your recovery."

Her head snapped up and she glared at me. The child persona was gone and the angry young man had taken its place. "You don't know what's best for her. I know she can't be in a therapist's office. When she goes there, bad things happen even if they are just memories. If you don't take care of her, I will. She either comes here or you won't see her again." Donna's voice had a threatening tone now and I wasn't sure what she would do. I was pretty certain she wouldn't hurt me.

This was the reason therapists are taught to see clients in professional settings with other colleagues around. *I* felt like the child now, a bad child, trapped in a tiny hallway and unable to get away. Though I probably wasn't in any physical danger, I'd lost control; I was no longer the therapist. I knew I had to make Donna leave my house.

"Donna, it's time for you to go." I tried to steady my voice. "My husband will be home any minute now …"

As quickly as he had come, the mean young man disappeared and the child persona was back. Donna looked up at me through her lashes with a coy half-smile. "Give me a hug first."

I put my arms around her, feeling resigned and powerless. I was not in control of the relationship between Donna and me. In fact, I hadn't been in control for a long time. Finally, she let me go and looked up at me with a smile, this time of satisfaction. She'd won and she knew it. "Okay, I'll see you in your office next week." She practically skipped out the door.

Usually Donna called me several times a week. The week after the hugging incident at my house, she called me several times a day. She used every ploy to get me to allow her to come back to my house. "I can't stand it, Mary. I can't sleep. I know what will happen in your office. All those memories of Dad. What he did. Please. Don't make me."

And on another call, "I need to sleep. Promise me I can come back to your house sometime."

"Sometime, Donna. Not this week."

"But sometime. Promise. And promise you'll always be here to take care of me."

"Donna, it's not time to talk about that. There's still a lot of work to do. We'll keep working on the issues together."

I had stopped trying to persuade her to transfer to another therapist. It was easier for me to keep on seeing her, even with all the difficulties, than try to convince her that I was no longer doing her any good.

The calls went on. She couldn't sleep; I couldn't sleep. I'd had these feelings before, but couldn't remember when. My back hurt. My head ached constantly. I wanted her gone—I almost wished she'd die, anything to let me go. Rationally, I knew this wasn't about her and that something was very wrong with me. I was too ashamed to be honest with Dr. A about it or talk to the consultant I'd hired to assist me with the more difficult cases. I didn't want to admit that a client had the kind of control over me that Donna did.

Although Donna hadn't talked me into letting her come back to my house, she managed to change our appointment so she'd always be the last client in the evening. Every session was a fight for control as she tried to get me either to leave the office with her or to continue the session beyond the time I'd allotted. Donna's symptoms weren't getting any better and I felt that in the process of trying to heal her, I was getting sicker. I didn't know what she wanted from me any longer. I suspected that she had stopped seeing me as her therapist and saw me now as her friend. Perhaps Donna, a lesbian, was even hoping we would eventually become lovers.

Early in our marriage, George and I could share what we felt with each other, but we were not at that place now. Sometimes when I told George what was happening to me with Donna he was supportive. Other times, he was too tied up in his own stuff to take time for mine. He'd make some sort of short, abrupt statement such as, "Just deal with it" or "If you don't like it, quit." Quitting didn't feel like an option to me at the time and I didn't know *how* to deal with it.

As I drove home from work each evening, I'd feel a rising sense of anxiety. Would George be happy and accepting of me or angry and judgmental? He rarely talked to me about what work was like for him, perhaps because he didn't think I would understand or be available, given my own work concerns. Later, I was able to see how difficult his job had become and to understand how much he hated the long freeway drives every day in rush-hour traffic. He merely wanted a peaceful home and a satisfied and happy wife to come home to. During those years, he rarely had either.

One Monday afternoon as I sat in my office wingback chair and Donna perched on the edge of the couch across from me, her angry young man persona was going on and on about what Donna needed from me and what I was doing wrong. I was so tired and felt so helpless, I could barely keep my eyes on her face as I listened. Then something strange happened: I saw Jeff. I hadn't thought about him in years, hadn't even spoken about him to anyone other than to Tuck when I was still in high school and—briefly—to Dr. A and George. But now Jeff peered out at me from Donna's eyes, spoke to me through Donna's mouth. As I watched, Jeff's face flashed over hers and then disappeared, over and over. I gripped the arms of my chair. I had to end the session and call Dr. A. I was hallucinating and surely having a nervous breakdown. I sucked in my breath and pushed my back against the chair. I had to hold it together until I could get Donna out of the office and put in an emergency call to Dr. A.

When our time was up, I stood and said she had to leave as I had another commitment. We went through the usual "I'm not leaving until I get a hug" struggle. But Jeff had disappeared and even though I was thoroughly shaken, I no longer thought I was in imminent danger of a breakdown. After we set up her next appointment, Donna finally left and I called Dr. A's office. Dr. A assured me that I probably wasn't having a breakdown, but he agreed to see me that evening anyway.

Once in his office, I explained what had happened.

He nodded and smiled. "Mary," he said. "You're not having a nervous breakdown. You're finally ready to deal with what Jeff did to you. You'll resolve this now. And as for this client of yours, it's time we figure out how to transfer her to another therapist. There is nothing more you can do for her."

For two months, Dr. A and I worked on my own painful abuse history. It was hard for me to understand that what Jeff had done to me was rape, with all the subsequent damage that rape victims suffer. Because he was my boyfriend at the time and because rape under those circumstances is labeled "date rape," it was easier to blame myself than if I'd been raped by a stranger. The powerlessness I felt with Donna was similar to the powerlessness I'd felt during the years I'd been involved with Jeff. Although there was nothing physical going on between myself and Donna, her manipulative techniques—her fluctuations between tears and angry verbal rebukes and threats of harm to herself or me—were the same methods Jeff had used to get me to do what he wanted, to be the person he wanted me to be.

Because I was now able to see the connection between Jeff and Donna, and see how damaging my relationship with Donna was to my own mental health, I could start the process of transferring her to another therapist. I found a woman who had the credentials and experience to work with patients suffering from dissociative disorders. She was willing to take her on as a client and I brought up the transfer again with Donna. As expected, she pulled out all the stops to get me to change my mind and keep her, just as Jeff had done years before when I tried to break up with him. Donna used every tool she'd learned to keep herself alive and sane during her long years of childhood abuse. I couldn't have followed through with her transfer if I hadn't had the support of my own therapist and wasn't doing my own emotional work.

Even after Donna started seeing the new therapist, her behavior toward me continued to escalate. Now that I was able to recognize the similarities in the personalities and our relationships, Donna reminded me of how difficult it had been to break the ties with Jeff. Donna continued to call me but now she took the position that because I was no longer her therapist, I could be her friend. Becoming friends with a former client is clearly against the rules laid out by all professional counseling organizations and there are good reasons for those rules. I explained this to Donna, but she still tried to establish a friendship with me. She'd show up at my private office or at The Children's Place. I felt safer at the agency because it was a locked facility and the receptionist could tell her I wasn't available. But in my own private practice office or in my house, I had no such protection. I never knew when I'd see her car sitting at the end of my cul-de-sac when I returned home. Though she never threatened, I worried about the safety of myself and my family. She left presents at my front door, such as homemade pies or cookies. I was pretty sure her gifts were safe, but George and I threw the food in the trash anyway and I hated myself for becoming so suspicious of a woman I'd worked with for so long.

The situation with Donna could be considered the proverbial straw that broke my back. I was ill, physically and emotionally. I was in recovery from alcoholism and trying to rebuild my family. I had spent several years by now treating sufferers of horrible childhood abuse, both children and adults. The world felt very unsafe and ugly to me. The thought of the ugliness of what people did to each other poisoned everything I came in contact with. And now it seemed I had a stalker.

I grasped at anything that would take me away from Donna and all the rest of it, even briefly. I could no longer use alcohol or any other mind-altering drug. I couldn't—wouldn't—turn to men. I tried a variety of hobbies that were fun and could take my mind off what was ugly and painful in the world.

I frequented quilt shops and gazed at the bright and beautiful fabrics neatly arranged in color-coordinated rows. I signed up for classes in decorative arts and painted cute wooden figurines and birdhouses. I joined a romance writers' group and fantasized about writing books where I could control the endings—where I had the power to make situations turn out happily for everyone.

I returned to my childhood coping mechanism of making up stories as a way to calm myself long enough to fall asleep. The details of my stories changed, but there was one constant: I was always living in a cozy cabin in the woods.

FIFTEEN

Life-Giving Waters

In October 1991, a month before I found the cabin I would eventually buy in Colorado, I attended a retreat at Arrowhead Village in the San Bernadino Mountains in Southern California. The retreat was put on by a Catholic nun friend of mine who was also a fellow recovering alcoholic. While I enjoyed the small group meetings and the food and fellowship of the retreat, what I loved most was its location.

The lodge where the retreat was held had knotty pine paneling and floor-to-ceiling windows overlooking a lake fringed with evergreens. The air at that time of year was crisp and fresh and fragrant with wood smoke and pine. We slept in small cabins under thick blankets and ate local food and rich desserts. Surrounded by the beauty of the natural world I felt at home again, something I hadn't really felt since leaving Iowa. I walked and wrote and thought and prayed. I prayed especially to feel as if I belonged somewhere again.

At the beginning of the retreat, Sister B led us through an exercise that she said would help us leave our 'real' world behind for a couple of days. She asked us to write private letters to God, turning over any concerns that might prevent us from immersing ourselves completely in the retreat experience. She suggested we include in our letters any question or problem we'd like guidance on or an answer to by the end of the retreat.

We wrote our letters and put them in a basket provided by Sister B. This she placed on a temporary altar in our main meeting room. In my letter I asked God to help me find a spiritual home. When I wrote the request, I was thinking more about a church or social community where I would feel most comfortable. Since joining AA, I hadn't felt connected to my party-loving friends or my quite conservative fellow Lutheran parishioners. But I didn't yet accept AA as my new spiritual home either. I wanted God's guidance on finding a place where I could be most completely *me*.

At the end of the retreat, we gathered together as a group—there were about 50 women present—and Sister B returned our letters. We sat silently in our circle and read them over. Then Sister B passed a second basket containing folded slips of paper on each of which was typed a short scripture reading. She suggested we quickly take one without looking at it, say a prayer of thanksgiving for prayers answered and read the passage silently to ourselves. My scripture said: "I will lead you to life-giving waters."

At first I thought this was verification that God would lead me to a church home or some other group that would feel life-giving and nourishing, the way water is to all living things. But God was not so metaphorical. Within the month, I was led directly to *real* water, the waters of the Cache La Poudre River running through Fort Collins and Poudre Park in Colorado. Little did I realize at the time exactly how life-giving this river would become, not just for me, but for my family, as well. I did not know then how much of a spiritual home it would turn out to be.

The only way to describe my feelings after I bought my little bungalow in the canyon is to compare them to how I've felt when I've fallen in love with a person. Whenever I was away from the canyon I missed it terribly; it was almost a physical ache. My thoughts slid between ideas such as how I wanted to fix up the cabin or what it would be like to walk beside the river in the spring or fall. Happy, comforting memories of my grandmother came out of nowhere while I did mindless tasks such as ironing or washing dishes. And whenever I returned to the canyon, I'd get the same butterflies in my stomach I'd had when I was about to see a lover. I'd turn the car onto Highway 14 going west and feel the catch in my throat, knowing it would be only minutes until I'd be driving over the cattle gate. And as soon as I felt the familiar rumble under my tires, I'd let out my breath with a deep sigh. It was like being in the arms of the one I loved again.

In the first year I owned the cabin, the house was more a fantasy home for me than a real one. It was almost a thousand miles from my California door to my Colorado door and not an easy trip to get there. I wanted to close the door on my California life, be done with it once and for all, and embark on a new adventure in Colorado. I just hadn't figured out how to do that yet. In order to get through my days at work in California, I imagined life for myself in Poudre Park. When I was a teenager, I often imagined living in a cozy, safe cabin in a forest with a loving partner. Now the cabin I envisioned was my little house in the canyon. But this time in my fantasy there was no partner. Though I'd been in one relationship or another with a man since I was 15 years old and I was currently married, I'd finally learned that a man could never be my answer. I had always looked to men to give me what I thought I lacked, whether it was love or safety or self-esteem. And of course, I'd always been disappointed. I now understood that we always set ourselves up for disappointment when we expect someone else to do for us what we can't or won't do for ourselves, but I had no idea yet how to provide for myself the love and esteem and safety I constantly sought from others. All I knew was that, for a while, I needed to be alone somewhere rural and beautiful.

I was in California—not Colorado—the day I closed on the cabin and acquired my little piece of Poudre Park. I'd hired a lawyer in Fort Collins: the same lawyer my grandmother had used some 40 years earlier to buy her house in the canyon. And Aiden, now quite old and close to retirement, admonished me just as he had my grandmother then: "You're paying too much for this and I can't for the life of me understand why you would want a house way up there anyway." Still, he reviewed all the paperwork thoroughly, filed documents at the appropriate times and generally did what was necessary to make sure the house would be legally mine on December 11, 1991.

Although George was a lawyer himself, he wanted nothing to do with the closing. "You wanted this, you handle it," he said. He was also upset because I had signed the contract before having a lawyer look at it. "Once you've done that you're stuck. Good or bad, you've agreed to what's laid out in the contract. No lawyer can help you now," he told me.

I felt stupid and foolish, and I knew he was right. If I'd made a mistake, I was going to have to live with the consequences. And although the money Mom was giving me to buy the house seemed small compared to the cost of most houses, it was a lot of money to us. It was more money than either Mom or I had ever spent on anything before. I tried not to think about it too much and instead focused on the outcome I intended: to have a safe and cozy cabin of my own in a beautiful natural spot beside "life-giving waters." Instead of worrying about whether Mom's monetary gift should have been invested rather than possibly squandered on an old house, I thought about what it would be like to own a place where I could breathe and move and feel anonymous, a place where I could feel happy and carefree again. I was beginning to realize that I had rarely felt any of those things since we'd left Iowa five-and-a-half years before.

George continued to make the occasional derogatory comment about my buying the house. First he agreed when Dad said, "Well! We're certainly not going to let the two of you (meaning Mom and me) go anywhere alone together again!" One day George told me that a woman in his office had said—in what I assumed was a patronizing tone of voice—"Oh yes, I went through that type of emotional upheaval once, but I got over it before making any huge mistake." I thought she was implying that I obviously hadn't given myself time to get over whatever "emotional upheaval" I was going through before making *my* huge mistake.

For Christmas in 1991, George, Brad and I drove to Chicago to spend the holiday with Mom and Dad, not realizing it would be our last Christmas with Dad. We left Brad in Illinois so he could visit with his father for a while before returning by plane to California and George and I drove to Colorado, where George would see the cabin for the first time.

We arrived in Poudre Park on a snowy, cold, moonless night. No streetlights brightened the way up the canyon and most of the houses along the road were set far enough back that they didn't provide much light either. The last ten miles of our drive were dark, isolated and a bit spooky. George leaned forward and peered through the windshield, trying to discern what the area around our new second home looked like. All we could see by our headlights was the snow-covered road twisting a few feet in front of us and fog-shrouded evergreens rising on either side. George wasn't talking, which meant he was either really angry or intrigued. I hoped for the latter.

George was very tired and so was I; we both needed a break from life in California. Although he apparently enjoyed his career more than I did mine, a life lived inside a fluorescent-lit office for 40 to 60 hours a week, with long drives on commuter-choked highways, was probably not what he would have chosen for himself if he hadn't been raised to be super-responsible and a good provider for his family. George is a gifted designer, builder, craftsman and gardener. If he can envision a project, he can develop and build it. Physically, he's big and energetic and needs lots of action. He isn't happy constrained by walls and desk chairs, nor for that matter, by organizational policies. Though he wasn't admitting it at the time, the Colorado Rockies fit him better than tract-home neighborhoods with residents who follow the rules and like to participate in community affairs.

As we drove that last stretch of road, I hoped he would find something to love about this place that I had loved so much as a child and was falling in love with all over again. I hoped he would find a way to be more himself here, just as I knew that I would in this beautiful and—to me—sacred space.

We pulled up in front of our new house, opened the front door and brought in our sleeping bags and suitcases. The house was cold and dreary and empty. We had no furniture and were going to have to make do with the camping equipment we'd brought along until we could get to town and at least buy a bed. George flipped on lights and looked around our new little house. The previous owners had made sure the house was well-stocked with firewood, so we made a fire in the woodstove and turned on the pump for water. Then George found the trapdoor in the floor outside the bathroom that led down to the basement and the trapdoor in the closet that led up to the attic. Unwilling to wait until morning light, he explored both.

"Whoever remodeled this house didn't bother to put any insulation in the attic," he said. "At least, not as far as I can see. I'll have to fix that before we leave." He continued to prowl, stomping on a floorboard every so often to test its soundness or flipping on a light to see if it worked, or opening a cupboard or closet door to peer inside. Coming up from the basement, he said, "There's been water down there. Must be a leak. We won't be able to store anything in *that* basement." He got down on his hands and knees, looked under the kitchen sink and said, "Mice. I bet this place is full of them."

I pulled out a few snacks and we rolled out our sleeping bags on the floor. "Is there anything you like about it?" I asked. Though an inspector had gone over the place before the closing and assured me that nothing major was wrong with the house, George had found lots of little things wrong in the first hour we were there.

"Well, it has a nice layout and the loft is pretty good," he said. "It's pretty crappy paneling though. I wonder why they painted it white?"

The house was warming up, we'd had something to eat and I wanted to get to sleep so I could show him the yard and take him down to the river the next morning. I was sure he'd love Poudre Park as much as I did when he saw it in the light and experienced the vastness of the surrounding mountains. Tomorrow we'd go to town to buy supplies and a few basic pieces of furniture. Once we began to make this little house into a home, I was certain George would see it more as another adventure than as just one more burden.

We slept on the living room floor in front of the roaring woodstove. Exhausted by our long drive from Illinois and my concern over Dad's health, I slept deeply. I vaguely heard George throw another log on the fire once or twice, but when I woke up, he was still sleeping. I was standing at the French doors looking onto the backyard, which was surrounded by a high privacy fence, when I heard his voice behind me. "The first thing we've got to do is take down that fence. What were they thinking?"

"Timothy told me the fence made them feel safer. He also said they are master gardeners. I bet we'll have all kinds of blooming things out there in the spring."

"Not likely. This isn't good soil for growing things."

We took turns taking showers in the tiny bathroom. After I'd dressed, I found George standing in the front yard looking at the neighboring houses. "They certainly don't have any neighborhood association regulations around here, do they?" he said.

"Well, that's great, isn't it? You hate neighborhood associations and all their stupid regulations."

"That's true. But these are hardly houses. They look more like fisherman shacks."

I looked around me and for the first time saw the little town through eyes not blinded by romance and memory. George was right. In the light of day and the dreariness of winter it looked pretty rundown and dumpy. Perhaps this place would never mean anything to George. Perhaps it would be one more thing we wouldn't agree about, one more interest we wouldn't share, one more bone of contention. But at that moment, I didn't care. I loved all of it, every ramshackle house, every old car, every pile of debris in every yard. It might not be what one would call attractive, but it felt so human, so natural, so different from the plasticity of Orange County, California.

On the last day of 1991, I awoke to a stillness that could only be described as not of this world. As George slept, the silence infused me with a powerful sense of awe. Morning had broken, but no car passed on the highway. At this time at home in California, the sound of traffic on the road nearby—about the same distance from our house as Poudre Canyon Highway was from the cabin—would already be a constant irritating drone. Here in the canyon, no breeze even rustled the trees. The river, still flowing beneath a blanket of snow and ice, was silent. As I fixed coffee and tried not to awaken George, I imagined what it would be like to stay permanently or at least spend most of my time here. It seemed almost too good to be true. But I was sure about one thing: I was not cut out to live the jam-packed, anxiety-ridden life I was living in Southern California. As I looked out at the tree-covered ridge beyond the river, I suspected I'd found the place where I could most be myself, where my creativity would blossom, where *I* would blossom.

On the first day of 1992, George and I drove up the canyon to Steamboat Springs, a ski resort town about four hours from the cabin. As we drove west along Highway 14, both of us fell silent, each lost in our own thoughts. I looked out the window at the river, at the rocks just beneath the water's surface, and felt a stab of memory and grief. The grief was for my grandmother, for the woman she was and the simple unconditional love she gave me and for a simpler, happier time when I was still a child and she was still alive.

Just before George and I entered the Narrows, where the river is particularly turbulent during the spring and summer months and the walls of the canyon are especially steep and rocky, I saw a warning sign about steep grades and sharp curves. I wanted to ask George to slow down, to find the words and tone of voice that would help him understand how his fast driving scared me, but I was too afraid of making him angry, even of making him wish I'd never bought the cabin—that old loop we'd fallen into so many times before. So I gripped my door handle, forced myself to take long, deep breaths and said nothing. I wanted to be able to talk to George as we had when we were first together, but I didn't think I could. I had the sudden but familiar sharp sense of having lost him somewhere during all we'd been through over the 12 years of our marriage.

After we made it through the twisting labyrinth of the Narrows, the canyon opened up. The walls had a smoother, softer shape and finally gave way to spacious, snow-covered meadows. Clumps of aspens appeared as we continued west and gained elevation. Most of the ridges to the south were heavily forested with pine, but pine trees were sparse on the mountains to the north and the land was covered with small bushes and scrub oak.

The farther west we traveled, the stronger the sense I had of years falling away, of myself becoming younger and freer. The air was crisp and I rolled down my window and breathed in the fragrance of the pine meadows, despite letting in the cold winter air as I did so.

The drive from our cabin to Steamboat Springs wound through what had to be some of the most beautiful country in North America: pine forests, deep rocky gorges and expansive meadows laid out beneath a deep blue, cloudless sky.

We passed Dadd Gulch to the south, just east of the 93-mile marker and once again the meadows gave way to forest that hugged both sides of the road. The land opened up once more after Indian Meadows Lodge. For a while, at 7,250 feet above sea level, we had vast views. We cruised through the tiny town of Rustic, entered a large U-shaped valley and saw a sign for the Fish Hatchery. Another sign pointed out the start of the Roaring Creek Trail and I made a mental note to return in the summer to hike the trail and find the roaring creek it was named for. As we continued to drive and climb, to 8,100 feet now, there were more aspen trees and I made another mental note to return the following October to see them in all their brilliant, autumnal golden glory.

At Blue Lake Trailhead we hit 9,500 feet and the temperature outside the car dropped ten degrees. It was windy and we were the only car around. Although I still prayed we wouldn't have car trouble, I'd lost my fear of George's driving. I was glad he was with me and I settled into my usual sense of oneness with the land, with my sense of the rightness of the place, of my decision to buy the cabin.

As we passed Joe Wright Reservoir on the left we were reaching tree line. I felt dwarfed by the grandeur of the world now spread out before and around us. Suddenly, I had a strong feeling of lightness, of buoyancy, of all my responsibilities, commitments, anxieties and stressors blowing away in the wind that buffeted the car. Clients, AA sponsees, troubles and worries of all kinds were far behind. And I also sensed that the spaces in me—and between me and George—could be cleaned out and refilled, this time with awe, exuberance, renewed hope and love.

We made the peak (10,276 feet) at Cameron Pass and started down the other side. Cameron Pass remains unblemished wilderness, with the mountain ranges of Medicine Bow to the south and Never Summer to the north. Though Cameron Pass had been surveyed several times for possible train routes through the Rockies, no railroad company had ever laid track along this route through the mountains.

We passed the Moose Observation Center, now closed for the winter, and entered the tiny town of Gould at the 56-mile marker. After Gould, the valley opened up even more. In this part of the high country we seemed to have left the mountains behind, but we were actually on top of them. Old ranch buildings falling into disrepair were bumps beneath the snow. The sun was bright and, in places, the fields were shadowed by enormous white clouds floating in the deep blue sky. We were both happy and relaxed and hungry now. We passed through Walden, disappointed by the options for food in that small town, and hurried on to Steamboat.

But Steamboat Springs depressed and disappointed me. While I thought the land between the mouth of the canyon at Ted's Place and Steamboat was some of the best of Colorado, Steamboat Springs was the worst. Row after row of condominiums and ski runs chopped up the natural habitat. The high cost of living had forced the locals out as wealthy part-time skiers came in. Old but charming buildings had been torn down or redone into fancy new ones with false Western fronts. As I passed two women wearing fur coats and fur boots, I made a crack to George under my breath about the furs looking better on the animals who'd worn them first. My mood had swung from the exhilaration I'd felt on the drive to grumpiness. As far as I was concerned, Steamboat was as materialistic as Orange County and I had no desire to stay overnight or ever return. After eating lunch at a noisy, busy restaurant on the main strip and checking out a local bookstore and coffee shop, we drove the four-plus hours back to Poudre Park.

George and I left Poudre Park on January 4th. We hadn't bought any tables or chairs or beds, but the little house felt like home to me nonetheless. I didn't want to leave. Back in Orange County I would be facing a lot of unanswered questions: what to do with my private practice clients, especially Donna, whom I felt I could no longer handle; what to do about my practice in general; what to do, in fact, about my whole career. I needed to figure out whether we could afford for me to live part of every year in Colorado. How would I support myself? I was so tired of counseling other people that I didn't think social work was a career option any more, even if I could work part of the year in Colorado. What about our marriage? Could George and I live separately part of the time and still maintain a marriage? My brother and his wife had managed it successfully for 11 years, but could we? Despite not knowing the answers to these questions, I understood that I had to get out of Southern California and into Poudre Park, at least on a semi-permanent basis. My happiness, my peace of mind and perhaps even my health depended on it.

SIXTEEN

A Life
Freely Chosen

As soon as we were back at our house in its extravagantly landscaped, well-maintained California neighborhood, within walking distance of a grocery store and restaurants and "freeway close" to everything else, George pointed out the downside of the cabin in Colorado. It was too far from town, too small, required too much work to fix up and was in a rundown neighborhood with weird neighbors.

The first part of 1992 was a roller coaster. My emotions were up and down. My relationship with George was close and then distant; we loved and we argued. At one point, I told him I liked our house in Orange County, but hated the traffic. He snapped back, "That's life." I raged that it was his life. I didn't want to be here, I'd been happy in Iowa. Back and forth we teetered. I knew I loved him and didn't want to be with anyone else, but I wanted a life of my own. One I'd chosen; one in which I could live where I wanted to live, simply and surrounded by nature. I wanted a place where I could rest my eyes, look out beyond my window and not see another person or house or vehicle. And I wanted George to want all that, too, to share my dream. I didn't know if I could close my practice and spend part of every year in Colorado without his full support.

My feelings and thoughts about my clients also swung back and forth. At one moment I felt compassion for them: they had difficult lives in which they felt trapped. They didn't have the tools to get out, emotionally, mentally or financially. On one hand, I believed I had answers for them. On the other, I wondered if I was hurting my clients by creating too much dependence on me. Sometimes I felt like a trapped animal that would willingly chew off her leg for freedom if necessary. And other times I felt too weak and exhausted even to imagine making such a difficult and all-encompassing life change.

George periodically gave me a glimmer of hope that he was at least thinking about moving to Colorado with me. Perhaps he could obtain a position as a patent attorney at Colorado State University in Fort Collins, he suggested. He joined an organization of university patent attorneys so he would hear about job openings. My hopes rose only to fall again when he later said that he wouldn't leave his company or California.

When things got too difficult at home, I'd walk through the neighborhoods around our house. Gazing upon the blooming bougainvillea, the well-tended lawns and flower gardens and feeling the soft breeze on my face, I believed I was crazy to want to leave this place that others thought of as paradise. Few, if any, of my friends would understand my need and love for a place as wild, untamed and harsh as Colorado. One friend, a native Californian, assured me I'd never leave Southern California. And if I did, he said, I'd be back: "Who would leave California by choice?"

Brad wanted to leave, too. He was in his last semester of high school and had been accepted at the University of Iowa. As soon as he knew he had the opportunity to return to Iowa, he wouldn't even consider another school. In his mind, he was going home. I wanted to go home, too; my home was now in Colorado, even if I had an official California address. For the first time in my life, I wanted to be in a particular place, not because of a husband or parent, or even a school or job, but because that place was calling to me.

In February, Mom and Dad went to Barbados on vacation. Although Dad's health wasn't good and his doctors warned him against traveling out of the country, he couldn't stand the idea of, as he put it, just sitting around waiting to die. "You can get me home if I have another stroke," he told Mom and she assured him she could.

One of Dad's dreams was to travel with the Windstar Cruise Line. He'd heard about Windstar's luxurious motor-sail yachts with unique rigging that enabled the crew to change the ship's operation from motor to sail in a matter of minutes with just the push of a button. Mom liked the casualness of the cruise line and the reports of its great food.

Mom and Dad ended their cruise in Barbados and stayed again in the honeymoon suite of their favorite small, locally owned hotel. A couple of days after their arrival, having had brunch in the hotel dining room, they went for a late morning swim. Still in the water, Dad told Mom he was tired and was going back to the room. Mom stayed in while he walked slowly out of the water. As soon as he reached the beach, Dad collapsed. Mom noticed the commotion on the beach as lifeguards worked to save Dad's life. By the time she reached him she knew he was dead, though the lifeguards wouldn't say so and continued to work on him until the ambulance arrived.

That year—1992—Dad died; Brad graduated high school and left California for college in Iowa; we now owned a second residence in Colorado; and I quit my private practice. For several years afterwards, I fought emotional issues I feared I wasn't strong enough to bear. Although I was still working part-time at The Children's Place, I became obsessed with trying to figure out an enjoyable way to make money so I could leave social work altogether. I read books like *Do What You Love, the Money Will Follow* and *Earning Money without a Job*. Unhappy and exhausted myself, I was incapable of working day after day with unhappy people who had chaotic lives. Though Donna had been transferred to another therapist, she hadn't been the only client I'd had with seemingly insurmountable problems. One client was doing everything she could to keep her ex-husband from their children: despite an absence of suspicion on anyone's part but hers that he'd sexually abused their little girl and boy, she was determined to enlist me in her cause to prove that he had. The rage she directed at him for leaving her was so powerful that it affected all of us who had contact with her on a daily or weekly basis.

All I wanted to do was paint or quilt or write stories with happy endings. I'd pour acrylic paints onto a plate and smoosh them around with a palette knife and meditate on the beauty and creaminess of the mixture. I couldn't, however, actually paint anything; I couldn't watch the news or read the paper. And I felt different and alone as I watched George and our friends drink alcohol to relax every night—as I had once done—while I tried to stay sober.

I turned more and more to the Christian faith and my belief in God. I read the Bible and various meditation books daily, writing long involved journal entries about how a particular Bible passage fit my life as it was on that day. I saw God as talking directly to me, counseling and guiding and comforting me on all I was going through. I shared little of this with George, because when I did he insisted the whole religious thing was silly and a crutch, that no one with any intelligence would believe all that garbage. Though I suspected he was right, at least about the way I was *using* God and the Bible, I couldn't stop myself. I clung to the Bible and my faith the same way I'd held onto alcohol in the past.

I wasn't able to get to Colorado at all during the first six months we owned the cabin. In California, I struggled with self-hate and the belief that I didn't measure up to those around me. I was the odd duck, the sore thumb, the stick-in-the-mud. One night, after a party to celebrate the 40th birthday of one of our beautiful women friends, a party where everyone but me had too much to drink, George wanted to make love. The smell of alcohol on his breath brought back memories of numerous nights when I'd been the same way. The idea of having sex with an inebriated partner, even my husband, sickened me and I pushed him away. He slept in the guest room that night—his choice—and I stayed in our big king-sized bed alone, feeling very much like I was the one who'd been bad. After that I wanted little to do with him or with anyone for that matter. I wanted to be left alone to study the Bible and talk to God.

I continued to wrestle with how to make money doing something other than counseling, the only profession for which I was trained. I never seriously thought of getting a job in a store or a school. I was exhausted and sick much of the time and wanted as little to do with people as possible. Finally, a friend and I came up with the idea of starting a business selling our crafts. George commented that it would take years of hard work just to recoup all the money I'd put into it already. I could barely finish anything I began, so how could I build up sufficient inventory to have enough to sell? I felt ashamed and gave up on the whole idea of trying to make my living as a professional craftsman. I knew I had switched addictions from drinking to dreaming: dreaming of careers that would be easy and fulfilling and successful. But when it came down to doing the hard work and facing the judgment and failures that inevitably come with any new endeavor, I always gave up before I'd barely begun.

California for me became a symbol, a reminder of failure. I was not one of the beautiful and successful people while I believed my husband was. I didn't have an exciting, fulfilling and lucrative career that I believed so many other people—and George—had. And because I was certain George *was* what I was *not*, I worried he would leave me for someone who was more like him. I was not one of the perfectly put-together mothers who drove her children to school in her Volvo station wagon or Mercedes coupe: I was the recovering drunk who couldn't maintain the career she'd worked so hard to obtain because she didn't know how to set healthy boundaries or take care of herself. I was the one who couldn't make a consistent effort to create another business. At least, in California, that's who I believed I was as I compared myself to my neighbors and friends and even to my husband.

In Colorado, whenever I managed to spend some time there, I felt like a different woman, one who was perfectly capable of living a self-sufficient and gratifying life. The instant I passed over the cattle gate and entered the canyon, I was transformed—in my head, at least. And years later, when I was living permanently and year-round in Colorado, I'd go back to California for a visit and discover that I didn't look at my friends and the residents of Orange County the same way I had when I lived there, the way I had before the canyon exerted its power over me. When I looked at some of the friends and colleagues I'd once envied, I saw unhappy people who appeared to dress, act and buy more in order to impress others, rather than to please themselves. I saw men and women pushing themselves to live as they thought they should, rather than how they truly wanted to live. They hadn't changed, but I had. Because I was then living, at least in part, a life more in keeping with who I was, I no longer saw others as better than me.

After Brad graduated from high school in June of 1992, I took my first extended trip to the cabin. Mom had flown in from Illinois for the graduation ceremony; she, Brad and I drove to Colorado together. I'd never taken such a long car trip without George. It was a bit scary, but exciting at the same time. Taking steps like that and handling whatever was needed at the cabin was the only way I knew to get stronger. Grandmother had taught me that in 1962, when I thought I wasn't even strong enough to get out of bed.

The three of us arrived in Colorado on June 26th after a good drive. We'd had no car trouble or arguments; Brad shared the driving. But as soon as we arrived, I was upset. George had torn down the privacy fence when we were out in December and I noticed that the neighbors to the southeast of us were using the back of our property as a parking lot: the clear view from my back windows to the mountain across the highway was blocked by old cars. I might as well have stayed in California. Suddenly, I regretted buying the cabin. I'd been too hasty. George was right again: I'd acted impulsively and now I'd have to live with the consequences. Clearly, one of those consequences was inconsiderate neighbors who parked their cars on someone else's property without permission.

I decided to consider the cabin a vacation home only, nothing more, a place I would visit once in a while to recuperate from the fast pace of

Orange County. I'd visit whenever it got hard to breathe—or think.

After Brad and I went home to California, I returned to my part-time position at The Children's Place to supervise interns, but no longer worked directly with clients. Burned out as I was, this was a huge relief. I also helped my friend, Sister B, establish a new retreat center for, as she called them, "the overworked and overwhelmed of Orange County." Sister B knew I was unhappy as a therapist and suggested I make an appointment with her friend, Sally, for career counseling. Sally led a group for adults who wanted or needed to change careers and I signed up for it. One morning during the class, Sally gave us a battery of personality and career aptitude tests. Later, she met with each of us privately to discuss the results.

I arrived at her office for my appointment feeling somewhat afraid. What if Sally told me I was suited for only one occupation and that was social work? I knew I listened well and often could motivate people to make positive changes in their lives, but I no longer wanted this type of profession. I wasn't sure what I wanted to do, but I knew I had to do *something*: I needed the income.

Sally sat at her desk and fingered a stack of papers I assumed were my tests. She looked at me with a curious grin on her face. Finally, she said, "Well, I've never come to this conclusion with a client before." She hesitated.

"What?" I asked. Was she about to tell me I had no aptitude for anything?

"It seems to me that the best occupation for you is to be a creative writer, particularly a novelist, living in a cabin in the woods somewhere. Preferably by yourself."

I stared at her as she hurried to explain. "I want to assure you that this conclusion doesn't come from just one test. I mean, there isn't any result that actually says *this woman should be a novelist living alone on a mountaintop*. But given our interviews, the tests and your history, I'd say that life would suit you perfectly. Not sure if it would be self-supporting, but it certainly would be right up your alley."

This was the first time since I'd tossed my dream of being a writer into

Eileen Miller's garbage can along with my Beatle book that I could even slightly imagine myself as a serious writer. Sally was saying the words I most wanted to hear: that she saw me living in the mountains and crafting a creative life for myself. The tests I'd taken had validated the dream that was barely on my radar anymore. In Sally's office that glorious afternoon, I changed my obsession from "how to make money without a job" to "how to become a published author."

Soon after, one Saturday in January of 1993, I let a friend who was also interested in developing a career as a writer take me to a Romance Writers of America chapter meeting. Having grown up in a somewhat snobbish literary family, going to a gathering of romance writers was almost as difficult for me as stepping into an AA meeting for the first time. But once there, as I listened to a speech by popular and well-educated romance writer, Jane Ann Krentz, I was in tears. Perhaps it really was possible to make a living as a writer. Perhaps there was something to romance writing. Perhaps the reading of romances was not bad for women at all, might even be good for them. Could I be of service to others and still do what I most wanted: write fiction? I joined the organization that day, started to read romance again for the first time since high school and decided I'd make my living as a writer of popular women's fiction.

I threw myself into the world of romance fiction, read one romance novel after another, and attended every meeting and workshop of my RWA chapter as well as the next two national conventions. I joined a critique group, wrote several full-length manuscripts and submitted work to our annual contest. But every step of the way I fought inner demons who bemoaned my lack of talent, who berated me for picking such a frivolous genre and who told me that, no matter how hard I tried, I'd never make it as any kind of writer, much less as a popular novelist.

No longer a practicing therapist, I still filled my days with needy people or with friends I met for lunch or shopping, so I wouldn't have to do much writing or confront the brutal inner critic who invariably showed up at my desk. And I told myself that the reason I wasn't successful was because I had no real time or space to pursue my craft. As soon as I could spend more time in Colorado, things would be different; then I would be able to do the writing I wanted to do, to become the successful writer I wanted to be.

Several times a year, when I did get to the cabin in Colorado, I carved out time to write and study the craft. Still, I rarely wrote. I told myself that if I wasn't interested in reading romance, I'd never be very successful at writing it. I switched to writing personal essay and poetry, and sent off several completed manuscripts and poems to various markets, but eventually I gave up on that, too. My nasty inner voice prevailed. She convinced me I didn't have what it took to be a *real* writer.

Whenever I went to the cabin in Colorado, crossing over the cattle gate was like crossing into another reality. As soon as I felt the familiar rumble beneath my tires, I relaxed; my breath was deeper, my body more expansive, lighter. Dwarfed by the steep canyon walls around me, I was unnecessary to anyone but myself and, if she was with me, to my dog, Romi. No one knew me or cared what I did or didn't do with my day: I could spend it in bed or on the living room couch, watching the birds and trying to figure out, by flipping through my red Audubon bird book, what type each was. I could drive into town and around Fort Collins assured that no one would recognize me or ask me to share my time with them.

In the canyon, everything and everyone seemed suffused with the same light I'd seen in George when I fell in love with him. The trees, the rocks, the ridges glowed with a golden light. But the people did, too. Dan, the man with the Beatles haircut and a pet raccoon, had it. My neighbor to the east, a little old man who suffered from dementia and repeated the same sentence over and over whenever he saw me, had it. And Luke and Ramona, the couple next door to the west, glowed with the light, too. Although Luke had "issues," neighbors told me, issues caused by tours of duty in Viet Nam and a series of tragedies when he was young, I never worried that he might hurt me during one of the episodes caused by his chronic post traumatic stress. I loved the economic and age diversity in my new neighborhood. I felt at home with these people.

Several of my new neighbors had lived in the canyon long enough to have known my grandmother. They welcomed me warmly and nodded knowingly when I mentioned a sense of coming home.

Other beings who lived in the canyon were suffused with that light, too: the deer that romped in the snow behind my house at midnight; the bears who would come to the bird feeders and crab apple trees in late fall; the white mergansers that flew up and down the river in summer; the evergreens, the cottonwoods, the river rocks, everything. And perhaps most surprising was that, for the first time in a very long time, I felt the glow inside. It burned within me and gave me energy and strength to work long hours in my yard, weed-whacking the tall grasses that hadn't been cut since I'd owned the property. It gave me strength to buy furniture and move it into the cabin myself and to clean and sort, and sometimes, it even gave me the strength to banish my inner critic and write.

Whenever I managed to get to the cabin by myself, I'd settle into a routine that someone looking in from outside would probably call the life of a hermit. I didn't go to AA meetings or to church; I joined no organizations. I didn't do volunteer work, as was my custom in California. While I was in Colorado, I was very careful not to commit to anything or anyone. Each morning, I'd awake without benefit of an alarm, fix coffee and a light breakfast and settle down on the couch in the big room to watch birds or read. The only sound I'd hear for the first hours of the day would be birdsong, the burble of the river if it was running in spring or early summer, and the occasional car or truck on the highway beyond my window. I had no television and I never turned on the radio or CD player. I wanted and needed complete silence.

Later in the day, I walked. If Romi was with me, I took her along. Occasionally, my neighbor Cindy joined us. We always walked west up the canyon along the highway, passing the old man who sold bundles of firewood, stacked beside his front porch, to campers. As we passed, he nodded. Sometimes if I was walking alone, I sat for a while on his porch with him. We didn't talk much, just about the weather mostly. On one of my visits, I noticed he was gone. Later, another neighbor told me that his children, worried about his living alone up the canyon, had moved him into a nursing home, where he soon died. "It's a pity," the neighbor said. "He'd have much preferred to die at home. His kids had different ideas."

Sometimes on my walks I turned away from the canyon highway, crossed the river and walked Hewlett Gulch. Sunshine, a golden lab, often saw me walking towards her up the hill and waited beside the path outside her home. She'd fall into step with me, wagging her tail, and walk as far as I wanted to go, zigzagging here and there, but always returning to wherever I was on the trail. She would turn around when I did and trot alongside as I made my way back. I liked having her with me as a deterrent for any mountain lion or bear that might also be out for a stroll. And I liked having a friendly companion who didn't talk, one who left me space for my thoughts. Those days, I had many thoughts on my walks alone in the canyon: *Could I live here full time without George? Would I want to? What would I do to earn a living? Could I make any money writing? Did I have what it took?* I also talked to God a lot as I walked. *What did God want from me? Was I following God's will? Or was I merely running away from responsibilities, taking the easy way out?*

When my visit ended and it was time to leave the canyon and return to California, I'd cry just as I would if I were leaving a human lover. I'd cry and talk to the canyon and to my little house and the trees in the backyard and the old carriage shed with its creaky double doors and musty smell. I'd tell them all how much I loved them and I'd promise to come back. I'd walk across the road to the river and say goodbye to it and cry there, too. I'd weep all the way down the canyon and as I drove over the cattle gate, wishing there was some way I could be in my little house in the canyon all the time and not just for a few weeks a year.

SEVENTEEN

Finding Joy in Tumbleweed and Antelope

In August of 1992, six months after Dad died, my mother bought a condominium in Fort Collins. She hired an interior decorator and gave her free reign to completely redo the place. Once the work was well underway, Mom yearned to visit Colorado to see how the redecorating was coming along and to visit with me and Catherine and Evan. Mom and I arranged a time to meet, but failed to tell each other that neither of our places would be available to stay in: Mom's condo was in disarray because of the remodel and my friend Willa and her five children were vacationing in the cabin. When Mom and I met at Denver airport and discovered this, Mom said, "Let's go to the ranch! Catherine and Evan never do anything anymore. They'll be glad to have us."

On her last trip to Colorado, Mom had bought a new Mercedes coupe, the only make of automobile she and Dad had owned in the last 20 years. Though frugal in many respects, Dad loved that he was finally able to afford such a well-made and reliable car. I don't think Mom considered buying any other kind when she went car shopping on her own after Dad's death.

We took the airport shuttle to her condo, peeked in the front door to see how the remodel was coming along—everything looked torn apart—tossed our luggage into the trunk of Mom's new, but not-yet-broken-in white Mercedes and headed out of town toward the ranch, laughing about our silly situation: two homes between us but nowhere to sleep.

When we arrived at Catherine and Evan's house almost an hour later, there was nowhere for us to sleep there either. Other out-of-town guests had beaten us to their door, also stopping by unexpectedly earlier in the day. As we knew was her custom—and had counted on ourselves—Catherine had asked them to stay. We didn't want to upset her, so we said nothing about what we'd planned and left after a short visit. Once back on Highway 287, we looked *right* towards town and *left* towards Wyoming and I, driving the car, said, "Now what?"

Mom thought for a moment. "Have you ever been to Wyoming?"

"I have," I said, thinking of an AA Women's Retreat I'd attended several years before. The retreat was up by Yellowstone National Park, in the far northwestern corner of the state. "Wyoming is really beautiful, Mom. Let's go." The area around the Grand Teton and Yellowstone National parks *is* gorgeous and I remembered some places to stay there. I'd also been to Jackson Hole, a ski area with lots of hotels and motels. I decided this was going to be a lot of fun; we had a comfortable and safe new car and plenty of time before we needed to fly home. Mom smiled and nodded, settling herself more comfortably into her seat, and I turned left towards the state line.

Little did I realize that the only part of Wyoming that *is* beautiful and somewhat populated is in the western part of the state, a long way from where we were driving. Between the Roberts' ranch and the Yellowstone and Grand Teton National Parks lie 430 miles of territory with more antelope than people, a smattering of rundown motels that are few and far between, no cell phone service, maybe two pay phones, lots of wind and billions of tumbleweeds.

We drove around Wyoming for five days, taking little roads here and there rather than staying on major highways, calling George whenever we found a pay phone stuck to the side of a building in a place where the wind didn't blow too hard and staying in what had to be some of the seediest motels in the country. We stopped in small towns that hadn't seen a tourist in months and where people stared in open amazement at two women in a shiny new white luxury sedan pulling up in front of their café or store. A cattle drive down Main Street blocked our car in Cody, Wyoming, a delightful and truly "old west" town. Mom and I found a nice little motel there and spent several leisurely hours at the Buffalo Bill Museum.

The next day, we drove to Grand Teton National Park. Arriving at the eastern park entrance, we discovered it closed for the winter though it wasn't yet October. We stayed at a dude ranch that was also officially closed for the winter. Mom and I snuggled under wool blankets in a cute little cabin and talked long into the night. She told me how much Wyoming reminded her of Colorado when she was a little girl. She thanked me for taking her on this spur-of-the-moment trip; she told me she was glad I was her daughter. For the first time I could remember, I'd done something that truly pleased my mother.

After meandering the state's back roads for the better part of a week, we were ready to return to Colorado; we drove back by way of Casper, Wyoming. I knew Willa and her family would be out of my cabin and I wanted to have a shower in something other than a motel stall with broken tiles and rusty water. I wanted my own bed. I wanted a salad with fresh greens. I wanted to be able to talk to George without yelling over the wind while propping myself up against the side of a gas station. I wanted to get out of the car. What I didn't want to do was end this vacation with my mother. We'd never had such an easy and good time together for so many days. I hoped Mom's good feelings about me would last.

They didn't. One nice trip didn't erase all our problems, but it gave me a glimpse of what Mom could be like, what we could be like together. This was the mom I'd known on family vacations as a child: the mom who liked travel more than just about anything, the mom who could drop her concerns if there was a new locale to visit or new restaurants to try. During the next nine years, we continued to have our ups and downs. But eventually I was able to drop all past resentments and begin to love my mother for the woman she was, instead of wishing she were a different kind of mother. In the 14 years between our visit to Wyoming and her death, our relationship changed from "mother and daughter" to "friend and friend" and eventually we arrived where many do: in a relationship where she needed me to mother her more than I needed her to mother me.

EIGHTEEN

Letting Go

July, 1994

The 123rd annual Fourth of July picnic was coming up at the Roberts Ranch and Mom was determined I take her to it. I had a temperature of 101 degrees, but that didn't seem to matter to Mom—"Take a couple of aspirin, Mary, and it will go right down"—nor that the outside air temperature was 105 in the shade, nor that I couldn't stop coughing, nor that it probably wasn't the wisest idea for me to be around elderly Evan Roberts, who wasn't in the best of health himself.

My friend Judy and I had flown out from California a couple of weeks before to visit Mom at her condo in Fort Collins. Just before leaving California I'd noticed a strange tenderness in my hands and an unusual weakness in my muscles. While working out, I'd recently discovered I wasn't able to lift the same weight as usual or walk on the treadmill as long.

Judy and I borrowed Mom's car to drive to Iowa City to see our sons, who were both attending the University of Iowa; the pain in my hands and muscles worsened on the drive. By the time we reached Iowa City, I felt as if I was on fire and my eyes were almost swollen shut. I blamed the allergies I'd forgotten I was prone to during Midwestern summers. But it was not allergies I was suffering from. I had a high fever and a bad cough. Judy wanted me to see a doctor, but instead, I spent our few days there in a motel bed and let her drive most of the way back to Fort Collins. I decided that as soon as we reached Mom's condo I'd find an earlier return flight back to California. I'd planned to stay in Colorado for a week longer than Judy, so I could take Mom to the Robert's Fourth of July picnic. But I was too sick. All I wanted was my own California bed and my own California doctor.

When we reached Fort Collins, however, I learned that my returning to California early was not acceptable to my mother. She had every intention of making sure I went to the picnic at the Roberts' ranch with her. "It's only a few hours," she said. "You can stay in bed here in the condo just as easily as you can stay in bed in California. You shouldn't be flying now anyway, the way you feel."

"Please, Mom." I was practically begging her, while Judy stood in the doorway of Mom's living room and looked at my mother as if she'd lost her mind. "It's best if I get a seat on Judy's flight and go home with her. I need to see my own doctor."

"Fort Collins has perfectly good doctors if you need one. But you're being dramatic. You've got a cold. A good night's sleep and you'll be fine in time for the picnic."

I hoped she was right. Dad had only been gone a little over a year and Mom was still immersed in her grief. She needed me; she needed Catherine and Evan Roberts, too. She wanted me to take her to the party. I could do that for her. I *would* do that for her.

Judy left on July 3rd and Mom and I spent the day baking homemade rolls "just the way Catherine likes them," Mom said. I had pleased her by sending Judy off on the airport shuttle while I stayed in Fort Collins. I swallowed Excedrin with the intensity of an addict, four to five tablets every three to four hours, and drank cough syrup like a drunk downs vodka. While Mom pummeled and squeezed the bread dough, I cooked potatoes for potato salad and chopped cabbage for coleslaw and took every chance to lie down on the couch.

With potato salad, coleslaw and fresh baked rolls in hand, Mom and I met Catherine and Evan and a couple of their friends at the ranch. We loaded the food into the Roberts' sedan and set off for the picnic. I thought we were going to a large gathering at a house on the ranch belonging to David, Evan's son by another marriage, but instead Catherine drove down a narrow track, heading for a secluded part of the ranch that neither Mom nor I had been to before. I learned later that the main picnic was, in fact, taking place at David's house—Catherine had chosen to have her own picnic instead of attending David's annual celebration.

I was fortified with aspirin, but our ride over bumpy roads in the intense heat of a Colorado July did nothing to help how I felt. I closed my eyes and prayed to get through the day. "Please, just don't let me throw up," I whispered to myself. I sat in the back seat between Mom and Catherine's full-figured friend, Dell, and concluded that throwing up was a real and terrifying possibility.

After what seemed an interminable length of time, Catherine stopped the car in an isolated section of their 18,000-acre ranch. The location she'd chosen for the picnic *was* beautiful, I thought, as I looked for somewhere cool to sit. A spot under a couple of cottonwoods by a gently flowing creek was about all the shade there was in the open expanse of field. I spread out the blanket and announced a bit abruptly that we would be having our picnic there.

After lunch, Mom insisted on a tour of the area while I pleaded with God to let the damn picnic be over. With my stomach as upset as it was, I was afraid to eat anything and merely sipped on a couple of lukewarm Cokes. After what seemed like days rather than only hours, we climbed back into the car and lurched our way towards the hill that would lead us home. But halfway up the road, the car jerked to a stop: we were stuck in a couple of deep ruts between two droopy and very thirsty trees. I leaned my head against the back of the seat, closed my eyes and thought longingly of death. Mom, Dell, Dell's husband (whose name I don't think I ever learned), Evan and I extricated ourselves from the car and Catherine steered, while 80-year-old Evan and his 70-if-he-was-a-day friend pushed somewhat impotently at the back of the car. I wobbled over to a rock and sat down. Mom wouldn't look at me.

Finally and only God knows how, Evan, his friend and Catherine managed to free the car. Then, after a slow and torturous tour of that particular section of the ranch, our offshoot of the 123rd annual Roberts Ranch picnic was over and Mom and I were on our way back to the condo.

I returned to California on my scheduled flight feeling slightly better and thinking that perhaps I'd beaten whatever it was I'd had the last couple of weeks. I went to Dr. O, our family doctor, just to make sure and after a series of tests, he told me I was recovering from double pneumonia. I still had a serious kidney infection, however. This was the beginning of numerous visits to my doctor: I'd recover briefly and then get sick again. The soreness in my hands traveled into other joints and it was painful to move.

Dr. O eventually admitted defeat. "Frankly, I don't know why we can't get you well and keep you that way. Your lab tests are all out of whack," he said. "I think it's time you see a specialist. I'm sending you to a rheumatologist I know personally and respect. He'll figure out what's wrong."

Dr. H, the rheumatologist, diagnosed me with systemic lupus erythematosus, an inflammatory auto-immune disorder that can attack various organs of the body. Lupus was attacking my joints, kidneys and the lining around my heart and lungs. He later diagnosed me with the lupus-related symptoms of fibromyalgia, arthritis, Sjogren's Syndrome and secondary Raynaud's phenomenon. I started a long process of frequent blood tests, various prescription drugs and monthly appointments with him. Dr. H also gave me a bone density test to make sure my bones were healthy enough to handle steroids, in case I needed them to control the lupus. The bone scan indicated that though I was only 45-years-old I had the bones of an old woman; I had severe osteoporosis of the back and hips.

Dr. H was shocked and unable to hide his dismay. "If we don't get this under control," he said, "you'll be in a wheelchair by the time you're 55!" Of all the diagnoses I'd received over the last couple of weeks, this one upset me the most.

While I was going through my physical difficulties, George was facing his own problems at work. Fred, the boss he'd loved and who was a father figure to him retired, aged 75. While almost everyone expected George would replace Fred as the Intellectual Property Counsel, the company chose an attorney from a private law firm to fill the position. Although disappointed, he was more saddened by the changes in the company's management philosophies and treatment of employees in the legal department. The company appeared to be headed towards minimizing the policies George and Fred had considered important for maintaining a challenging and enjoyable work environment. At the same time, the company was reassessing its corporate structure and divesting itself of various business units. The future of George's department was uncertain and the changes to the company bred anxiety about the future. When it was suggested he take a position with the company purchasing one of the business units, George realized that no matter what he chose to do his future career was limited. Under those circumstances and with the changes in his department, George didn't want to stay with the company, but couldn't yet see any other option.

In the last few years, two of George's colleagues at the company had died tragically. One was in his late forties when he suffered a massive heart attack on a business flight to Japan; the other died on US Air Flight 427, which crashed just prior to its expected landing in Pittsburgh on September 8, 1994. Both had had a strong impact on how George viewed life and work, especially in light of the significant turmoil occurring as the company reorganized. Perhaps it was only natural then that my illness and George's change in status and opportunity at the company triggered his search for a different—a calmer and more peaceful—way to live.

It didn't take us long to agree that finding another kind of life was what we both wanted.

"I think I can negotiate an early retirement package that will allow us to live relatively comfortably without jobs, hopefully for the rest of our lives," George said. "We'll never be able to afford it if we stay in California, but perhaps if we sell our house here and move to the cabin in Colorado we can make it work."

We didn't have a mortgage on the cabin and property values in California had increased since we'd bought our house there. After selling our California house and paying off its mortgage, we'd have some cash left over. George would be 50 in a few months and he figured that, if he could hold on until then, we'd only need to worry about covering the five years before he could start collecting his retirement. If he played his cards right, perhaps his boss would *pay* him to leave, providing a severance package that would hold us until George turned 55; he had stock options from the company that would give us a cushion, too. Perhaps I could make a little money with art or sewing or writing, since moving to Colorado would give me long, uninterrupted days in a quiet, secluded place in which to work. It sounded heavenly.

George urged me to move to Colorado as soon as the California house sold. When I protested that I didn't think it was a good idea for us to be apart that long, he insisted. "It will make it more real to me," he said. "If I know you're out there and our house here is gone, I'll have no choice but to follow through with leaving the company and come out there, too. I'll rent a studio apartment close to the office and fly to Colorado often. And you can sometimes come here."

We put the California house on the market, figuring it would be quite some time before it sold; we had a full-price offer within the week. Then the prospective buyer changed his mind and we were instantly $5,000 richer, as he forfeited his earnest money. I saw it as a sign that we were on the right track, doing what we were supposed to do in this next stage of our lives. George worried we'd lost a good deal, but a week later we had another full-price offer and the house sold within the month. It was time for me to go to Colorado and for George to move into the small furnished apartment he'd found close to his office.

In October of 1996, I loaded up my car with the bare necessities and my old and arthritic dog, Romi, and headed off alone to Colorado. Married friends from Iowa, Bob and Sue, planned to spend the first week with me. Although I'd hoped to be there alone at first, I was also glad to have the company. Bob could help me with some of the heavier jobs around the house, while I shared my feelings around this huge, life-changing event with Sue.

They arrived at the cabin almost at the same time as Romi and I. We spent my first evening in my new permanent home catching up on news and recuperating from our long drives. Romi seemed stiffer than usual; I hoped it was merely the result of 18 hours on the road and she'd soon be back to her slow, but relatively normal self.

The next morning, Romi refused to move. She wouldn't stand up or even attempt to sit. I carried her outside and set her down on the grass. She struggled to stand, but couldn't get her hind legs straightened beneath her. She'd had back and hip problems in the past and I thought perhaps the long car trip had made those problems worse. I watched her all day, hoping she'd get better. Because I was so concerned about Romi, it was hard to concentrate on Sue and Bob or on any of the chores I'd hoped to accomplish while they were able and willing to assist.

I remembered Colorado State University in Fort Collins had a highly rated veterinary school. It was late in the evening by the time I realized Romi needed professional help, but I called the vet hospital anyway. When I described the severity of the situation—that Romi couldn't stand even to pee and merely wet wherever she was (not like her at all and probably causing her great shame)—the receptionist told me to bring her in. Sue and Bob urged me to let them ride along, but if the news about Romi was bad I wanted to be alone to feel whatever I needed to feel.

I carried Romi to the car and we drove down the canyon, she lying silently on the seat beside me, her head resting on her front paws. I found the hospital easily and carried Romi into the quiet, dimly lit waiting room. The only other person there was a young woman sitting behind the admittance counter. She took my name and told me kindly to have a seat; someone would be with me shortly. I held Romi on my lap, speaking gentle words of reassurance as much to myself as to her. I petted her soft coat and tried not to cry. George had given me Romi as a surprise a few years after my last ectopic pregnancy in 1982—after the doctors said it was too dangerous for me to get pregnant again, after I knew adoption was out of the question and that Brad was the only child I'd ever have. Romi was a perky, blond, cocker spaniel puppy then. She'd been at my side through recovery from alcoholism and my recent difficult, painful months of active lupus. She'd been with me through the hard years of graduate school and when I left the home, friends and family I loved in Iowa for a new life in California. I couldn't bear the thought of losing her now, just as she, George and I were starting our new life together in Colorado.

Finally, we were led into an examining room where CSU's on-call veterinarian confirmed my worse suspicions. "The only way for Romi to regain full use of her hind legs is through major back surgery," he said, looking at me with the same kindness shown by the young receptionist. I remember thinking this man was awfully young to be a veterinarian. "However," he continued, "I wouldn't recommend the operation for her. She's old and not in very good physical condition. I think it's too risky and even if she made it through the operation, the recovery would be brutal."

I could hardly look at him as I whispered, "Then is our only option to put her down?"

He nodded. "Of course it's your choice, but I'd say it's the kindest thing to do for Romi."

His assistant, a girl of no more than 21 or 22, started to cry. She rubbed Romi's back as I stroked the dog's head. I was surprised and touched. "You don't even know Romi and you're crying."

"I can tell she's a really, really good dog." She was sobbing now and rotten as I felt, her tears made me smile.

I reached out and touched her hand. "Honey, you've got to toughen up or you'll never make it as a veterinarian."

As Romi and I were leaving the hospital, I stopped by the desk and made an appointment to bring Romi back the next day. The doctor had warned me that this was something we couldn't put off: I knew that if I didn't make the arrangements right then I'd never go through with it and

Romi would suffer. I'd talked to George before calling CSU, explaining Romi's condition and my fears. He had told me to trust my instincts and that I'd have his support whatever I decided. As difficult as it was for George and me, I knew this was the right decision for her.

Bob and Sue wanted to accompany us to the vet clinic the next day, but I couldn't let them. I wanted to be alone with Romi one last time. We left for our appointment early, so I could take her through the Mac-Donald's drive-through. Romi liked to eat and I knew there would be nothing she'd like better than a MacDonald's hamburger and fries as her last meal. I tried not to cry as I put in my order and picked it up at the window. Though I didn't know the area well, I wanted to take her out of town and let her eat her sandwich outside the car. Off College Avenue, I turned right on Drake and drove past the vet hospital where we'd been the night before and would return soon, out to Overland Trail and past the Colorado State football stadium. I wasn't sure where I was going, but I felt I'd know the right place when I got there. I did. I turned off the road into an empty parking lot beside a pond. I parked and with the MacDonald's bag in hand, I scooped Romi into my arms and carried her up onto a grassy knoll overlooking the water. It was a beautiful sunny Colorado morning with a bit of a breeze rippling the surface of the water.

Romi didn't seem to care where she was. All she wanted was whatever was in the white bag that smelled so good. I laid her on the grass, sat down beside her and opened the bag. She nuzzled my hand as I broke off pieces of the hamburger and fed them to her. Then I fed her the French fries one by one. When everything was gone, she stuck her head in the bag to make sure it was empty and licked my hand. I looked at my watch. I barely had time to get her back down the hill for our appointment.

I hadn't cried yet that morning, but when I arrived at the vet hospital, now filled with people of all ages and dogs of all breeds and a few cats in carriers, I broke down. I could no longer pretend this wasn't happening. I held Romi on my lap and buried my head in her neck and sobbed. I knew people were looking at me and were probably very understanding and sympathetic. These were dog and cat people, like me. The people around me stopped talking and the room went quiet except for the occasional whimper, bark or mewl from the animals. I didn't care. Romi was the only one that mattered to me and soon I'd be leaving the clinic without her. I was afraid I wouldn't be able to do it.

A young man, most likely a college student, touched my arm and guided me, still carrying Romi, over to a large floor scale. He weighed her and led us down a hall to a large room with a mattress on the floor. There were several other people in the room, preparing the injection they would soon give to Romi. I focused on nothing but Romi and that large mattress.

The room was dim and soft music was playing in the background. Everyone seemed kind and gentle. I sat on a chair with my dog on my lap and looked at the mattress. "Some people like to lie down with their pets and hold them when we administer the injection," someone said. I couldn't stop crying or looking at the mattress. I'd been with pets before as they'd been put to sleep: I knew what to expect. But I'd always held them up on an examining table. This was very different: the room felt too much like home; the people around me were being too kind. There was no institutional, medical feel to it. I didn't know if I could handle it this way. I was usually too private, too afraid of others seeing the depth of my emotions, but before I fully realized what I was doing, I had placed Romi gently on the mattress. Then I sat down beside her, rubbing her back. I couldn't watch as they placed a rubber tube around her hind leg.

The young man knelt beside me. "Why don't you lie down with her?" he suggested.

"I can't," I said.

"Yes, you can," he said. "Later you'll be glad you did."

I lay down.

"Hold her," the young man said.

I pulled her into my chest. I held her as I would hold a baby or a young child. I stroked her head that was soon wet from my tears.

"Are you ready?" the young man asked. The two women in the room with us had introduced themselves when we'd come in, but I'd felt I was in a bubble or very far away when they spoke to me. Still, I knew one of them was a doctor. Both of the women were now motionless, one holding Romi's leg and the other holding a syringe and hovering over Romi's lower body with it. They were obviously waiting for me to give the okay.

I scrunched down so my head was next to Romi's. I wanted her to see me, to know I was with her. I wanted to be looking at her the last time she closed her eyes.

Still crying, I nodded to them. I think I whispered to Romi that I loved her. I know I thanked her, for loving me, for being my best friend all those years. And at the very last moment, right before she closed her eyes for the last time, Romi did something she'd never done before: she looked at me—*really* looked at me. She looked straight into my eyes. She'd always been the kind of dog that never did that, the kind of dog that wouldn't look you straight in the eye, as deference to you as head of the pack. But that day she did. And with that one look I think she thanked me. For letting her go. For not letting her suffer. For being good to her now, the way I'd always been.

NINETEEN

The Healing
Power of Solitude

I cried for what seemed like months after Romi died. I felt very alone. Although George and I talked often on the phone, he wasn't able to visit me in Colorado as often as we'd expected and the couple of times I stayed with him in his little studio apartment in California I sensed an awkwardness between us. He was eager to tie up the loose ends of his work life and move to Colorado. And he grieved the loss of Romi, too. She'd been an integral part of most of our marriage and we felt her absence acutely.

Alone in Colorado, I rarely went to town. I knew that if I wanted to connect with people I could check out AA meetings and my California AA sponsor was urging me to do that. She worried I'd go back to drinking without a local AA connection and with the isolation of living alone in a cabin so far from town.

I almost went to an AA meeting the day Romi died. After making plans to have her body transported to a pet cemetery east of town for cremation, I left CSU and drove to the Serenity Club on Mulberry Street, where I knew an AA meeting was scheduled to begin at noon. I arrived a little late and realized I couldn't bring myself to walk into a roomful of strangers, knowing all eyes would be on me and that they'd probably imagine I was a newly sober woman crying over my latest drunk. I pulled my car into a parking space and stared through the club's window at the backs of the people sitting in the room. It was the most I could bring myself to do. Still, I was comforted by that one small action. I consider AA people *my* people, no matter where in the world they're located, but I wasn't ready to connect with them in Fort Collins yet. I left the parking lot before the meeting was over.

I didn't attend AA meetings in Colorado until after George moved there permanently. I'm not sure why. It might have been because AA members have a wonderful way of gently bringing people out of themselves. Usually this is good, because it facilitates healing from the self-absorption of addiction. But I didn't want that now: what I needed most was to reconnect to myself and to the God I believed in. I somehow understood that to reach my next level of healing I needed solitude, as much solitude as I could manage before George arrived.

I did have a few acquaintances in Poudre Park: Dan across the road, and Cindy, and Luke and Ramona. But for the most part I begged off when they asked me over, preferring to stay by myself in the cabin. I drove into Fort Collins or the smaller but closer town of La Porte only when I needed groceries. I had no television and though sometimes I could pick up the public radio station, most of the time I couldn't. My dream had come true: I wouldn't be returning to California, but I wasn't attempting to create a life here either.

I'd never before been alone for an extended period of time. I'd gone straight from living with my parents to living in a college dorm, and from there I went to living with a husband and later a child. After my first marriage ended, I added a new husband and stepson to the family almost immediately. Until I bought the cabin, I'd never even been on a trip alone. From early childhood on, I'd been adept at reading the moods and needs of the people around me and doing what I thought I needed to do to please or take care of them. And most of the time, I was very good at figuring out what others thought I should do about my life and then doing it.

What I didn't know how to do very well was *read the real me.* I was 47 and I had no idea who I really was. I'd always craved solitude and at the same time worried there was something wrong with me for wanting it so much. I'd often heard in AA meetings that you have to be careful about isolating: that isolating is a warning you're shutting people out; refusing to be accountable to others; preparing to pick up that drink again. And American society is an extroverted society with the underlying belief that you can't be happy and mentally healthy unless you have strong intimate relationships and an active social life. Up until the moment I arrived in the canyon, I had always forced myself to be social in order to fit in, to feel I was like everyone else. Until 1987, alcohol put me in the right frame of mind to socialize with others; now I was sober, but burned-out and exhausted. I didn't want to make the effort to socialize or connect with anyone.

I felt there was something inside me I was trying to grasp, but couldn't quite reach. Or as if *someone* inside me was trying to reach me. When others were around, I could almost sense that internal *someone* withdrawing, becoming less and less willing to show herself. I didn't want that to happen. I think now that the "someone inside" who was trying to reach me was a smarter, larger part of me; perhaps my intuition, my soul or even my higher power. That part of me, whoever she was, knew the real Mary and what the real Mary wanted and needed, apart from the expectations of others or the standards our culture has set for women. The trouble was that this woman within usually spoke in a quiet whisper and mostly I refused to take the time or make the space and silence necessary to hear her. Then she'd get fed up and cause a great big fuss by drinking too much or striking out at the people around me or making my body ill so I'd have no choice but to listen. I'd paid a high price by not paying attention earlier.

When I moved to Colorado, I knew I needed to make a silent, open space in which to hear that voice before it had to scream at me again. The canyon bearing the spirit of my Grandmother was the perfect place and the period before George joined me there was the perfect time. I didn't want to waste a minute of it by spending time with others.

I also wanted to find out if what I was feeling was something other people felt; whether or not it was normal. I've always turned to books to find answers and this time was no exception. *Solitude: A Return to the Self* by Anthony Storr became my guidebook as I explored this new terrain. Storr provided assurance that solitude was the path to self-discovery and awareness of my deepest needs and feelings. His examples of creative people like Kant, Trollope and even Beatrix Potter, who needed to withdraw from others in order to fully realize their creative, individualistic selves, reassured me that I was on the right track, that my need for a period of seclusion was actually healthy and necessary for me to become a whole and mature individual and to connect with the creative being within me.

I was also in the process of shifting from one kind of external life to another. Southern California is a high-energy, brightly lit—often materialistically focused—metropolitan area, while Poudre Park, Colorado, is a drowsy hamlet populated mostly by people who aren't much interested in high-powered careers and by elderly retirees, some of whom had sold their farms in Nebraska and come to the mountains to finish out their lives. Now it took up much of the day to visit grocery stores, restaurants, movie theatres and malls which, in California, were in close driving distance of our home. In California, I focused on having a career and so did George. In Colorado, my days were empty and when George arrived *our* days would be empty. We'd have few friends, little entertainment or distractions, no impulsive shopping. And there would be no Romi. For the first time in our marriage, it would be just the two of us—*alone*. As the months went by, me in Colorado and George in California, the reality of our decision slowly sank in. What had we done?

Ever since Mom and I had rediscovered Poudre Park, living in the canyon in Colorado had been a dream for me. Whenever a situation wasn't going well in California, I could fantasize about chucking everything and moving to the canyon. It was a pipedream, something I thought I wanted but never believed I could have.

My first indication that living full-time in Poudre Park might not be all I'd hoped and expected it to be came when I woke up one morning to discover a mish-mash of automobiles, campers and tents parked haphazardly all over the back half of our Poudre Park property. Occasionally, the neighbors behind us had used our back lot to park their car or truck, but this was different altogether: it had been transformed into a campground overnight.

I hurriedly dressed, barely able to contain my anger. The older couple who lived adjacent to our rear—usually empty—lot was standing in my yard, laughing and talking with various members of the make-shift camp. I went outside, walked up to the little group and trying to keep my voice from shaking, asked them to explain what all the people, vehicles and tents were doing in my backyard.

My neighbor, Harvey, was clearly surprised and a little taken aback by my question. "We have an agreement with the previous owner of your house to use the back field for our family reunions. We mow the lawn and he lets our kids and their families camp out here several times a year. And," he added almost as an afterthought, "he allows me to park my own vehicles here *all* the time."

Speechless, I stared at him. How could he think that what the old owner had promised would apply when a new owner moved in? Did he think his right to park in my backyard passed on with the deed? Surely not.

"Harvey," I said, "I didn't move to the country from Southern California to look out at a used car lot. I am the new owner of this property. From now on, I'll mow the lawn myself and I'd appreciate it if you didn't park your vehicles on my property. I'm sorry, but I won't allow your family members to park here either."

Before Harvey could try to change my mind, I turned around and walked back to the house. I like to be hospitable, but Harvey and his family had gone too far, assumed too much, overstepped too many lines.

And I knew that if we didn't set up boundaries now, at some point he could legally argue a right to the back property and obtain the power to take it away from us.

The next morning there was a note on the windshield of my car: "We are neighborly around here. And we are Christians." It was signed, "Harvey."

Another sign that Poudre Park might not be the peaceful sanctuary I'd dreamed about came one quiet Friday afternoon around five o'clock. I was lying on the living room couch, lazily considering what I'd have for dinner, when suddenly I was catapulted to my feet by the crash of cymbals and the boom-boom-boom of a bass drum. I walked around the house, looking out each window and trying to figure out where the racket was coming from. When I couldn't, I called my friend, Cindy.

"Oh that's just Luke," she said calmly. "He only lets himself drink on Friday afternoons. After a few beers, he gets pretty sentimental about the life he used to live and the band he played drums for. You can practically set your clocks by it. If you hear drums and cymbals, it must be Friday afternoon at five."

Cindy laughed. "Just hope he passes out before he starts shooting off the guns."

Once I knew what to expect on Friday afternoons, I made sure I started off on my walk well ahead of the drums and cymbals. I walked the same way each time—west along the main road—so wrapped up in whatever issue I was mulling over that I wouldn't notice my surroundings. But soon I'd realize I was out of Poudre Park and alone on the road. In the autumn of 1996, very few cars went up and down Highway 14 even on a Friday afternoon. I could walk for an hour or so and only see one or two passersby. As I walked, the sense of seclusion intensifying with each step, I'd shove my hands into my jacket pockets, throw my head back and breathe in the cool fragrance of pine and mountain river. I'd close my eyes and let my body carry me forward with the sureness of a forest animal. I felt safe and at home, as if I belonged here, like the fox and deer, raccoon and bear; as if I had always belonged in this place between the rugged rock formations and the river.

It was on those walks that I started talking to the "someone" I imagined within me. At the time, I thought this someone was God. The conversations were fragmented, an isolated thought here and a somewhat connected response there, as if two very close beings were conversing. I never remembered later what these talks were about or what I'd discovered during them, but I would return to the cabin with a sense of completion, as if a problem I'd been struggling with had been, on some level, solved. I was developing trust in myself again, something I hadn't experienced for a long time and perhaps had never experienced. I no longer felt the need to check out my every move with anyone but myself.

As I walked the road I'd look up often, my eyes scanning the cliffs and the tops of trees and the sky above me. I wasn't searching for anything in particular, such as birds or animals. I was merely trying to soak it all up and somehow freeze it within, as you might capture a scene with a camera. Even as the beauty and perfection filled me, it was almost too much to bear. After a while, I'd have to turn around. I'd have to get out of the grandeur and fullness of it and back to the cabin where I could shut it out. It was as if I was ingesting a potent tonic: while the right amount was life-enhancing, too much at once was detrimental and it was easy at my current level of need to gulp it all in too quickly and feel overwhelmed.

Even on the days Luke wasn't drumming, a thought, a concern, a phone call or too much attention from one of my neighbors would drive me out of the cabin and the whole process would start over. Day after day I walked west along the canyon highway, thinking, looking and talking to this being within. My legs became stronger and so did my lungs in the thin mountain air. My body became more balanced and my feet, as they maneuvered the pebbly side of the road, more sure. I began to feel cleansed of the frenetic activity and crowds and drama I'd been part of in California. And, perhaps most important of all, I became more sure of how I wanted to live.

Whenever I returned to the cabin after walking the canyon road, I felt at peace, no longer worried about what my neighbors were doing or whether my friends and family back in California were happy and safe and getting along okay without me. The canyon had worked its magic on me and once again I believed our decision to move to Colorado permanently was the right one.

The cold can arrive in the canyon as early as September and bring with it a premature snow. Wet, fat flakes pile up into drifts several feet high and break the limbs off trees that haven't yet lost their leaves. Then, just when it seems winter has settled in for good, the weather changes. The Chinook winds carry in a wave of warm air from the plains, the snow melts and the residents of Poudre Park are once again out on the road in shorts and T-shirts.

This was how it was the first winter I lived alone in the cabin. From one day to the next, I wasn't sure what surprises the weather would bring and I welcomed it. Neighbors warned me that Poudre Canyon was no California. Winters could be rugged and hard and long and there was a "real good possibility," they'd warn me, that I "wouldn't last 'til spring." I couldn't understand what they were talking about and had no doubt I would make it through the winter just fine. Someone told me about a man who would bring out a cord of chopped wood for me: I called him and in the casual, informal manner that people did business here, he said sure, he'd bring it out first thing Saturday morning. And he did. I watched him as he backed his old, beat-up pickup truck into the driveway in front of my house and tossed the wood this way and that all over the drive. When he came to the door, I gave him a check, thinking he would return to the wood and stack it alongside the house, but instead he jumped in his truck and drove away with a nod and a tip of his hat. I spent the rest of the day stacking wood as Luke and Dan looked on, smiling to themselves and probably thinking again that I wouldn't last the winter.

But I had something they didn't know about: my grandmother. In the crisp cold of the canyon, I felt my grandmother with me. The feeling wasn't strong, not something I could put my finger on or say yes... there it is… she's here. It was more like an underlying, barely audible hum; a background to my world, like the soundtrack in a movie. Even with no one else in the cabin, even knowing I was completely alone for the first time in my life, I wasn't lonely or bored. Like Grandmother, I was making a home all by myself in this little town cradled by canyon walls on either side. And, perhaps because I had felt so safe whenever I was with her, I felt safe now. She'd led the way, made her home here first. When Jack had died and everyone told her she was making a mistake by coming alone to Poudre Park, she came anyway, sure in the knowledge that she was doing what she needed to do for herself, to grieve Jack's death and to heal from it. Now I was here, too. I was doing what I needed to do for me, to heal from my losses in the place where she had healed.

On the cold winter nights of that first year in the cabin, I would turn off all the lights and snuggle alone under blankets and down comforters. I would listen to the fire crackling in the woodstove and to the absolute and utter silence of the world muffled by snow beyond my windows and feel the same safety and happiness I'd felt years before as a little girl of eight, when I had snuggled against my grandmother's back in her big bed in the little house down the road.

During the days of that first winter, I relished the opportunity to do some of the same things my grandmother had done. Unlike her, I had an indoor bathroom and hot and cold running water. But like her, I loved watching the wildlife and putting out seed for the birds. Grandmother had been surprised when someone once asked her if living in the country was ever boring. "How could anyone be bored living in the country?" she'd said, "There's so much to do!" I felt the same. I loved stacking wood, bringing it in on a cold morning, starting the fire. I loved cooking breakfast and eating it as I watched the birds at the feeders. I loved the silence of no traffic noise and no dogs barking, no radios or televisions blaring. Just like my grandmother before me, I loved hanging laundry on an outside line to dry, forbidden in the Orange County subdivision where we'd lived. I loved it all and as the days went on I discovered that I wanted George with me, to share the peace and joy I was discovering in the canyon.

TWENTY

Finding Our Way
Back To Each Other

George's last official day at work was Friday, April 4, 1997. Two days later, on the evening of his 50th birthday, he pulled up in front of the cabin. I was so ready for him to arrive and thought he looked wonderful, even after his almost non-stop, 19-hour drive through five states. I looked forward to sharing all I'd discovered about the canyon in the last few months and wanted him to love it as much as I did. I hoped he wouldn't regret our decision to leave California.

On George's first night in Poudre Park, I snuggled up to him in bed, grateful for his presence, even while vaguely aware of the difficulties likely to come: difficulties that would probably include attempting to hold onto myself while melding my life to George's in this new place. I did what came easiest to me: I decided not to think about it.

While I tend to ignore a problem, George immediately homes in on it and considers how he can fix it. I'd rather not notice what's wrong and tend to leave things as they are. Almost immediately after his arrival, George was walking around the cabin and talking to himself about what needed to be done, just as he had when he'd first seen it six years before and on every visit to the cabin since. As he did so, I felt tired and overwhelmed and my defensiveness kicked in. I wanted to stand up for my new little house and community. And I wasn't ready to change anything about the cabin just yet: I loved the slight shabbiness of it, its worn places and bits of peeling paint here and there. I loved the sense that the canyon and its residents were comfortable, homey and real, not sparkly clean like the place we'd just left.

Mixed in with my happiness at having George with me again was a slight sense of foreboding, a feeling that something I'd enjoyed alone in the cabin would soon be gone. On some level, I knew I wasn't ready yet to share my space with George or anyone else, for that matter.

The cabin had become something more to me than just a building. It was my shell, simple and small enough to hold me closely so my un-protected self didn't bang around in it too much. And my shell house was positioned on a piece of property that gave me the solitude I needed, a place where the outside world couldn't easily intrude. Because no one but me occupied those small rooms, I could shut the door on whatever and whoever was outside and focus on what I thought and wanted and needed and believed.

When I'd first arrived in Colorado, it was as if I had no skin between me and everyone else, including or perhaps especially George. Between moving to Poudre Park and George joining me six months later, I had grown skin again in the confines of my temporary shell. I was learning how to be at least somewhat self-contained. When George finally joined me, that skin was new, easily torn and bruised. I didn't yet know how to protect it and I didn't know how to continue growing it with another human being living in my space.

Instead of negotiating with George the changes our new living sit-uation required for both of us to be happy and comfortable, I reverted to old behaviors and coping mechanisms, like focusing on the good and ignoring what's not so good. So when George arrived in Colorado and I began to feel edgy and itchy, I pushed those feelings down and focused on enjoying having my husband with me again. I thought about how my impulsive decision to buy the cabin had precipitated George's and my realization that we *had* the option to retire early and that a simpler and less expensive lifestyle was desirable. I thought how, though I no longer had the benefit of long, solitary days, I did have, for the first time in our marriage, the undivided attention and full-time presence of this man whom I so dearly loved. And I had a playmate now, a playmate who excited me and made me laugh, a partner with whom I could explore my beautiful surroundings more thoroughly.

George and I had had our difficulties over the years and through those years I'd struggled to hang onto a sense of an independent self in the presence of my strong, assured and very successful husband. Still, we'd managed to maintain a deep and abiding bond with each other, despite all our emotional ups and downs. George and I called it "touching," the only word we could think of to describe what went on between us. "Touching" was the term we used for the powerful connection that bound us together even when we weren't in one another's proximity. We certainly felt it when we were close to each other physically—sitting next to each other, making love or merely being in the same room—but we felt it even when we were far apart, even in different parts of the country. For me, George wasn't just a soul-mate but my conjoined twin, attached bodily to me at the heart, as close as my breath in spite of continents or oceans between us. This feeling was so strong I often thought no one had ever loved another person as much as I loved George. But the intensity of my feelings was a double-edged sword: it was difficult to believe that George could ever love me as much as I loved him and this set me up for major flashes of insecurity and fear.

Our passion flared during lovemaking *and* fighting, both of which we did often, and our life together was full of ups and downs. Once while we sat at the dining table in our house in Iowa, George had diagrammed how he saw our life together. He drew a straight line across a piece of blank white paper and then drew another line meandering over and under the first line. "This is our relationship," he said, pointing to the squiggly line.

"And it's the way I like it and want it to stay. We have deep lows, yes, but we only have those lows because we also have these highs."

I took the pen from him and drew another line on his diagram. My line ran along his curvy one, but my peaks were lower and my valleys were not so deep. "This is the way I want it," I said. "The lows we have now are killing me."

When George and I lived in California, I learned that to some extent I could manipulate our highs and lows. Guardedly, I'd watch George and try to read his mood. Then I'd try to *play* to it, mold myself into the kind of woman I thought this man in that particular mood would need. It seemed that when I did what I thought George wanted, we could usually avoid a fight.

I reverted to this somewhat dishonest behavior when George joined me in Colorado. Slowed down by my six months alone in the canyon and pretty much recovered from Southern California life, I found George often abrasive and jarring. Energized by his long-awaited freedom from the world of work, a freedom he hadn't experienced since he was 15 years old, George couldn't relax. I was six months ahead of him in learning how to be still and savor the long, empty days of our new life. Our dispositions clashed: my slowness irritated him and his intensity exhausted me. When George's energy was high and he was happy, he was spontaneous, acted on impulse and wanted me as his partner, his companion, in whatever he decided to do. I sensed his disappointment if I begged out of whatever adventure he was planning, so usually, in an effort to keep him happy with me, I'd drop my plans for writing or reading or watching the birds and go along with whatever he wanted to do.

Some days, George woke up grumpy and reclusive. I read those moods, too, and tiptoed around him, not asking for anything from him until I sensed he'd worked out whatever was on his mind. Sometimes I read him wrong or was irritated myself and then we'd fight, leaving both of us bruised, tender and unsure of what to do to restore our closeness, our sense of "touching."

I didn't want to make any changes to the cabin during those first months. I wanted to continue living the way I had before George arrived, but he was too much of a fixer, an improver, to leave things as they were. When he talked about painting the kitchen or what kind of tree to plant in the front yard or whether we should add a second story, I'd freak out, thinking we were going to do those things right away and worried I'd have no choice in the matter. I didn't understand yet that George was thinking out loud, mulling over possibilities. Sometimes I'd express a resounding and determined no, which would almost always initiate a fight, but usually, to keep the peace, I'd grudgingly agree to his improvement plans. Instead of clearly letting George know what I wanted or needed, I nagged at him or made subtle but cutting remarks, which would, of course, hurt and anger him.

George hadn't been in the canyon long before I realized with dismay that while I'd shaken off the mantle of Orange County intensity, he had brought it with him. I wanted him to experience the canyon calmly and deeply, the way I had over the last few months. I wanted to grab him by the shoulders and sit him in a chair and make him breathe deeply. I wanted to *make* him watch the birds.

Because it turned out so right, I often wondered if a power greater than George or me had inspired our move to the canyon. Because the small community of Poudre Park and its environs had changed little since my grandmother lived there, over 30 years before, I felt transported to a time when life was simpler and plump with the healing power of life with nothing much between you and the natural world. Perhaps this is why George also regained his equilibrium and strength, despite not having known my grandmother or the area before joining me there.

George benefited from living in the canyon and so did our relationship. Because I'd spent so much time alone and hadn't gone out of my way to make friends in town, George and I relied mostly on each other for company. We now found time not only for ourselves but for each other, time to rediscover what we loved about the other, what drew us together in the first place. Without good television reception or the close proximity of an active city or town, we depended on ourselves for entertainment and companionship. With George's desire to be on the go, doing something intense and physical a lot of the time, he took to climbing the mountains outside our door and often convinced me to accompany him. No one but George could cajole me into walking a terrifying path up the side of a mountain or convince me that I really could return home by way of a trail that looked as if one slip would surely send me plunging over the side into the faraway, rocky gully below. George had me scrambling over boulders, sliding around pockets of prickly shrubs, reaching from one bush branch to another to maneuver down the sides of steep hills. He could talk me into walking farther than I thought possible by convincing me that the top of the ridge was just the other side of that big tree up ahead. He'd grab me just before I sank, exhausted, into a patch of prickly pear or he'd catch me when I jumped down onto a narrow ledge or patiently wait as I climbed backwards down a slope, tapping my foot around to find the next firm foothold.

While I had never stopped loving George during all our difficult years in Illinois and Iowa and California, it was as if that love had gone underground. The canyon brought it once more to the surface. We were—as we used to say—"touching" again.

TWENTY-ONE

Found *And* Lost

Not long after George and I moved to Colorado, my mother phoned us from her home in Evanston, Illinois.

"I've been thinking," she said. "There's nothing left for me here. You and your brother are so far away." She hesitated. "And Dad is gone."

"Are you saying you want to leave Illinois? Live in Colorado year round?" I asked. My mother owned her condo in Fort Collins and stayed in it several times a year.

"I've already talked it over with Dave and he thinks it's a terrible idea. He says I'll lose quite a bit of money, but I can't seem to get the idea out of my mind." Dave had been Dad's financial advisor and he'd handled Mom's investments since my father's death. Neither my brother, Paul, nor I had wanted to take on that job though we worried that Dave didn't always represent Mom's best interests. Perhaps it was time to take a more active role in her affairs.

I thought for a moment. "What do *you* want to do, Mom? What is your *heart* saying?"

I don't think my mother had ever considered the idea that her heart knew the right thing for her to do. If she had, she'd certainly never talked to me in those terms. And I knew she was concerned that if Dad were still alive he wouldn't have wanted her to waste money.

She sounded a little choked up when she answered. "Mary, Colorado has always felt like home to me. I want to come home."

I understood.

I said, "Then come, Mom. The money doesn't matter at all. Come home."

Mom didn't let sentimentality stop her from giving away much of what she and Dad had collected over a lifetime together, nor did she seem to have any compulsion to hold onto many of Dad's personal belongings. She gave a few of his things to family members, such as the watch she gave Paul, but donated the rest of Dad's stuff to Goodwill. She asked if there was anything in her house that I wanted and, except for a few knick-knacks and one or two unique pieces of furniture, I said there wasn't. So she gave away most of her expensive and still-in-good-shape furniture and various odds and ends to the women who cleaned for her every week and to employees of the Presbyterian Home where she and Dad had lived the last few years of his life.

Within days of giving away her excess belongings, Mom called movers to pack up the rest and haul it out to Colorado. Paul flew to Chicago from his home in California and drove away her newish, low-mileage automobile (given to Paul along with Dad's watch) and she flew west. I didn't pick her up at the airport; instead, I met her at the Fort Collins condo where, independent as always, she'd had the airport shuttle drop her off. When I saw her, the look on her face told me she was tired but happy, that she knew she was finally where she belonged and that she felt at home.

After I stopped drinking and particularly after Dad died, I'd worked at repairing my relationship with Mom. It wasn't that we had what could be called a *bad* relationship, but I was too dependent on her approval, approval she found difficult to give. Giving praise and appreciation was not Mom's way—she came from stoic stock, stingy with their applause—and perhaps I needed more than most daughters did.

Mom still had the ability to wound me deeply with a disapproving look, raised eyebrow or a bored expression when I tried to talk about something important to me. Before she moved to Colorado, our infrequent visits with each other could be magical, like the week we'd driven around Wyoming or the day we, together, discovered Poudre Canyon again after so many years. But now we were living within 25 miles of each other and I couldn't continue to be so sensitive about how she treated me or what she did or didn't say.

Dad had been gone five years when Mom moved to Colorado and she'd made her peace with his death. But the back-and-forth travel between Illinois and Colorado had become increasingly difficult and she was often confused. When she was in Illinois, she thought about Colorado and when she was in Colorado, she worried about her home in Illinois. Now she was happy to be in one place, close to me and to Catherine and Evan. At 78-years-old, my mother was ready to start a new chapter in her life in the part of the country she loved most.

Mom spent lots of time with Catherine and Evan. They talked about the old days and about Grandmother and Jack. Mom entertained them in town on Sunday afternoons and drove herself up to the ranch to stay for several days at a time. Before Mom went there, she'd make up a batch of fresh rolls and a cake or pie to take. Sometimes I went along, too, and felt very much at home on the ranch. Though I hadn't been there since I was a child it felt familiar. Catherine honored the past and wanted to keep the old days on the ranch alive as much as she could. She deeply loved the natural world and believed, like the Native Americans who'd been there before her, that land could never be truly owned by anyone. Catherine said often that God loaned us the land to use during our brief lifetimes. She believed that humans are responsible for protecting and maintaining the land, charged with preserving it in its natural state for future generations.

When she wasn't at the Roberts' ranch Mom stayed close to home, shopping in the Old Town area of Fort Collins, visiting the library, making the rounds of independently owned stores, like The Cupboard and Toddies Grocery Store. Unlike Evanston, Fort Collins had a small-town feel that Mom liked and in which she felt comfortable. Sometimes she and I drove around outside town for a day: up Rist or Poudre canyons or even west on Highway 34 along the Big Thompson River to Estes Park. As I drove, Mom talked about her childhood. She repeated favorite stories over and over. Her long-term memory was good, but her short-term memory (remembering which stories she'd already told me, for instance) was failing rapidly. I was worried, but because I didn't know what to do about it I'd just listen to her talk. I'd watch as Mom, slightly hunched over on the seat beside me, struggled to come up with something to talk about. Then she'd smile as if she had suddenly remembered something of great importance, sit taller in her seat and relate a story she'd already told me, sometimes only moments before, often using the exact words in identical sequence.

Mom often told the story of the time she and Catherine and Evan started out for a brief drive up the Poudre and continued until they meandered into Wyoming, never seeing another car along the way—"Can you imagine?"—and because it was so late, decided on the spur of the moment to get a motel and spend the night. Or she'd repeat her story about the families of the field hands who worked on the beet farms when she was a child: "Every woman had a party dress hanging on the back of the bedroom door and the men... Well, at least one of them would end up bloody on a Saturday night." Or she'd say, "There was nothing Mother and Jack liked better than breakfast picnics. Jack would wake up early and announce, 'Mildred, pack the basket. Bring plenty of eggs and bacon. We'll find a pretty spot down by the river, make a fire and have a table with the best view in town.'"

Hearing Mom repeat the same stories over and over as if she didn't remember she'd just told them frightened me. Was this the beginning of Alzheimer's? I also worried about the amount of alcohol she drank. When I was growing up, Mom and Dad enjoyed their evening cocktails, but they never had more than one or two drinks. Later, long after Paul and I left home, Mom did sometimes drink too much. Even before Dad died, I rarely called her in the evenings because her level of intoxication made conversation difficult, but her drinking problem was more apparent to me after she moved to Fort Collins. Clearly inebriated, she would often say hurtful things if I called her around dinnertime. The next day she'd have no memory of our conversation. If I dropped by the condo early in the day, I would sometimes notice four or five spoons lined up in a row on the kitchen counter. This was her way, she said, of keeping track of how much she drank.

"I limit myself to three drinks, Mary. That means when I put the third spoon out, it's time to stop."

When I pointed out that there were five rather than three spoons on the counter, she'd look confused, as if something didn't quite compute. Then she'd brush it off with, "Oh well. I guess I decided to have a couple more."

Mom and I spent a lot of time together when she first moved to Colorado, but gradually I stopped seeing her as often. Once she'd settled in and made a few new friends and found a church, I didn't feel as responsible for her. Mom and George had moved to Colorado during the same year and I'd gone from having no family around to having two very strong and opinionated family members close by. Though I loved them both, I searched for opportunities to spend time away from them.

When I was living in the canyon alone, I had looked to myself for validation. I started to trust that my wants and needs, thoughts and opinions mattered just as much as George's and my mother's. Now they were both around again, I sometimes felt I was disappearing, losing myself. And though Mom didn't do it quite as much as she used to, she still had the tendency to dismiss my interests as silly or unimportant.

I'd hoped that our simultaneous moves to Colorado would bring us closer and heal our relationship; when that didn't happen, it was easier for me to stop thinking about it, stop wishing it was different and merely stay away from her as much as possible.

Mom had made friends with a couple about her age, Poppy and Dick, who owned a condo in the same neighborhood. I'd given them my phone number in case of an emergency. One day, after Mom had been living in Fort Collins for a couple of years, Dick called me to say he was worried about her. I hadn't seen her in a while and felt a little guilty. Dick said he'd seen her trying to take a bag of garbage down to the trash bins; she was walked hesitantly, as if she might be weak, and had difficulty catching her breath. He'd even seen her stop and lean against a parked car for a few minutes, as if to regain her strength. It was just like my mother to be in trouble, but not ask for help.

Admonishing myself for staying away from my own mother so much, I immediately drove into town. I let myself into her apartment and found her sitting on the living room couch. I was shocked to see how gray and breathless she was, though she assured me nothing was wrong. I felt her forehead: it was clammy and hot. I called her doctor, who directed me to get Mom to the hospital immediately. Though she complained that I'd exaggerated the severity of her symptoms to the doctor, she slowly and with a great deal of help from me, got dressed and into my car.

During the 15-minute trip to the hospital, Mom gently scolded me for "making a mountain out of a molehill" while I silently chastised myself for being so oblivious to what was going on with her health. She had no one but me and I'd let her down. Although she was playing down her symptoms, I was frightened; her breathing sounded heavy and raspy and she was obviously very weak. She leaned her head against the back of the seat and closed her eyes. I asked her questions, trying to keep her awake as I drove. I was beginning to fear she might die before we arrived at the hospital.

As I pulled up to the curb outside the emergency room, the security guard hurried over to the passenger side of my car and opened the door. "Do you need a wheelchair?" he asked. I said yes at the same time Mom said no, but the guard took one look at Mom's drawn, gray face and went for the wheelchair.

Perhaps because of how she looked or her age or the fact she was wheeled into the hospital instead of walking under her own power, we were taken immediately past other waiting patients and through a set of double doors into a large room with cubicles separated by curtains. A nurse entered one cubicle at the same time we did; she helped Mom out of the wheelchair and into a bed. Mom had stopped arguing with me and was quiet now; she lay back on the thin pillow and closed her eyes.

The nurse covered Mom with a warm blanket, for which she was weakly thanked, took Mom's vital signs and asked us both a series of questions. Then she left us alone. I sat beside Mom's bed and wondered again if she was dying. I was terrified. Suddenly I knew that though she often frustrated and hurt me, I couldn't imagine life without my mother in the world. I didn't want to let her go.

A young man with sandy blond hair and wearing light blue scrubs joined us. The thought crossed my mind that he'd feel more at home on a ski slope than in a hospital.

"Do you have pain anywhere?" he asked Mom.

"My chest hurts when I breathe in," she said. "But not badly. My daughter is a little dramatic, I'm afraid." She looked over at me and smiled weakly.

The doctor had Mom turn on her side. He thumped her back and listened to her chest. "Let's make you feel better," he said after completing his brief examination. He turned to me. "I'm going to order some X-rays of her chest and we'll see what's going on. She's running a fever and it's probably pneumonia, but let's take a look so we know for sure."

After the doctor left to make arrangements for the X-rays and the nurse had helped Mom change into a hospital gown and left again, Mom looked up at me and said, "Is my breast cancer back?"

The question surprised me: she'd had no sign of cancer for 37 years and I didn't know she thought about the disease anymore.

"Mom, no," I said. "The doctor thinks you have pneumonia. But let's wait to see what the X-rays show before we jump to conclusions about anything." I was probably saying that more for my sake than hers.

After the X-rays were taken and Mom was back in her emergency room cubicle, the pro-skier-looking doctor joined us. He slipped two

X-rays onto a screen on the wall and flipped a switch to backlight the photos. He pointed to a white area on the screen.

"Mrs. Porter," he said. "This is a mass in your right lung. I think we should admit you to the hospital for a few days."

"I understand," Mom said. "My breast cancer is back."

The doctor raised an eyebrow at me, as if to ask what that was all about.

I stepped closer to the bed. "No, Mom. What he's seeing is in your lung, not your breast. This isn't breast cancer."

"Mrs. Porter, it looks like you've had pneumonia for a while. That can cause fluid to build up in your lungs. Sometimes the fluid solidifies," the doctor explained. "I've talked to your internist and she wants you admitted. You stay here and rest until your room is ready."

I wanted to call George and tell him what was going on, but the look on Mom's face alternated between terror and resolve. I didn't want to leave her when she clearly felt so scared.

"I've had one breast removed. It's okay if they remove the other one." She laughed a little. "I don't need my breasts anymore."

"Mom, it's not breast cancer."

I knew that what I said made no difference. In her mind it was 37 years earlier and she was in another hospital being told she would undergo surgery for a lump in her breast. For months, I'd been trying to ignore the signs that my mother's mind was going; now I couldn't. Her short-term memory was almost non-existent, especially during times of stress and I could no longer deny the severity of the situation.

If Mom recovered from this present illness, we had to move her out of the condo and either into a retirement home or in with us, where she could be watched more closely. Would she see the necessity of moving? Would she understand she was no longer able to live alone? I dreaded having her live with us and I knew she wouldn't like it anymore than I would. But perhaps she was dying and there would be no decision to make. At 79, overweight and diabetic, that might well be the case.

Shortly after Mom was formally admitted to the hospital and in a private room, her regular physician, Dr. H, came in to see her. She told us that after talking with the emergency room doctor, she had consulted with Dr. Mark G, a well-known local thoracic surgeon. "He's one of the best," Dr. H told us.

Mom looked confused about why we would consult a heart surgeon. "I don't know what a heart surgeon is going to do about my breast cancer," she said. "And it doesn't matter anyway. I knew I couldn't live with breast cancer. I'm ready to die—I've had a good life." She closed her eyes and sank deeper into the pillow.

"No, Mom. You don't have breast cancer. It's a mass in your lung, probably caused by pneumonia…." I trailed off. I didn't know what to say. Exhausted, I wanted to go home, see George and call my brother.

Dr. H touched Mom's arm. "Betty," she said, leaning over the bed and speaking quietly. "We don't know yet what the problem is, but I don't think whatever it is will kill you now. I've ordered a biopsy of the mass in your lung for tomorrow. After we have the results of that and Dr. G has had a chance to review them, we'll talk with you about all our options and come up with a plan. Okay?'

"There's no plan necessary," Mom said. She didn't bother to open her eyes. "I've had a good life, I'm ready to die. Ready to see Dwight again."

Dr. H gave me a look that I read as a warning not to argue with her. I was too tired to attempt it anyway. I bent down and touched my cheek to Mom's. "I'll be back in the morning. We'll decide what to do then."

She didn't respond; she was already asleep.

Paul agreed to come out as soon as he could make arrangements; he planned to stay at Mom's condo so he'd be close to the hospital. It was as if George, Paul and I had come to our senses overnight. We'd all been denying that Mom was failing and losing her independence. Paul hadn't been checking up on her often either and whenever I'd brought up concerns about her with George he'd say he didn't think her memory was any worse than it had ever been. We'd all wanted to believe that, but now we acknowledged the truth and rallied around. We were on the same page: we'd help Mom recover from whatever was making her so sick and then consider our options. We all agreed that if Mom recovered, she could not continue to live alone.

I arrived at Mom's hospital room the next day before the needle biopsy of the mass in her chest. She was still convinced that the mass was probably cancer and was in her breast, not her lung.

George called to tell me he'd heard from Paul. He planned to arrive late that afternoon and George would pick him up at the airport so I could stay with Mom all day.

An orderly arrived and with the help of a couple of nurses transferred Mom from her bed onto a gurney. Mom apologized to the young orderly and nurse for not being able to get onto the bed on her own. It hurt me to see how fragile she was.

I asked if I could accompany Mom to where they would perform the needle biopsy and the orderly said yes. I walked alongside the gurney, listening to Mom weakly ask the boy about his interests and his job. I realized that, no matter how sick she was, she felt she needed to do this in order to be polite—she needed to show interest. I tried not to think about how little interest she'd showed in me or Paul when we were the same age as this boy. I wondered why she considered it polite to take interest in the lives of strangers, but not in those of your own family members. Ashamed of thinking such thoughts when she was so sick, I turned my attention back to Mom and the present circumstances.

Later that afternoon, Dr. G entered Mom's hospital room. He walked over to her bed and, after introducing himself to me, did a basic, quick physical assessment of her vitals before pulling over a chair and sitting. He nodded to me, as if to tell me silently he understood I was an important player in this drama, but he would be focusing his attention on Mom. I backed away a little and leaned against the wall. It felt good not to be the one trying to convince Mom she should do one thing or another for a change.

"Betty," Dr. G said quietly, "you are very sick right now. It looks like the fluid that builds up when someone has pneumonia has jelled in your left lung. It is now a fairly solid mass and there is no easy way to remove it. Do you understand?"

I watched Mom as she looked at the doctor's handsome and kind face. Her eyes were very big and her mouth was set in a hard line. She nodded. "You're saying I'm going to die."

Dr. G appeared taken aback by Mom's statement. "No, Betty, I'm not saying that at all. In fact, I can fix this. I can make you well, but it's going to mean major surgery."

Mom had been telling me all day that she was ready to die, that she didn't want to do anything to prolong the inevitable. Now I watched as she held Dr. G's hand and listened to him talk. She nodded slightly.

"So you're saying I'm not dying?"

"I'm not going to pretend this isn't a major surgery," Dr. G went on. "It is. It will require you to be in intensive care for several days, on a ventilator and you'll be in the hospital for a week or so after that. There's some risk with all surgery, especially at your age."

"I'm not dying?"

"No. Not if I can help it," he said. "I'm going to fix you."

"Okay," she answered, leaned back against her pillow and closed her eyes.

I couldn't believe it. For two days, George and I had tried to tell her she wasn't dying and that she didn't have breast cancer and she hadn't heard us. She'd repeatedly told us she didn't want to prolong the inevitable. In five minutes Dr. G had turned all that around.

He stood up. "The nurses will prep you for surgery in a little while. I don't want to wait. We'll do it tonight."

"Okay," Mom whispered, "if you think it's best. But I want to sign one of those forms that say you won't resuscitate me."

Dr. G sat down again. "Betty, I don't want you to sign that form. It may be necessary given the kind of surgery we're doing that we will have to resuscitate you. If you sign the form, we won't be able to do it and that would be a shame. I can save you. You *will* live through this operation. You have good years left ahead of you."

"Okay," she said.

I was shocked. Mom had had a DNR scotch-taped to her refrigerator for months, perhaps even years, so that if anything happened to her and paramedics were called, they'd see the DNR and not perform CPR. Dr. G had not only convinced her to let him operate, but also convinced her not to sign a do-not-resuscitate form.

I called George and told him the surgery would take place soon. He needed to get Paul to the hospital from the airport quickly so he could see her before the operation. I wasn't as confident as Dr. G that she would have the strength or state of mind to live through it.

TWENTY-TWO

The Four of Us
or A Game of Bridge

Mom's recovery was lengthy and difficult. Though I was the one who mostly focused on her day-to-day care, George and Paul did what they could to support and care for Mom *and* me during this time. Their gentle and quiet support reawakened and strengthened the love I'd always had for these two very special men. My relationships with my brother and my husband were long-term, of course, and had been fraught with difficulties at times in our history. Paul's instant response to Mom's crisis, without question despite their painful past relationship, and the concern in his voice *for me* as well as Mom, resuscitated the powerful love I'd always felt for him, but rarely let myself acknowledge. Watching George take care of my mother—cajoling her into doing physical rehabilitation exercises and going out of his way to visit her, first in the hospital and later at the inpatient rehab center—reminded me why I'd fallen so deeply in love with him. I saw once again that whenever there was any crisis or need, George was always right there doing what had to be done, taking no credit for it, bringing no attention to himself. I was grateful that, regardless of the pain we'd caused each other over the years, we'd never made the mistake of ending our marriage. And I was grateful that our choice to move to the canyon and Mom's choice to join us in Colorado had given all of us the opportunity to rediscover the powerful love we had for each other, a love never extinguished, but was on occasion very deep underground.

After a brief period of recuperation, first in a nursing facility and then at our house, Mom ignored our advice and returned to living in the condo by herself. She had recovered physically from the surgery, but her short-term memory was worse than ever. Paul, George and I knew it was not safe for her to live alone: she might tumble down the stairs or forget to turn off the stove or take her medications. She didn't want to live with us and we traveled too much for that to be a viable option. I was constantly frustrated that she couldn't—or wouldn't—recognize what her refusal to move into a facility was doing to all of us. Why didn't she understand that she would be safer, happier and more secure in a care facility and that such a move would make George's and my life so much easier, too? My constant low-grade anxiety about it all adversely affected my relationship with her, but still she refused to look at retirement homes and insisted she was perfectly capable of living alone in the condo. Although I suspected she was no more capable of making that kind of decision than she was of living alone, I often felt Mom was, once again, being selfish.

One day, without thinking how it would affect Mom, I mentioned that George and I could no longer travel together while we knew she was living alone. A shocked look crossed her face, as if she'd realized for the first time how her actions affected George and me.

After a moment or two of stunned silence, she said, "Travel is one of life's greatest joys. If I'm keeping you and George from traveling, then it's time for me to move into a nursing home."

I felt terrible and wished I hadn't mentioned it. "Not a nursing home, Mom. There are wonderful assisted living facilities that would be perfect for you."

Mom interrupted me with a wave of her hand. "Whatever. It's time I leave the condo. I've been selfish. Let's find me a place to live that will allow you and George to travel together again."

And that was the end of the discussion.

I made a list of facilities I thought she might like and we began the task of visiting each one together. It wasn't until we found Good Samaritan Retirement Village south of Fort Collins that Mom acknowledged the amenities of an assisted living facility might outweigh the benefits of staying in her condo. She especially liked Good Samaritan because she could have her own two-room apartment, prepare her own meals if she wanted to and pretty much be left alone unless she needed help or wanted company. She also liked Good Samaritan's requirement that she check in morning and night and that, if she didn't, someone would come to her room to make sure she was all right. This gave her a sense of safety that other independent living facilities and her own condo did not. A fortuitous chain of events allowed Mom to move into Good Samaritan almost immediately after she'd made up her mind to live there; she didn't have time to regret her decision.

As soon as she'd signed on the dotted line and paid the deposit, I felt instant relief and a sense of freedom. Once Mom had moved into Good Samaritan, I could enjoy my time with her without having to worry about her safety: her basic needs would be met. She could socialize if she wanted to and eat healthy meals she didn't have to prepare for herself. My main responsibility now was to deal with the numerous prescription medications she took. Every week, I filled pill boxes and wrote out elaborate instructions for her, but that was minimal compared to what I'd managed for her before she moved into Good Samaritan. Now I could enjoy visiting my mother without feeling like a police sergeant interrogating a frightened suspect, asking what she'd been doing and where she'd been the night before.

After Mom moved into Good Samaritan, her short-term memory loss proved to be somewhat of a blessing. She quickly forgot about the condo that had meant so much to her and started to believe she'd lived at Good Samaritan for years. If I forgot and said something about how she'd only lived there for a month or so, she looked at me as if I were the one who had lost her mind.

I now visited Mom for fun; I loved taking her on outings because she enjoyed them so much. We went to church, where she would praise the choir and complain, sometimes quite loudly, about the sermons. We went on drives together, like we had after we first moved to Colorado. I drove her around Horsetooth Reservoir or up the Poudre to Rustic or Glen Echo. She no longer tried to remember things as she had before the surgery: she merely enjoyed the present moment, the day she was spending with me. Our relationship became very basic: though I now had a mother who was mentally impaired, I also had a mother who truly appreciated me in a simple way, perhaps the way a child appreciates someone or something. She never forgot to thank me for coming, for taking her out, for doing some small task for her. It was as if I had never been the daughter who disappointed her or was interested in things she found silly or boring. Now I was the daughter who showed up and took her on drives in the country and prepared her medications and handled any small annoyance that might come up with the staff at Good Samaritan. The tables were turned: I was more her mother now than she mine. And that was okay with me. Because I knew she was safe and her basic daily needs were met by people paid to do that, I could be the kind of daughter I wanted to be and enjoy Mom for the woman she was, instead of wishing she was someone else—a different kind of mother.

George was very involved with Mom, too, and I was deeply grateful. He'd stop over at Good Samaritan to see her on the spur of the moment, do small repairs around her apartment, straighten it up a little, talk to her simply so she could follow. Another kind of man might have only done these things to look good in his wife's eyes, but not George. Usually, he didn't even tell me he'd be stopping by at Mom's and sometimes I'd discover him there, watching a television program with her or talking about the stock market or something she didn't really understand. He knew it didn't matter what he talked about: she liked his company, liked the sound of his voice.

One of the reasons Mom originally chose Good Samaritan was because it had various levels of care: when she eventually required more assistance, she'd only have to change apartments, not move to an entirely new facility. When her mind had deteriorated to that point, we moved her into an assisted living apartment on the second floor. Within a year, we moved her again; Mom's mental and physical capacities had declined so rapidly, she now required the care only given on the nursing wing of the first floor. At first, she shared a room with another woman, but because Mom loved privacy and solitude, we moved her again into a private room when one became available. In her new room, she could look through a large picture window onto a small yard with a beautiful maple tree. George installed a grouping of bird feeders and from then on made sure they were always full of seed. Mom's new living space was a fraction of the size of her previous homes, but whenever we visited her there she never failed to thank us for her beautiful room, her comfortable bed and the feeders that attracted so many pretty birds to her window.

In the spring of 2006, Mom's doctor, the physician who cared for many residents of Good Samaritan, told me she had esophageal cancer. There was nothing to do other than make her comfortable and call in Hospice to help her—and us—to manage the last months of her life. We withheld this diagnosis from Mom; her dementia was now so bad we didn't think she'd understand and the knowledge would only frighten her. I didn't want to lie to Mom or pretend everything was okay if the subject arose, but Paul, George and I decided not to tell her she was dying unless she asked.

I watched as her body rapidly deteriorated. The cancer affected her ability to swallow and we had to start her on soft foods; even those were difficult for her and watching her choke and vomit when she tried to eat anything was almost beyond bearing. The staff at Good Samaritan and everyone on Mom's Hospice team were angels to me. Sometimes it got to be too much and I'd leave Mom's room and go to the nurse's station at the end of the hall, where the nurse or aide on duty would give me her undivided attention and support as I despaired over the imminent loss of my mom. They would answer my questions and explained what was going on in my mother's body as it shut down and prepared itself for death.

Paul flew out from California as often as he could, whenever I asked. The problems my brother and I had had as teenagers were long over and we'd been pleasant toward each other as adults, but a distance, a formality, between us had remained. Now that formality disappeared. As we let Mom go, we reached out to each other. I felt close to him again. I knew our renewed close connection would most likely last the rest of our lives.

George was with Mom a lot, too, and he watched over me with such tenderness and ferocity that I felt, as I had when I first fell in love with him, that no one had ever or *could* ever love me the way he did. Over and over, I was reminded of what real love is all about and how I had received the exquisite gift of it from George.

The three of us—George, Paul and I—united into a team during the time of Mom's dying. We connected in ways we never had before. At first, it was just the three of us—as if we knew what was happening but Mom didn't and she couldn't share with us the experience of her own dying. Then one morning, when I was alone with her in her room at Good Samaritan and the sun was streaming in through her big picture window and the birds were chirping at the feeder, she looked up at me with clear, understanding eyes and said, "Mary, I'm dying, aren't I?"

I hesitated. I started to deny it.

She looked at me with a steady, clear gaze. "Tell me the truth, Mary. I'm dying soon, aren't I? I want to know."

"*Yes*," I said.

In that moment, Mom's dementia disappeared forever. Perhaps it was because she suddenly had a focus; perhaps the recognition that she would soon die was so big it wiped out all the frivolous daily concerns that had cluttered and confused her mind. Suddenly, all she wanted was to be with Paul, George and me and hear our ideas about death and God and a possible afterlife. As she settled into the process of letting go of life on this earth, she showed me how death could come with grace, dignity and even humor.

Each day of September, 2006, the last month of her life, I never knew what to expect. Sometimes she wanted to tell me what she remembered of the deaths of others close to her. She liked to talk about the death of her maternal grandfather, the grandfather she had lived with in Iowa after her parents divorced. Mom had been in college when he died. A week or so before his death, she'd asked him, "Grandfather, are you afraid to die?"

"Of course not," he told her. "I'm going to see my mother and father and all the people I loved who passed on before me. That is a glorious thing, not something to fear!"

I knew Mom was hoping her grandfather was right and that she would see him and Dad and Grandmother and her younger brother, Bob, who had died several years before.

One day, when George, Paul and I arrived in her room, Mom told us we had to leave right away. She was agitated and insistent. When we questioned her and wouldn't leave immediately, she grudgingly told us that a friend of hers—an elementary school nurse who'd died several years before—had come and given her a "death pill." Mom said that in a few minutes, the pill would start to work and she didn't want us around to see her die. Without openly questioning what she said, we stayed in the room.

"The pill must not have been strong enough," she said eventually, great disappointment in her voice. "I didn't know it would take so long to die," she said, sadly. It seemed dying was now something she was looking forward to.

In the week before Mom died, when her body looked like a small mound of sticks beneath her white blanket and the ponytail a Hospice nurse had fashioned at the top of her head pulled her gray skin taut over her high cheekbones, I spent most of my time sitting quietly by her bed as she slept. She looked tiny and frail. Why hadn't I noticed before how small her hands were? The hands of a child.

I worried that she was suffering even in sleep, that a body with cancer had no choice but to suffer as it died and I wished for an end to her suffering. Sometimes I wanted her to die more quickly and I felt guilty for wanting that. I watched her as she slept and thought about this woman who was my mother, and how loving her had sometimes been hard and painful, but how, sometimes, it was the easiest thing to do.

Then she would wake up, smile quickly when she noted my presence and say the same thing she said every time she woke up: "Am I still here? I didn't know it would take so long to die."

Near the end, she asked if I believed in God and I told her I did. What I didn't say was that I found it easier to withstand the ups and downs of life when I believed in a god, though I wasn't sure one existed. Another time, she asked if I believed in an afterlife and I assured her I believed in that, too. I told her about my experience in the year following my friend's death in Vietnam—how I'd sensed his constant presence—and how I had believed ever since that our souls go on after our bodies perish. Whenever we talked about these kinds of things—subjects we had never talked about before—she'd turn her face away and nod, as if considering what I'd said. Our conversations were short intermissions between longer periods of sleep. I think she thought death would only come for her while she slept and she was eager to experience this new adventure.

Paul and I were sitting beside Mom's bed one afternoon when the Good Samaritan's on-staff minister entered. He looked as if he were about to make himself comfortable and stay a while. He asked Mom if she was in a "right relationship with God." Mom cut him short with a wave of her hand. "Can't you see I'm talking to my son and daughter now? Please come back at another time." Paul and I glanced at each other and smiled; her strong voice did not match the obvious condition of her body.

Another day, when Mom was discouraged because it was taking her so long to die, I said, "Mom, think about it like waiting for a train." Because she had always loved to travel, I figured this was a metaphor she could easily understand.

"You're excited to begin the journey," I went on, "but you have to wait for the train. You know trains. They arrive on their own time schedule and are often late."

She smiled and closed her eyes. "I'll wait for the train," she said.

Another time she told me that some old college friends were calling her from the top of a cliff. Although she hadn't seen these friends for years and they were long dead, she easily recognized them. "Come on, Betty," they said, extending their arms down to her. "Hurry up. We're waiting for you."

"I'm trying to reach them, Mary," Mom told me. "But the cliff is so steep and they're so far above me."

"Ask them to come partway, Mom. Ask them to give you a hand up."

"Okay," she agreed and closed her eyes once again, hoping for sleep.

After a couple of days, her dreams changed. Now her friends weren't on top of a mountain, they were at a bridge table: three friends, one empty chair. "Come on, Betty," they said. "We need you for a fourth."

One day, after telling me the story of her grandfather's death once again, Mom asked if I was afraid to die. Without thinking about it, I said, "No. I'm not afraid to die. But I am afraid to live in this world without you."

And my mother looked at me and said, "Honey, you will never live in this world without me. I will always be with you. I will always be looking after you."

I said, "I love you, Mom."

And for the first time I could remember, she said, "Oh, honey, I love you too."

The day before Mom finally succeeded in sitting down at her friends' heavenly bridge table, her Hospice team chaplain told Paul and me that Mom was very near death. She suggested we make arrangements for at least one of us to stay with her around the clock. I decided to spend the night in the relatively comfortable armchair in her room while Paul went back to Mom's condominium, where we'd been staying. He assured me that all I had to do was call and he'd return within the hour. Mom didn't wake all that night nor the next day. Paul returned early in the morning and George came from home to be at Mom's bedside, too.

We stood vigil in our own ways: Paul and George reading the New

York Times and quietly discussing the news of the day and the stock market; me attempting to read a book while keeping an eye on Mom's infrequent, slight movements. We left the room only rarely. I wanted to look at Mom's face as much as possible; though she didn't look like the mother I'd known, I wanted to burn her image into my mind. I didn't want to forget her. No matter how much she and I could irritate each other, we were never out of touch for more than a week or two during my entire 57 years of life. I wanted to be able to pull up her image after she'd gone. I expected there would be times I'd need it for comfort.

The staff at Good Samaritan supplied a constant round of snack food and drinks on trays and her Hospice team kept us informed about what Mom was experiencing. They reminded us that she could have pain medicine anytime we requested it: if we saw her grimace or struggle, we had only to let them know and they'd give her an injection. The Hospice chaplain came often. She stood by Mom's bed and passed her hands gently above Mom's body without touching her as she murmured, "It's okay to let go, Betty. Paul and Mary are here. They are strong enough to let you go now, too."

Mom never opened her eyes or spoke again, but I sensed she knew we were with her and that she understood what the chaplain was saying.

At six o'clock on the evening of September 28, 2006, Paul and I decided it wouldn't hurt to make a quick run to a nearby Thai restaurant for a decent dinner. We had just sat down and ordered our food when Paul's cell phone rang. It was George. Paul handed me the phone.

"You don't have your cell phone with you," George said.

I was confused; what was he talking about? "I guess I left it in Mom's room. Why?"

"Good Samaritan tried to call you. They couldn't reach you so they called me. Your mom's gone," he said, gently.

I didn't understand what he was saying. I handed the phone back to Paul. George told him the same thing and while they were talking, his words sank in. Mom had died when we left the room. The Hospice chaplain had said that the moment of death is a choice and that people who enjoyed solitude often chose to die alone. Mom had always liked her solitude. She'd tried to rush us out of the room when she thought her friend had given her a *death* pill. I should have realized then that when the time came for her to die, she would want to be alone.

Paul closed his phone and we looked at each other, unsure what to do next. She had died; there was nothing we could do. Should we eat or would that seem cold and insensitive while Mom lay dead in her bed just a few miles away? Paul made the decision and paid for the food we hadn't eaten. We returned to Good Samaritan.

The staff had changed Mom's bed and put her body back into it. They'd dimmed the lights, taken away the trays of half-eaten food, emptied the wastebaskets and generally made the room look nicer. Mom looked nicer, too, more relaxed. We entered her room quietly, as if we didn't want to disturb her. I went over to the bed and gently touched the blanket spread across her. She looked as if she was only sleeping.

Good Samaritan's acting chaplain, Jim, quietly joined us.

"Some families like to have a brief bedside service," he said and we looked at him, not understanding.

"The mortuary will be coming soon to pick up Betty's body. I thought perhaps, before they do, you'd like me to say a few words…"

Paul wasn't religious. And I didn't feel a prayer service by Mom's bed would make any difference to either Mom or God. But some sort of closure seemed in order. Paul and I looked at each other and nodded. Jim left the room to make a few preparations and to gather some of the others.

Within minutes, we were joined by several staff members who were still on duty and who had cared for Mom over the years. Jim led us in a prayer and said a few words about Mom and how kind she'd been to him. Several of the staff said similar things. Paul and I remained silent; we didn't know what to say. Neither of us cried. I felt very tired and, though Jim's words were meaningful, I was ready to go home. I was ready to go home to George and the dogs.

When the brief bedside service was over, I bent over and touched my cheek to Mom's forehead and Paul patted her arm. Everyone else had quietly left so we could be alone with her one last time. Still we didn't say anything. There wasn't anything left to say; we'd said pretty much all of it in the weeks since we'd been told of her impending death.

Finally, we gathered our belongings and left. Two young men from the mortuary were standing in the hall outside the room; both were very good-looking and wore dark dress suits. I asked them how they were going to transport Mom to the mortuary. They looked surprised, as if I'd asked a strange question given the circumstances. One said that they'd take her out very inconspicuously. I understood; they didn't want to upset the other residents. I didn't ask any other questions. Paul and I walked through the quiet halls and out into the autumn night. We arranged to meet the following day to go to the mortuary together and make funeral arrangements.

Paul got into Mom's car and drove to her condo to get some sleep. I got into my car to drive up the canyon to George.

TWENTY-THREE

Full Circle

On Saturday, April 10, 2010, George and I drove out of the canyon and turned north onto Highway 287. We were going to Livermore Community Church to attend a surprise party for Catherine Roberts' 90th birthday. Alongside her husband, she'd spent 70 years working their ranch, her feet firmly planted on the hard earth and her heart strengthened by loyal friends, a strong faith in God and probably good genes, all of which had brought her to this ripe old age. She still lived alone in the house she had shared with Evan from the early 1940s when they married until his death, at the age of 94, in 2002.

Neither George nor I was looking forward to this party; we hadn't seen Catherine in a while and I doubted we'd know anyone there other than Catherine and her stepson, David. George and I aren't party people: we prefer getting together with one or two other couples for deep conversation than making small talk with a large group of virtual strangers. But I felt I had to go. If Mom were still alive she would have thought it important to attend and, if she had some way of knowing what I was doing, she'd be pleased that I was representing her at a party for Catherine.

Several of Catherine's friends had taken her into Fort Collins for lunch while the guests gathered secretly at the church. George and I arrived early enough to mingle with the men and women who had known Catherine, some of them, like me, all of their lives and others only briefly. We felt a bit out of place among so many people we didn't know who clearly had strong friendships or family ties with each other, so we mostly hovered around the edges of various groups, listening to the men talk about this warm and sunny party day in April after a long winter and their herds of cattle. "Baby calves," they said, "are popping up all over the valley." The men, regardless of age, wore cowboy boots and hats, blue jeans and dress shirts or sport coats. Catherine's stepson David—75 but looking at least 20 years younger—wore a western-style suit, boots and a belt with a large "R" inscribed on the buckle. The women, dressed in casual pantsuits or fancy embroidered jeans and boots, talked in separate groups about gardens and grandbabies.

A tall busy woman in a black pantsuit, whom no one seemed to know particularly well, finally herded the party attendees to a spot outside the front of the church to await Catherine's arrival. As I leaned against the railing alongside the walkway, a woman of about my age introduced herself and asked how I knew Catherine, since obviously I was not from the small, tight-knit Livermore community. After several minutes of conversation, we figured out that her grandfather was the man I'd taken my first steps to 60 years before.

The story of my taking those steps had grown to mythic proportions in my family. My parents had been assured by my pediatrician that nothing was physically or mentally wrong with me, but I'd stubbornly refused to walk—I wouldn't toddle toward Mom, Dad or Grandmother no matter how they pleaded and cajoled—until the day I met Mr. Sloan. When I was 14 months old and Mom was pregnant with Paul, Mom and I traveled from Hawaii to Colorado to visit Grandmother. Shortly after our arrival, Grandmother took us to the Sloan Ranch for a party. While everyone was busy talking, I had climbed off my mother's lap and walked without stumbling over to Mr. Sloan. I crawled into his open arms and sat beaming on *his* lap while everyone laughed. Supposedly, Grandmother had whispered to Mom, "There's not a female alive who can resist Wes Sloan!"

Finally, Catherine arrived at her party in a mini-van driven by an old friend. As she climbed out of the vehicle, she stopped and gazed at the now quiet gathering on the church lawn. She had on the same brunette wig she'd worn for as long as I could remember. Today, it sat slightly askew on her head, but that didn't diminish her regal demeanor. Because of her assuredness, her self-confidence, Catherine had always appeared taller than five feet. She was wearing her usual slacks, a white shirt and a summery vest and leaned on a cane because of hip and knee problems, the only outward sign that she was a 90-year-old woman. She looked 20 if not 30 years younger than she was, with just a few lines on her round face.

Smiling slightly but not appearing particularly surprised, Catherine made her way along the walk to the front of the church. Reaching her friends and neighbors, she shook their hands and quietly asked about families, ranches and livestock. At first, the group seemed a little taken aback at Catherine's lack of surprise, but they quickly shook off any confusion and ushered her into the church's fellowship hall for food, fruit punch and renewed conversation. I wasn't surprised at Catherine's outward calm or apparent lack of enthusiasm; like my mother, she was not given to wearing her emotions on her sleeve. But I knew she was deeply touched, just as Mom would have been under similar circumstances.

The fellowship hall was decorated with balloons and flowers. Round tables and chairs were arranged into a semi-circle in front of a long head table and podium. Large gold letters spelled 'Happy Birthday Catherine' in an arc on the wall behind the head table. Someone who didn't know Catherine well must have expected her to sit in front of the crowd and possibly give a speech. I found a chair at a table near the back of the room and, while George looked for something for us to drink, I struck up a conversation with a friendly-looking older woman sitting next to me. I found out that, before she was born and before my grandmother and Jack moved to the Roberts' Ranch, her parents had worked there and lived in the same house my mother, Jack and Grandmother had occupied in 1942. Despite knowing hardly anyone at the party, my family and I had many underlying connections to the people gathered around Catherine.

After Catherine had made her way around the room thanking well-wishers, her eyes sparkling and her smile never wavering, she sat in an armchair next to the door. People lined up to talk to her and I stood at the end of the line, waiting for my opportunity to wish her well. When my turn came, I knelt down beside her and took her cool hands in mine. She pulled me close and kissed me first on one cheek and then the other. "Isn't this wonderful?" she whispered. "So many people." I looked around: over a hundred guests now squeezed into the relatively large room and more were coming in the door. Catherine asked how our recent trip to Florida had been. I was a little surprised she remembered we had gone there—to visit George's parents—since I hadn't talked to her in months. Then she said, "I wish your mother were here."

My eyes stung with unshed tears. "I miss Mom so much, Aunt Catherine," I said. "And I miss Grandmother, too."

"So do I, Mary. And Evan."

I thought about how Catherine and Grandmother had traveled from Denver to Honolulu and stayed with my parents for the month of August, 1949. "It feels so right to be here at *your* birthday party," I said. "After all, you came all the way to Hawaii to be with Mom the day I was born."

Others were waiting behind me to wish Catherine a happy birthday; I could feel rather than see them shifting from side to side, waiting for me to move on. I squeezed her hands and let go. She touched my face and I stood and walked away from her as she turned to her next guest.

George looked at me with compassion. After so many years together, I knew he understood.

Catherine and the Poudre Canyon are my last links to Grandmother and Mom. Like them, Catherine will also soon be gone. Most, if not all of the children who grew up on the ranches in this part of Colorado have moved away. In a while I'll be gone, too. Only the land will remain.

EPILOGUE

June 10, 2012.

My cell phone rings at 5:30 a.m. and wakes me. Groggy after a mostly sleepless night, I grab it from the floor beside me. George and I are sleeping on an air mattress in our friends' house; the dogs sprawl on the floor close by, also exhausted from our ordeal the night before. It had only been a little over five hours since we'd phoned Barry and Karen from Ted's Place and told them a wildfire was threatening our home. They had immediately offered us a room at their house, urging us to stay with them as long as necessary.

Now Kellie, Tony's wife and another of our community's volunteer firefighters, is on the other end of the line. It sounds like she's crying. "Mary, we saved your house." Before I can respond, she repeats the words I so want to hear: "We saved your house. It's standing right now, but it's not out of danger. We don't know what will happen later."

"Oh, Kellie, we were so worried, about the house, but mostly about you guys…"

"We're okay. We're hanging in. But I've got to get back. I'll try to call you sometime this afternoon." Kellie hangs up and I turn to give George the news.

Later, we learned that Kellie and Tony and three other firefighters for the lower Poudre Canyon fire district had evacuated the entire lower canyon in just under an hour and gone on to save as many of our houses as they could. Because the fire tore into the canyon faster than the authorities thought possible, the reverse 9-1-1 call we expect in case of emergencies like this never came: neighbors helped by calling other neighbors or, if the phone service was already lost as was the case for some, pounding on front doors until everyone was notified. The residents on the north side of the highway had more time than those on the south side, but they were in a hurry to get out of the canyon, too. Professional firefighters were tied up fighting the High Park Fire, as it was later named, at its origin southwest of Rist Canyon. So when it came to fighting the fire in *our* canyon and protecting *our* homes, only five men and women were there to face the conflagration slamming into our community. Tony, Kellie, Rachel, John and Mike used their training, skill and wits to save all but 19 of the homes in the canyon that night. They saved our house twice and later on in the week a third time, sometimes by using what amounted to an old-fashioned bucket brigade, sucking up water from the river into the fire truck and transporting it across the road and up the driveway to our house. That first night, five volunteers took a stand against the firestorm with only two old fire engines and an ambulance.

Before the High Park Fire was 100 percent contained nearly a month later, one rancher had lost her life, 259 homes had burned to their foundations and 87,284 acres were blackened. It was a terrible spring and summer for Colorado: at one point there were ten wildfires burning around the state at the same time. Beetle-kill, drought and days of intense heat had caused what our governor named, at one point, "a perfect storm."

This perfect storm became the deciding factor in an issue that George and I had been grappling with for a while. A month before the fire, we had purchased a house on the central coast of Oregon and had planned to divide our time between the two places. I'd felt unsettled for a couple of years and had a vague underlying sense that we needed a change, that the time to leave Colorado was coming. George seemed to feel it, too. Our marriage was strong; Mom had lived out the end of her life in the state she called home; she and I had healed our relationship; my brother and I were closer than ever. And I had grappled with the issues of my childhood and young adult years and come to understanding and acceptance.

When driving up and down the canyon in the couple of months after we were allowed back into our homes, I grieved at the sight of leveled homes, hillsides of blackened trees and bushes and the river running black with sludge and soot whenever it rained. Though I reminded myself that wildfires were natural and necessary occurrences in the healthy lives of forests and that we'd understood the risks when we moved into such a beautiful rural area, the canyon felt different to me—no longer home.

Perhaps it was time to close the door on this period of our lives: close the door on the 15 years we'd spent in this dry and rugged section of the Rocky Mountains and open another door on a moist and fertile hillside overlooking the Pacific Ocean. George had often mentioned how he'd like a view of an ocean somewhere and living within sight of the Pacific would be coming full circle for me. I understood that the healing we'd come to Colorado to achieve was now complete. Together we could move on.

ACKNOWLEDGMENTS

They say it takes a village to raise a child and I'd say it takes a village to write and publish a book. *Above Tree Line* would not have been born without the support, input, and assistance of many.

The following have assisted in the bringing-to-term and birthing process: Barbara Achey, Mary Allen, Amna Ahmad, Bobbie Ambruzs, Karen Bailey, Bobbi Benson (Wild Ginger Press), Diana Dallape, Marianne Elliot, Linda Fitzgerald, Janet Gelenter (editor), Elizabeth Hill, Judy Kallal, Sharon Lee, the late Sarah Lollar, Jennifer Louden, Ruth McCully, Joannah Merriman, Tara Mohr, Patricia Morris, Christina Pettan-Brewer, Joanna Powell-Colbert, Jana Rezucha, Nancy Stilson-Herzog, Heather Taylor (photographer), Vicky White and Laura Van Etten. If I have missed anyone here, I deeply apologize. I hope you know who you are and how grateful I truly am.

Most of all, I want to thank my beloved men: My husband, George, and my two boys: Jon and Brad. I love you now and always.

Made in the USA
Charleston, SC
18 September 2014